BENEDICT DE SPINOZA: AN INTRODUCTION

Benedict de Spinoza:
An Introduction

REVISED EDITION

Henry E. Allison

Yale University Press
New Haven and London

Designed by Nancy Ovedovitz and set in Times Roman type by
The Publishing Nexus Incorporated, Guilford, Conn. Printed in
the United States of America by Vail-Ballou Press, Binghamton,
N.Y.

Library of Congress Cataloging-in-Publication Data

Allison, Henry E.
    Benedict de Spinoza.
    Bibliography: p.
    Includes index.
    1. Spinoza, Benedictus de, 1632–1677. I. Title.
B3998.A42 1987   199'.492   86-24583
ISBN 0-300-03595-0 (alk. paper)
ISBN 0-300-03596-9 (pbk. : alk. paper)

10   9   8   7   6   5   4   3   2   1

Contents

To Norma, Eric, and Renee

Preface

The present work is a substantially revised version of my *Benedict de Spinoza* (Boston: Twayne, 1975). The new title is intended to reflect the aim of both the original and the present version: namely, to provide a comprehensive introduction to the thought of Spinoza. I have completely rewritten the three central chapters dealing with the *Ethics* but have made relatively minor changes in the rest. I have also omitted the epilogue dealing with the historical influence of Spinoza's thought, which was too brief to serve any useful purpose.

As an introduction to Spinoza's philosophy, this work is intended primarily for the general reader or student with some background in philosophy. Nevertheless, I hope that it may also be of interest to the more advanced student and perhaps even to the specialist. My goal continues to be to present a clear, complete, and balanced picture, one that will give the reader a sense of the breadth as well as the depth of this unique philosophy. I have tried, therefore, not only to provide an accurate account of Spinoza's main doctrines and the historical context in which they arose, but also to explain as clearly and concisely as possible the main arguments that he offers in support of these doctrines. Although criticism of these arguments is not neglected, it is usually subordinated to sympathetic exposition. My general procedure, particularly with regard to the central arguments of the *Ethics*, is to indicate where the major difficulties lie, or at least where Spinoza's critics think they lie, and then to suggest some possible Spinozistic responses to these difficulties.

In the preface to the first edition, I claimed that the main virtue of my book is that, more than similar works, it helps the reader to follow the actual course of Spinoza's argument. I had in mind primarily the excellent and well-known work of Stuart Hampshire, *Spinoza* (1951). I felt then, and I still feel, that, in spite of its many valuable qualities, Hampshire's work does not make sufficient contact with the text to be of very much assistance to the reader who is struggling to follow the often tortuous course of Spinoza's thought. Two other major English-language works on Spinoza have appeared recently: Jonathan Bennett's *A Study of Spinoza's Ethics* (1984) and R. J. Delahunty's *Spinoza* (1985). Although I have sharp disagreements with each of these authors, particularly Bennett, I have learned much from them and have tried to incorporate this in the new edition. But since neither of these works really attempts to provide a comprehensive account of Spinoza's thought, I do not believe that they make my own effort redundant.

The major changes in this new edition are the result of my attempt to rethink the argument of the *Ethics* in light of the most important secondary literature of the past decade, as well as some of the earlier literature that I failed to consider in the original edition. In addition to the above-mentioned works of Bennett and Delahunty, this new literature includes the second volume of Martial Gueroult's magisterial work, *Spinoza II, L'Ame* (1974), which deals with part 2 of the *Ethics*, and a number of important articles, many of which are contained in the spate of collections of essays spurred by the tricentennial of Spinoza's death in 1977.

My study of these works, which collectively constitute a decisive advance in Spinoza studies, led me not only to change my mind on many specific points—too many to mention here—but also to devote considerably more attention to some of the more problematic doctrines and arguments of the *Ethics* than I did in the first edition. Consequently, I now give a fairly extended treatment to a number of crucial points that were more or less glossed over initially. Nevertheless, I have tried not to lose sight of the fact that this work is still intended as a general introduction. Thus, in spite of what I take to be significant improvements, I am keenly aware both that there is considerably more to be said regarding the topics to which I have devoted the most attention, and that many other significant aspects of Spinoza's thought continue to receive a relatively superficial treatment.

Apart from the omission of the epilogue, the organization of the book remains the same. The first chapter offers a brief account of Spinoza's life and of the circumstances underlying the publication, or lack thereof, of his various writings. The second sketches the basic features of seventeenth-century thought that are directly relevant to an understanding of Spinoza's philosophy and attempts to provide an initial, nontechnical characterization of the main thrust, or "spirit," of this philosophy. The next three chapters, which form the heart of the book, deal with the central themes of the *Ethics*—that is, with Spinoza's metaphysical, epistemological, psychological, and moral theories. The sixth chapter deals with Spinoza's political philosophy, while the seventh outlines his views on the nature of revealed religion, particularly Judaism, and his then revolutionary method for interpreting the Bible.

In the original edition I cited, with some modifications, the Elwes translation of the *Ethics*. In this edition, however, I have made use of Edwin Curley's translations of both the *Ethics* and the earlier writings contained in the first volume of his edition of *The Collected Works of Spinoza* (1985). Curley's translations, together with his impressive editorial apparatus (which includes extensive notes and a glossary-index), makes this edition an indispensable tool for any serious English-speaking student of Spinoza. For Spinoza's correspondence, only part of which is contained in the first volume of Curley's edition, I have continued to make use of *The Correspondence of Spinoza*, translated by A. Wolf; for the *Political Treatise* and the political portions of the *Theological-Political Treatise* I rely, as before, on A. G. Wernham's *Benedict de Spinoza: The Political Works*; and for the theological portions of the *Theological-Political Treatise* on R. H. M. Elwes's *The Chief Works of Spinoza*, volume 1. References to the *Ethics* are usually given directly in the text and are to the definitions (D), axioms (A), and propositions (P), together with the demonstrations (D), corollaries (C), and scholia (S) attached to the latter. For example, IIP40S2 refers to the second scholium of proposition 40 of part 2. References to the part are omitted when it is clear from the context. References to the other writings of Spinoza are given in the notes. For those interested in consulting the original, I include references to the standard edition of Spinoza's works: C. Gebhardt, *Spinoza Opera*.

I am indebted to many people for their help in the preparation of this new edition. First, I would like to thank Edwin Curley for pointing out to me a number of errors and confusions in the first edition. I am also particularly grateful to my colleague Nicholas Jolley and my research assistant Michelle Gilmore, each of whom read carefully and commented on a semifinal draft of the chapters dealing with the *Ethics*. My debt to them on specific points of interpretation is acknowledged in the notes. Special thanks are also due to Catherine Asmann, who patiently saw my manuscript through the various stages of preparation. I would also like to thank my editor, Jeanne Ferris, for her enthusiastic support of this project and for her assistance in its completion. Above all, however, I must thank my wife, Norma, who not only continued to support me in every conceivable way, but aided materially in the preparation of the manuscript.

Finally, thanks are due Princeton University Press for permission to quote from Curley's *The Collected Works of Spinoza*; to Clarendon Press, Oxford, for permission to quote from Wernham's *Benedict de Spinoza: The Political Works*; and to George Allen and Unwin, London, for permission to quote from Wolf's *The Correspondence of Spinoza*.

BENEDICT DE SPINOZA: AN INTRODUCTION

CHAPTER 1

The Life of Spinoza

I The Jewish Community in Amsterdam and Spinoza's Life within It

Baruch de Spinoza was born in the city of Amsterdam on 24 November 1632.[1] His parents were members of the community of Jewish immigrants who had been living in the Netherlands since 1593. Spinoza remained within this community until his excommunication from the synagogue in 1656. This excommunication was undoubtedly one of the pivotal events in Spinoza's life. Not only did it make official and permanent his break with the Jewish religion, which he had long since renounced anyway, but more important, it resulted in a complete rupture with his family and the abandonment of any thought of a commercial career, thereby making possible a life devoted exclusively to the pursuit of philosophy. In order to understand this event, however, we must consider not only Spinoza's own character and beliefs, but also some of the salient characteristics and history of the unique Jewish community in which he grew up.

This community was composed largely of descendants of the Marranos, also called "New Christians" or "crypto-Jews." These were the names given to the Spanish Jews who were forcibly converted to Christianity by the Inquisition in the late fifteenth century. After their "conversion," which was usually, but not always, merely nominal, many of these Jews had risen to positions of great prominence in the intellectual, economic, political, and even ecclesiastical life of Spain. Precisely because of their success, however, they were again persecuted by the Inquisition and expelled from the country. The first stop in this new diaspora was nearby Portugal, where, even from the beginning, life was far from pleasant. Moreover, when the Inquisition officially arrived in that country in the late sixteenth century, the Marranos were once again subject to wholesale persecution and were forced to flee. The logical place to seek refuge was the Republic of the Netherlands, which had recently declared its independence from Spain and was engaged in war with that country. Not only did the young Dutch republic share with the Marranos a hatred of Spain and the Inquisition; it was also the most enlightened country in Europe at the time and allowed some measure of religious toleration. Furthermore, this was the time of the formation of the East India and West India companies and the emergence of the republic as a great commercial power. For this reason both the capital and the commercial abilities of the Marranos were welcome, and because of these they were allowed to settle in Amsterdam, which, with their help, soon became the commercial center of Europe. It should be noted, however, that even in the republic, religious toleration was far from complete. The political strength of the Calvinist clergy was far too great to allow that. Thus, although the first of the Marrano settlers arrived in Amsterdam in 1593, it was not until 1619 that they received official permission to hold public worship, and not until 1657 that they were granted citizenship.[2]

As a direct result of this experience, many of the leaders of the community were highly cultivated men, although their culture was more Iberian and general European than Jewish. Their native languages were Spanish and Portuguese, and they had been educated in Spanish universities. Furthermore, their commercial adventures had brought them into contact with a wide variety of peoples, and this tended further to inculcate a cosmopolitan rather than a ghetto outlook. Nevertheless, their commitment to Judaism was quite sincere.[3] As Spinoza himself noted, their common experience of suffering and persecution served only to reawaken and strengthen their adherence to the Jewish faith and to intensify their resolve to affirm and preserve their Jewish identity as a people chosen by God.

In addition to this religious factor, economic interests also served as a powerful unifying force in the community and as a source of shared values. It has been claimed that the Amsterdam Jewish community was not only a religious group, but also "a virtually autonomous socio-economic entity which negotiated with other nations, cities and Jewish communities."[4] This may be somewhat of an overstatement; nevertheless, the facts remain that the community was a tightly knit economic group, that as a result of the capital and expertise of some of its members the community as a whole was fairly prosperous, and that commercial success was a focal point of community concern.

As one might expect, all this was reflected in a basically conservative political stance. Externally, the Jewish community was a strong supporter of the House of Orange, the Stadtholders who had served as its protectors. Power within the community was concentrated in the hands of the wealthy commercial leaders. The synagogue was the real seat of this power, and its ruling council functioned as a virtual dictatorship, exercising almost absolute control over all aspects of community life. Dissent was prohibited, and the publication of allegedly libelous writings or the expression of disrespect for the presiding authority was punished by excommunication.[5] Such control was rendered necessary not only by the desire of the commercial oligarchy to remain in power, but also by the precarious position of the community within the republic. Having recently escaped from the clutches of the Inquisition and keenly aware of the far from liberal attitude of the Reformed clergy, the community was understandably anxious to keep its own house in order. The danger to the community was exacerbated by the activities of notorious heretics such as Uriel Acosta, who was excommunicated in 1640. In many ways a precursor of Spinoza, Acosta not only aroused the wrath of the leaders of the community by ridiculing their religious practices and materialistic values, but also openly denied the immortality of the soul, an act that was guaranteed to arouse the attention of the Reformed clergy.

Both Baruch de Spinoza's grandfather Abraham Espinoza and his father, Michael Espinoza, were among the leaders of the community. His father in particular was a fairly prosperous, although not wealthy, merchant and held several honorary positions. Thus Spinoza was by birth part of the commercial establishment and was undoubtedly instilled with its values as a child. Apart from the fact that the Espinoza family suffered a number of domestic sorrows, with Michael outliving all three of his wives and all but two of his six children (Baruch and Rebecca, an older half-sister), not much is known about the philosopher's early home life. Nevertheless, we do have considerable information concerning his early education. This was entirely religious in nature, and it took place at the Jewish boys' school in Amsterdam, of which Spinoza's father was a warden, and which all the boys in the community attended as a matter of course. This school consisted of seven grades with a precisely prescribed curriculum. In the early grades the students began to learn prayers in Hebrew and were introduced to the study and translation of the Hebrew Bible. In the higher grades they studied Hebrew grammar and selections from the Talmud and the later codes. At the final stage they were introduced to some of the great medieval Jewish philosophers, such as Maimonides.[6] It was thus within this purely religious context (secular subjects being taught at home) that Spinoza received his first introduction to philosophical thought. He soon repudiated much of what he learned, but some of it exerted a considerable influence on his intellectual development and became integrated into his final philosophical position.

Not even the briefest account of Spinoza's education would be complete without some mention of his teachers. Foremost among them were the rabbis Saul Morteira and Manasseh ben Israel, two classical representatives of Marrano culture. At the time, Morteira was the senior rabbi in Amsterdam. Born in Venice around 1596, he had studied medicine under Montalto, the Marrano court physician of Marie de Medici. Upon Montalto's sudden death in 1616 he had gone to Amsterdam in search of a Jewish cemetery for his teacher. While there he had accepted a call to the rabbinate of the older of the two synagogues in existence at that time. A third synagogue was established two years later, and when all three were amalgamated in 1638, Morteira was appointed senior rabbi, a post in which he served until his death in 1660. Although his orientation was basically medieval and orthodox, he had had some training in philosophy, and as a result of his experience at the Medici court, he obviously knew something of the world. It is reported that when Spinoza was only fifteen years old, the rabbi had marveled at the boy's intelligence and predicted a great future for him. It must therefore have been with a heavy heart that he presided over the court of rabbis that excommunicated Spinoza in 1656.

Manasseh ben Israel, a major figure in seventeenth-century Judaism, was a far more positive influence on Spinoza. Born in Lisbon in 1604, he had been brought as an infant to Amsterdam, where he lived almost all his life. He became rabbi of the second Amsterdam synagogue in 1622, started a Hebrew printing house in 1627, and in 1640, when about to emigrate to Brazil, received an appointment to the senior department of the Amsterdam Jewish school. It was in that capacity that he taught the young Spinoza. In 1655 Manasseh went to England on a special mission to Oliver Cromwell for the purpose of securing the readmission of the Jews to England. He remained there for two years and was thus absent from Amsterdam at the time of Spinoza's excommunication. He died soon after his return in 1657.

Exceedingly well educated in secular subjects, Manasseh ben Israel was the author of numerous, albeit not particularly original, philosophical and theological writings. These are replete with references not only to traditional Jewish writers, but also to figures such as Euripides, Virgil, Plato, Aristotle, Duns Scotus, and Albertus Magnus. He also had many Gentile friends, corresponded with people of the stature of Queen Christina of Sweden and Hugo Grotius, and sat for a portrait by Rembrandt. His great legacy to Spinoza was to introduce him to this rich secular culture. It was in all probability Manasseh ben Israel who first induced him to undertake the study of Latin, non-Jewish philosophy, modern languages, mathematics, and physics.

Contrary to Manasseh ben Israel's intentions, however, Spinoza's study of these secular subjects led him to abandon completely all

Jewish beliefs and practices. Spinoza's secular studies were begun
under the tutelage of Francis Van Den Ende. An ex-Jesuit, bookseller,
diplomat, and classicist, Van Den Ende had opened a school in
Amsterdam in 1652 to instruct the sons of the merchants of the city in
Latin and the sciences. As his background suggests, he was quite an
unorthodox figure and acquired considerable notoriety as a free-
thinker, atheist, and political radical. As a result of this notoriety, he
was eventually forced to close his school. In 1671, while living in
France, he was involved in a revolutionary project for founding a
republic in which all men would be equal. The project backfired, and
its leaders, including Van Den Ende, were imprisoned and later
executed.

Under Van Den Ende, Spinoza not only studied Latin and the
sciences, but was also introduced to the philosophy of Descartes, as
well as to the underground world of free thought and radical politics.
More than that, he and Van Den Ende became intimate friends, and
after the death of Spinoza's father in 1654, Van Den Ende took him
into his own house, asking in return only that Spinoza occasionally
help with the instruction of his pupils. Spinoza is reported to have said
years later that he had wished to marry Van Den Ende's daughter,
Clara. He apparently lost out to a wealthier suitor, however, and so the
only reported romantic episode in Spinoza's career ended in disappointment.[7]

Although he continued to appear occasionally at the synagogue, by
living at the home of Van Den Ende, Spinoza had, in effect, already
removed himself from the Jewish community. This removal reflected
his growing alienation from Jewish beliefs and practices, as well as
from the materialistic, commercial values of the community. For
Spinoza the philosopher, this alienation was a spiritual and intellectual
affair, grounded in his recognition of the inadequacy of the rational
foundations of biblical religion and the rabbinic tradition and the
emptiness of a life devoted to the pursuit of wealth. This process was
certainly accelerated by Spinoza's contact with Van Den Ende and his
circle and by his study of philosophers such as Descartes and possibly
Giordano Bruno, but its roots undoubtedly lie in his childhood experience and his first encounter with Jewish thought.

The "official" break with Judaism was forced on Spinoza by the actions of the leaders of the Jewish community. Both the motives of the rabbis and the actual course of events are the subject of some dispute. Strict doctrinal orthodoxy has never been a central concern in Judaism, and it certainly would not have been in the Amsterdam community. Likewise, as men of the world, the rabbis would not have been upset by the mere fact of Spinoza's association with Gentiles. But because of all they had suffered for the right to practice their faith, they would have been deeply offended by any aspersions cast on the uniqueness and significance of the Jewish people and their way of life. In addition, they would have been concerned by any reports that Spinoza was adversely influencing the youth of the community, or that his heretical views, which were fairly close to those of Acosta, might become public knowledge. Finally, as a recent interpreter has suggested, the rabbis' concern might have been aroused not by Spinoza's theological beliefs, but by his alleged revolutionary activities and associations.[8]

In any event, an investigation was launched. This led first to the charge that Spinoza had been contemptuous of the Mosaic law, and sometime in June 1656 he was called before the council of rabbis to answer this charge. He promptly denied it, only to find new charges brought forth concerning his views on the authority of the Bible and the doctrine that the Jews were the chosen people. This time Spinoza could not deny the charges, and instead he submitted a written defense of his beliefs. Unfortunately, this document has been lost, but it is generally believed that many of its arguments appear in the *Theological-Political Treatise*, which Spinoza published some fourteen years later. Needless to say, this defense did not satisfy the rabbis, and he was excommunicated for a period of thirty days. This temporary action was probably taken in the hope that he might still repent. He did not, and on 27 July 1656 the final and permanent ban was pronounced against him publicly in the synagogue. In response to this news Spinoza is reported to have remarked:

> All the better; they do not force me to do anything that I would not have
> done of my own accord if I did not dread scandal; but, since they want it
> that way, I gladly enter on that path that is opened to me, with the

consolation that my departure will be more innocent than was the
exodus of the early Hebrews from Egypt. Although my subsistence is
no better secured than was theirs, I take away nothing from anybody,
and whatever injustice may be done to me, I can boast that people have
nothing to reproach me with.[9]

This led to his permanent isolation from the Jewish community. One
of his first acts was to replace his Hebrew name, Baruch, with its Latin
equivalent, Benedict, by which he has come to be known in the history
of philosophy. He also left Amsterdam for a time to stay with friends at
Ouwerkerk, a small village just south of the city. He soon returned,
however, and seems to have spent most of the next four years in
Amsterdam. As the above passage suggests, Spinoza was very much
concerned at the time with the question of earning a living. With his
father deceased and the estate willed to his half-sister Rebecca, he was
totally without financial resources. Moreover, with a commercial
career now out of the question, he was forced to learn a trade. The
trade he chose for himself was the highly skilled one of making and
polishing lenses for spectacles, microscopes, and telescopes. He was
engaged in this activity for the rest of his life, and it was his reputation
in this field that first attracted the attention of leading figures such as
Christian Huygens, the mathematician and physicist, and Leibniz, the
philosopher. Unfortunately, the unhealthy nature of the work, which
made the inhalation of glass dust unavoidable, greatly weakened his
already frail constitution and probably contributed significantly to his
early death by consumption.

During this period Spinoza acquired for the first time a circle of
admirers. These men were largely followers of the Cartesian philosophy and members of the Mennonite and Collegiant sects. In contrast
to the rigid orthodoxy of the Reformed church, these sects offered a
simple, ethically oriented, nondogmatic form of Christianity, which
emphasized the role of reason and the necessity for toleration in
religious affairs. Although Spinoza could not share in their Christian
commitment, he must certainly have found much in common with
them. It is believed that he joined in study clubs with members of these
groups, in which they discussed Spinoza's own emerging philosophy,

as well as the dominant Cartesian system. In any event, it was to these men that he eventually communicated his own revolutionary philosophical doctrines, which he did not dare to make public. Within this group were some who figured prominently in Spinoza's subsequent career and what we have of his philosophical correspondence. They include Peter Balling, a merchant who translated Spinoza's Descartes' "Principles of Philosophy" into Dutch in 1664; Jarig Jelles, another merchant, who abandoned his business career and wrote a book showing that Cartesianism was compatible with Christianity; Lodewijk Meyer, a physician and apparent leader of the group, who wrote the preface to the above-mentioned work of Spinoza; Simon Joosten De Vries, still another Amsterdam merchant, who became a disciple of Spinoza and who, just before his own premature death, tried to make the philosopher his heir; and Jan Rieuwertsz, a bookseller in Amsterdam, who published the writings of Spinoza, as well as of many other unorthodox authors.

II The Rijnsburg Years, 1660–1663

Sometime early in 1660, Spinoza left Amsterdam for the village of Rijnsburg, which is located about six miles northwest of Leiden. The move was probably made at the suggestion of his Collegiant friends, as the village contained the main headquarters of the sect. Its purpose was no doubt to give Spinoza time and repose to pursue his own philosophical reflections, something he was not always able to do in the bustling city with its many distractions. This change of environment proved to be highly beneficial; for it was during this period that Spinoza not only produced his first philosophical writing, but actually worked out the main lines of his mature system.

Among these early writings is the Short Treatise on God, Man and His Well-Being. Although written originally in Latin, like all Spinoza's writings, this work has come down to us only in a Dutch translation, and it was not published or generally known until its discovery in the nineteenth century. This rather strange fate for the work of such a major figure as Spinoza is no doubt due to the caution of the philosopher, the loyalty of his friends, and the mistaken assumption of the editors of his posthumous works that it was merely an early, discarded draft of the *Ethics*. Spinoza composed it for the circle of friends with whom he had been discussing philosophical issues, not for general publication, and his caution is clearly reflected in the note on which it ends.

> So, to make an end of all this, it only remains for me still to say to my friends to whom I write this: Be not astonished at these novelties, for it is very well known to you that a thing does not therefore cease to be true because it is not accepted by many. And also, as the character of the age in which we live is not unknown to you, I would beg of you most earnestly to be very careful about the communication of these things to others. I do not want to say that you should absolutely keep them to yourselves, but only that if ever you begin to communicate them to anybody, then let no other aim prompt you except only the happiness of your neighbor, being at the same time clearly assured by him that the reward will not disappoint your labor. Lastly, if, on reading this through, you should meet with some difficulty about what I state as certain, I beseech you that you should not therefore hasten at once to refute it, before you have pondered it long enough and thoughtfully enough, and if you do this I feel sure that you will attain to the enjoyment of the fruits of this tree which you promise yourselves.[10]

This note of caution was well justified; for among the "novelties" contained in the work are the identification of God with nature and hence the repudiation of the Judeo-Christian doctrine of the creation of the world, the affirmation of the necessity of God's activity and thus the denial of any purpose in nature or of any divine providence, and the denial of the freedom of the will. On all these points, which remained central to his mature system, Spinoza had already clearly broken with the more conservative Cartesian position, which attempted to combine an understanding of nature based on the new mathematical physics with a basically theistic world view. Spinoza's friends, it will be recalled, were Cartesians, and this certainly underlies his admonitions to them not to reject his doctrines without careful consideration.

Although Spinoza had arrived at many of the fundamental doctrines of his philosophy, he had not yet determined the manner in which they could best be presented and demonstrated. This led him directly to a consideration of the problem of method, which was a central issue in seventeenth-century thought. Modern thinkers—that is, those who took as their point of departure the new, mathematical science of nature—were united in their repudiation of the essentially syllogistic method of scholastic philosophy and science. They differed profoundly among themselves, however, concerning what was to be put in its place. The issues involved are subtle and go to the very heart of the intellectual life of the period. We cannot hope, therefore, to describe them adequately here.[11] Suffice it to note that the broad line of division was between a basically inductive-empirical approach, as advocated by Francis Bacon and his followers, and a more deductive-mathematical approach, which was most forcefully advocated by the Cartesian school. The actual text of the *Short Treatise* shows us a philosopher torn between these two poles, casting about for an appropriate form in which to present his philosophy. For example, a priori and a posteriori proofs of the existence of God are juxtaposed, and straightforward narrative is combined with dialogue forms. It is only in an appendix, obviously written somewhat later than the main text, that we find a crude anticipation of the geometrical form of Spinoza's masterpiece, the *Ethics*.

The decision to side with the Cartesians in the advocacy of a deductive-geometrical method is reflected in the important, but unfortunately unfinished, essay *Treatise on the Emendation of the Intellect*. This work, which probably dates from 1661, was initially intended as a systematic treatise in which the discussion of method was to serve as an introduction to Spinoza's metaphysics. This discussion, in turn, is prefaced by a quasi-autobiographical prologue, which has often been compared with the opening of Descartes's *Discourse on Method*. In it Spinoza relates the concerns which led him to philosophy in a way that not only brings to mind many classical religious and even mystical writings, but also seems to reflect the spiritual crisis that he must have undergone after his excommunication. The basic theme is the quest for a true and lasting good. The "ordinary objects of desire"—that is, wealth, honor, and sensual enjoyment—are dismissed as transient and empty, and the true good is said to lie in "the knowledge of the union that the mind has with the whole of Nature."[12] The location of the true good in knowledge leads to a consideration of the best method for attaining this knowledge. The essay breaks off in the middle of the discussion of method and thus never gets to the metaphysical issues. Nevertheless, the completed portion delineates a conception of knowledge as a deductive system which naturally suggests the geometrical method as the most suitable means for ordering and demonstrating such knowledge.

Meanwhile, in 1662, Spinoza was visited by one Johannes Casearius, a student of theology at the University of Leiden. He came to Spinoza for instruction in the newest philosophy, and although Spinoza liked the young boy and was willing to help him, he was quite understandably hesitant about initiating him into his own thought. He decided instead to teach him the essentials of scholastic metaphysics as it was then being taught at most of the universities and to introduce him to the basic principles of Cartesian philosophy. Toward this latter end and in line with his recent methodological reflections, he put into geometrical form the second and a portion of the third part of Descartes's *Principles of Philosophy*. While on a visit to Amsterdam, Spinoza apparently showed this work to his friends. They promptly persuaded him to do the same thing with the first part of the *Principles* and to publish the entire work. Spinoza agreed to do so on condition that Meyer edit the work and add a preface explaining that the author was not in complete agreement with Cartesian philosophy. Meyer readily agreed, and it was published in 1663 by Rieuwertsz as *Descartes' "Principles of Philosophy,"* together with an appendix entitled "Metaphysical Thoughts." This was the casual origin of the only work of Spinoza's to appear in his lifetime with his name attached.

By then Spinoza was already hard at work on the *Ethics*, and he continued to work on it intermittently from 1662 until sometime in 1675.[13] As the correspondence with Simon De Vries clearly shows, his Amsterdam friends were in possession of a substantial portion, if not the whole, of the first part by February 1663 and discussed it in their philosophical club.[14] Their discussion led to some questions which De Vries, in his role as spokesman for the group, raised concerning the nature of definitions and their role in Spinoza's demonstrations. These questions were answered by Spinoza in two letters of March 1663, which not only show the stage of his thought at the time, but are important documents for the interpretation of his philosophy.[15]

Shortly thereafter Spinoza decided to leave Rijnsburg, probably for much the same reason that had brought him there in the first place— namely, the desire for peace and quiet. This move was necessitated by the constant stream of visitors who came to see him from Leiden. The most significant of these was Henry Oldenburg, whose interest in Spinoza is not only a good indication of the force of Spinoza's personality, but also of the reputation he had already achieved at that early date.

Oldenburg, a native German who was some twelve years older than Spinoza, was one of the more interesting figures in European intellectual circles of the time. Far from being a creative philosopher or scientist in his own right, he was nevertheless in constant touch with those who were. He specialized in the dissemination of information concerning the research activities of others and thus functioned as a vital link between scientists working in various parts of Europe. While on a diplomatic mission to London in 1660, he helped to found the Royal Society and served as its first secretary. During a visit to Leiden in 1661, Oldenburg was evidently told about the young philosopher and lens-maker, and, eager as usual to make the acquaintance of anybody who was in any way remarkable, he decided to visit Spinoza. This visit had a profound effect on Oldenburg and led to an important correspondence between the two men, which deals with both scientific and philosophical subjects. In the scientific realm, Oldenburg told Spinoza about the latest developments at the Royal Society, asked for news in return, and served as intermediary between Spinoza and the famous chemist Robert Boyle, founder of the "Corpuscular Philosophy." This led to a series of letters in which Oldenburg reported the results of Boyle's experiments on nitre (potassium nitrate) and other matters, while Spinoza responded with his own criticisms and reflections regarding Boyle's work. Oldenburg forwarded Spinoza's remarks to Boyle, but the exchange seems to have had little effect on either thinker. Boyle stuck to his empirical-inductive method, and Spinoza continued to advocate a more deductive model of scientific explanation. Moreover, the philosophical side of the correspondence was even less fruitful. In spite of his expressions of interest and constant requests for further explanation, which Spinoza readily provided, Oldenburg was never able to grasp the radical implications of Spinoza's thought. Consequently, when the real nature of Spinoza's unorthodox religious views became known to him after the publication of the *Theological-Political Treatise*, Oldenburg's interest cooled considerably and he ceased encouraging him to publish the *Ethics*.

III The Years at Voorburg, 1663–1670

Spinoza's next place of residence was Voorburg, a small village about two miles from The Hague. Its size provided him with the desired peace and quiet, and its proximity to The Hague, then the seat of the States-General and the capital of the United Provinces, placed him near powerful protectors who could make it possible for him to pursue and publish his philosophy without fear of harassment. Such protectors were to be found in the De Witt brothers, especially the younger and more powerful John De Witt, with whom Spinoza shared both a deep concern for the republican form of government and a strong interest in mathematics and physical science.

John De Witt was not only the leader of the republican cause against the royalist-federalist supporters of the House of Orange, but, as the Grand Pensionary of Holland, had also since 1653 been the effective ruler of the United Provinces. Moreover, at the time when Spinoza first settled at Voorburg, De Witt was at the height of his power. Having successfully extricated his country from a disastrous war with England that had begun before his ascendancy, he was not yet involved in the second English war, which started in 1665. In addition, by promising to withhold support from the Stuarts in England, he had gained, to some extent at least, the support of the House of Orange. Beyond that, he had managed to put the financial affairs of the country in order and to secure religious toleration and freedom of the press. But despite this, he had never achieved great popularity. The masses had always been supporters of the House of Orange and the monarchist cause; and De Witt's defense of religious toleration and of the supremacy of the civil power had earned him the bitter enmity of the Reformed clergy, who desired to establish a state church.

Although he was an ardent supporter of De Witt and the republican cause, Spinoza's central concern was philosophy rather than politics. After all, he had moved to Voorburg so as to be better able to continue his work on the *Ethics*; and from a letter to a friend, John Bouwmeester, dated June 1665, we learn that the work had advanced as far as what in the final version became the fourth part.[16] In September of the same year, however, we find Oldenburg chiding Spinoza: "I see that you are not so much *philosophizing* as, if one may say so, *theologizing*, since your thoughts are turning to angels, prophecy and miracles."[17] This suggests that in the interim Spinoza had informed Oldenburg that he had set aside the *Ethics* and was already hard at work on what was to become the *Theological-Political Treatise*. Spinoza confirms this in his response, in which he admits that he is currently writing a treatise on the interpretation of Scripture and lists the following reasons:

> 1. The Prejudices of the Theologians; for I know that these are among the chief obstacles which prevent men from directing their mind to philosophy; and therefore I do all I can to expose them, and to remove them from the minds of the more prudent. 2. The opinion which the common people have of me, who do not cease to accuse me falsely of atheism; I am also obliged to avert this accusation as far as it is possible to do so. 3. The freedom of philosophizing, and of saying what we think; this I desire to vindicate in every way, for here it is always suppressed through the excessive authority and impudence of the preachers.[18]

Behind the reasons given to Oldenburg is clearly a sense of urgency created by the political situation. In 1665 the republic was in a state of

crisis. The immediate cause of the crisis was the renewal of the war
with England and Sweden, as a result of which the Dutch forces were
so hard pressed that they had to employ French troops, an action that
served only to increase the popular discontent. In addition, the situation was greatly exacerbated by the actions of the Reformed clergy.
Still bent on Calvinizing everyone and resenting the liberalism of De
Witt's party, with its strong advocacy of religious liberty, the clergy
used the military situation as an occasion for mobilizing public opinion behind the young Prince of Orange and against De Witt. They did
this by citing the progress of the war as evidence of divine judgment on
the country because of the godlessness of its rulers. Furthermore, the
transfer of power to the House of Orange was claimed to be necessary
not only for the military, but also for the spiritual well-being of the
country.[19]

    Similar outcries had been raised earlier against that great champion
of liberalism and republicanism John Van Oldenbarnevelt, who, at the
instigation of the clergy, had been executed for treason in 1619. Thus,
De Witt and his supporters were well aware of the potential danger of
the situation, as well as of the urgent need for people willing to speak
out on the issue and to argue for the principles of republican government and religious liberty. Spinoza likewise saw this need; and it is
perhaps the strongest proof of the fact that he was not an "ivory tower"
thinker divorced from the cares of the world that he set aside his
lifework in order to do something about it. As a philosopher, however,
his concern was not simply to produce another pamphlet in favor of
freedom of thought, but rather to get to the very heart of the matter and
expose the foundations of the prejudices of the theologians that stand
in the way of such freedom. The basis for the clerical position was the
Bible, especially the belief that it was a divinely inspired, infallible
book which, as such, functions as the supreme authority on all matters
with which it deals. It was through an appeal to the Bible, thus
construed, that the clergy justified their repressive stance; and thus, it
was only by exposing the illegitimacy of this appeal that their position
could be undermined and freedom of thought defended.

    With this in mind, Spinoza returned to the study of Scripture and to the arguments against its alleged infallibility that he had raised some years earlier in defense of his beliefs before the rabbinic tribunal. The result is what is generally regarded as the first modern work on the Bible, the initial attempt at "higher criticism." Confining himself mainly to the Old Testament, with which he was obviously most familiar, he treats it in a thoroughly naturalistic and historical fashion, demonstrating that the various books date from different times and reflect widely different conditions and points of view. He combines this with a thoroughgoing critique of prophecy and miracles which shows that the authors of the biblical books were not men of extraordinary intellectual gifts. We are thus led to the conclusion that, aside from the inculcation of true virtue, which is the only divine aspect of the Bible, it contains no consistent message or set of doctrines. But if it sets forth no uniform teaching or any special speculative insights, it can hardly serve as an authority in these matters. Having undermined the authority of the Bible, Spinoza then proceeds in the final chapters to offer his positive arguments for freedom of thought and expression, as well as his negative arguments opposing any interference by a church in the affairs of the state.

The seriousness with which Spinoza approached this task is reflected in the time it took him to complete it: some five years, most of which were devoted to research into the text of the Bible, Jewish history, and the Hebrew language. Unfortunately, when the book finally appeared in 1670, the political situation had deteriorated to such an extent that there was little hope of its achieving its main purpose of providing an effective support for the policies of the De Witts and absolutely no hope of its achieving its subsidiary purpose of defending Spinoza against charges of atheism. Spinoza, keenly aware of the dangers involved and having given up any hopes of justifying himself in the eyes of the public, decided to publish the *Theological-Political Treatise* anonymously and under a false imprint (the place of publication being listed as Hamburg rather than Amsterdam). This stratagem proved to be completely ineffective, however, since his authorship was soon common knowledge, and both he and the book became the object of frequent and violent attack. Typical of these

attacks is a description of the work as a wicked instrument "forged in
hell by a renegade Jew and the devil, and issued with the knowledge of
Mr. De Witt."[20] The attacks were further intensified as a result of the
rapid spread of the work. By the end of 1670, there had already been
four reprints of the first edition in Germany and the United Provinces,
with many others under false titles. This naturally led to efforts to
suppress it, all of which were frustrated by De Witt. Thus, the project
that began as an effort to defend De Witt and his cause ended up
requiring defense in its own right. Spinoza was clearly disillusioned
by the whole affair and came to the realization that he could never
publish the *Ethics* during his lifetime.

IV The Years at The Hague, 1670–1677

In 1670 Spinoza moved once again, this time to The Hague, where he
remained until his death in 1677. Once again, he was probably
motivated by the desire for peace, and once again this desire was
frustrated, for these years proved to be the most eventful of his life,
especially in terms of his involvement in the affairs of the country.

Upon settling in The Hague, Spinoza returned to work on the
Ethics. The long period of neglect had brought with it the need and
desire for substantial revisions, and he worked on these revisions until
1675, when the book attained its final form. In the meantime, he was
either actually engaged in or contemplating a number of projects.
These included a Dutch translation of the Hebrew Bible, a scientific
treatise on the Hebrew language, a treatise on political science, a work
on natural science to supplement the very sketchy discussion in the
Ethics, and a new exposition of the principles of algebra. Of these
projects, the only visible fruits found at his death were the unfinished
texts of the *Hebrew Grammar* and the *Political Treatise*, and two
essays, "On the Rainbow" and "On the Calculation of Chances." The
first two works were published together with the similarly unfinished
Treatise on the Emendation of the Intellect, the complete text of the
Ethics, and a selection from Spinoza's correspondence in the *Opera
Posthuma*, which was edited by a number of his friends and appeared

in the very year of his death. As an indication of how Spinoza was generally viewed at the time, it is noteworthy that it was felt necessary to remove all names and other means of identification from the correspondence and to omit the names of the editors and publisher, as well as the place of publication. Not even the full name of the author was mentioned, and only Spinoza's inititials (B. D. S.) appeared on the title page.

Many of these projects were not completed simply because of Spinoza's ill health and early death. But political developments during the last years of Spinoza's life must certainly have been a contributing factor, especially in the case of the *Political Treatise*, which we shall consider in some detail later. The first and most shattering of these developments was the brutal murder of the De Witt brothers by a frenzied mob. This act was the culmination of a long series of events and of continued rabble-rousing by the clergy, but its immediate cause was the joint declaration of war against the republic by England and France in 1672. The resulting military crisis led to a popular outcry for the Prince of Orange to take over the country and save it from its enemies, as his father had done previously. Moreover, this was combined with a demand for vengeance against De Witt, who was treated as a scapegoat in the whole affair. This demand was satisfied on 20 August 1672, when a mob broke into the prison at The Hague, where John, who had resigned his post as Grand Pensionary of Holland on 4 August, was visiting his brother Cornelius, who had been arrested on a charge conspiring against the prince. Finding the brothers together, the mob murdered both of them, practically tearing them to pieces in the process and then hanging their mangled remains from a post.

When he heard of what had happened, Spinoza, for once in his life at least, lost all his philosophical calm. He is said to have burst into tears and then written a placard on which he expressed his utter abhorrence of "the very lowest of barbarians" who had committed this heinous murder. His intent was to place this placard near the scene of the crime, but fortunately his landlord, Van Der Spyck, realized the danger of the situation and locked Spinoza in the house.[21] Otherwise, it is quite probable that Spinoza would have suffered a fate similar to that of the De Witts.

The next major episode in Spinoza's life took place the following year and was likewise occasioned by the war with France. The French army, at the time under the leadership of Prince Condé, was occupying Utrecht. Condé was a man of liberal views, with an interest in science and philosophy. One of his officers, a Colonel Stoupe, who was a former Calvinist minister serving a Catholic king in the invasion of a Calvinist country, and who later wrote a pamphlet attacking Spinoza, informed the prince that the philosopher lived nearby and suggested that he might invite him to visit. Condé agreed and, through Stoupe, sent an invitation to Spinoza to visit him at Utrecht.

Spinoza seems to have regarded this invitation as a possible opening for peace negotiations and, being anxious to do what he could for the cause of peace, decided, after getting permission from the Dutch authorities, to accept. Thus, armed with the necessary safe-conducts, Spinoza traveled across enemy lines to Utrecht in May 1673. In the meantime, however, his host had been unexpectedly called away. Spinoza was invited to remain and await his return, which he did, and during this period he was treated well. While waiting, he was offered a pension on condition that he dedicate a book to Louis XIV. Spinoza respectfully declined, and when, after several weeks of pleasant conversation, the word came that Condé could not return, he decided to leave.

Upon learning of Spinoza's visit to the enemy, the people of The Hague immediately jumped to the conclusion that he was a spy or a traitor. They threatened to break into his house and murder him, just as they had previously murdered the De Witts. Spinoza came out of his house, however, and, confronting the mob directly, proclaimed his innocence and concern for the republic. Such frank and fearless conduct in this moment of danger must have allayed the suspicions of the mob, for they dispersed and left him alone.[22]

That same year Spinoza received another even greater honor, which he found considerably more difficult to reject than the offer of a pension from Louis XIV. In February 1673, the Elector Palatine, Karl

Ludwig, brother of the Princess Elizabeth who had befriended and corresponded with Descartes, offered him the professorship of philosophy at the University of Heidelberg. Karl Ludwig had spent many years in Holland and was a strong advocate of the republican philosophy of religious and economic freedom. The existence of a distinguished faculty, which included Samuel Puffendorf, the great authority on international law, and a Jewish rector, bears ample witness to the fact that these principles were in force at the University of Heidelberg, which Karl Ludwig had founded in 1652.[23] Moreover, the offer included a promise of absolute freedom of thought and expression, as long as he did not disturb the public religion. Despite his years of solitude and lack of experience with academic life, Spinoza was greatly tempted by this offer and the attendant opportunity to abandon his trade and devote more time to philosophy. Thus, he considered it for some six weeks before finally declining it. His reasons for this decision, as expressed in a polite letter of refusal to Professor Johann Ludwig Fabritius, the Heidelberg philosopher who had tendered the offer on behalf of Karl Ludwig, were a hesitancy to embark on a teaching career at that stage of his life and a characteristic refusal to compromise in any way the independence for which he had paid so dearly. Spinoza's affirmation of this latter point is worth citing in full:

> I think that I do not know within what limits that freedom of philosophizing ought to be confined in order to avoid the appearance of wishing to disturb the publicly established religion. For schisms arise not so much from an ardent love of religion as from men's various dispositions, or the love of contradiction, through which they are wont to distort and to condemn all things, even those that have been correctly stated. I have already experienced these things while leading a private and solitary life, much more then are they to be feared after I shall have risen to this degree of dignity.[24]

Although he decided to remain in the mode of life to which he had grown accustomed, Spinoza did increase his circle of acquaints. Indeed, the last years of Spinoza's life are among the most significant in this regard; for it was during this period that he first met and began a correspondence with the promising young scientist Ehrenfried Walter von Tschirnhaus and, through him, became acquainted with the great philosopher Gottfried Wilhelm von Leibniz, who at the time was in the process of developing his own philosophical system.

Tschirnhaus was a German count who had studied at the University of Leiden from 1668 to 1675, but he had served for part of this time as a volunteer with the Dutch army in the war with France. In 1674 he made the acquaintance of Spinoza's physician, Georg Hermann Schuller, who told him about Spinoza. Having already studied the works of Descartes, Tschirnhaus became immediately interested in Spinoza, began a correspondence, and visited him that same year. This correspondence is of considerable philosophical importance, since Tschirnhaus succeeded in pointing out many of the basic difficulties in Spinoza's system and elicited in return some significant responses from Spinoza. The following year Tschirnhaus visited London, where he met Oldenburg and Boyle, and the contact with Oldenburg apparently led directly to the resumption of the latter's long-interrupted correspondence with Spinoza. After leaving London, Tschirnhaus went to Paris, where he met the young Leibniz and told him of Spinoza's work, specifically about some of the doctrines in the *Ethics* which he had read in a manuscript copy. For his own part, Tschirnhaus later proved to be a man of some accomplishments in the sciences. He is credited with having discovered the tangential movement of circles and with the invention of porcelain. His main philosophical work, *Medicina Mentis* of 1683, was essentially a development of some of the views expressed by Spinoza in the *Treatise on the Emendation of the Intellect*.

In the meantime, hearing Tschirnhaus's reports, Leibniz became immensely interested in Spinoza's work. He had already read *Descartes' "Principles of Philosophy"* and in 1671 had sent Spinoza a copy of his "Notice on the Progress of Optics." In return, Spinoza had sent him a copy of the *Theological-Political Treatise*. Leibniz had also already read this work and had, in fact, described it as "an unbearably free-thinking book." Apparently, however, he had not known that Spinoza was its author. Now, after hearing about the *Ethics*, he was desirous of reading it for himself and requested Tschirnhaus's assistance in procuring a copy for him. Tschirnhaus wished to oblige, but could not show Leibniz his own copy without Spinoza's permission. When he wrote to Schuller in order to obtain this permission from Spinoza, however, it was denied. Spinoza, who as a result of his experiences had become increasingly cautious, simply did not trust Leibniz and suspected (quite correctly) that Leibniz, a German, was in Paris on a mission for the reunion of Protestants and Catholics, an effort which, if successful, would inevitably lead to the suppression of all liberal tendencies. Nevertheless, Leibniz did not give up. He came to The Hague in the fall of 1676 and managed to gain Spinoza's confidence. While there, he not only acquired a firsthand knowledge of the *Ethics*, but also engaged in frequent conversations with the dying philosopher. Because of the importance of Leibniz's own philosophy and its kinship in many ways with the thought of Spinoza, the interchange between these two men must be ranked as one of the major intellectual events of the seventeenth century.

Spinoza was by then declining rapidly. Nevertheless, he continued to be active and to go about his business until the end. This end came suddenly and peacefully at three o'clock on 21 February in the presence of Schuller. Numerous reports of deathbed confessions, frantic recantations, and requests for divine forgiveness began circulating immediately after the death was announced, and some seem to have gained considerable credence. It is clear from all the evidence, however, that Spinoza died as he had lived—that is, in accordance with his own description of a free man as one who "thinks of nothing less than of death, and whose wisdom is a meditation on life, not on death" (IVP67).

CHAPTER 2

Spinoza's Philosophy in Its Historical Context

S pinoza's *Ethica Ordine Geometrico Demonstrata (Ethics Demonstrated in a Geometrical Manner)* is an extremely difficult and forbidding book. Both its obscure, scholastic terminology and its stark, geometrical form provide formidable barriers to even the philosophically trained reader and undoubtedly help to explain the great diversity of ways in which the work has been interpreted. Thus, rather than plunging immediately into the argument of the work, with its strange format of definitions, axioms, and propositions and its bewildering talk of substance, attributes, and modes, it would seem far preferable to consider briefly the historical context in which Spinoza wrote and, in light of this, to introduce the central themes of his philosophy. This will be the task of the present chapter, and it is hoped that it will help to guide the reader through the more systematic and technical investigation that follows.

I The Roots of Spinoza's Philosophy in the New Science and Its Conception of Nature, and the Relevance of Descartes

We have already seen that, as a youth, Spinoza studied and was profoundly influenced by medieval Jewish philosophy. It is also generally assumed that, in the course of his development, he came under the influence of Renaissance philosophers of nature such as Bernardino Telesio and Giordano Bruno. A full-scale intellectual biography of Spinoza would thus have to deal with these and a wide variety of other influences—for example, the cabala—to which a Jewish intellectual living in seventeenth-century Holland would inevitably be exposed.[1] Nevertheless, for understanding the distinctive features of his metaphysical vision, the single most important factor is the development of the mathematical science of nature, which was occurring at a rapid rate during Spinoza's lifetime. Unlike Descartes, Spinoza was not a creative scientist, but, as his relationships with men like Huygens and Oldenburg clearly reveal, he was a keen student of contemporary developments in a number of sciences and of the fundamental problems of scientific methodology. This new science certainly inspired Spinoza's naturalistic approach to ethical questions, but, beyond this, it provided him with the basis, although not all the details, of his conception of nature. It is in the knowledge of the union between the mind and nature, so conceived, that Spinoza placed the highest good for man in his *Treatise on the Emendation of the Intellect*, and it is this same infinite and law-abiding nature that he identified with God in the *Ethics*.

The modern scientific conception of nature, like most philosophical conceptions, can best be understood by contrasting it with what it replaced.[2] This was the medieval view, in both its Jewish and Christian expressions, which was itself based on a precarious synthesis of Aristotelian physics and cosmology with biblical doctrines of God, man, and creation. According to this view, the world of nature was a cosmos in the original sense, that is, a finite ordered whole, in which everything had its determinate place and particular function. The earth stood at the center of this cosmos, and the allegedly incorruptible heavenly bodies, including the sun, revolved around it. The world was created by God, largely for the benefit of man, who was "made in His own image." The doctrine of the creation of the world ran counter to the Aristotelian view of its eternity, and this gave rise to some of the most difficult problems for thinkers like Maimonides and Aquinas who endeavored to synthesize Aristotle and Scripture. Nevertheless, apart from affirming the divine creation of the world, they basically followed Aristotle in conceiving it as composed of distinct types of substances, falling into fixed genera, or "natural kinds," each obeying its own set of laws.

The laws in accordance with which each substance behaved were dependent on its particular function, and this function, according to medieval thinkers, was assigned to it as part of God's providential scheme, which was directed essentially toward the salvation of man. Such a world was perfectly intelligible in principle, although not in fact, for naturally man was not privy to all the details of God's great plan. Nevertheless, the understanding available to man, which, thanks to Aristotle, was thought to be fairly extensive, was primarily in terms of the function or purpose of the substance under exmination. This function or purpose was characterized by Aristotle as the "final cause" in his famous analysis of the four causes, and such causes played a very significant role in scientific explanation. In more modern terms, the prime manner of explaining an event was teleological—that is, in terms of the end achieved. Consequently, the basic scientific question was "Why did X do something?" and the first place one looked for an answer was the peculiar nature or function of X. This would provide the final cause of the action in question. It was only if the action did not accord with X's function—that is, was "accidental" rather than "natural"—that one looked for an external cause. Thus, in accordance with this style of explanation, one might well think that one has understood why the rain falls when it is seen that this provides water for the crops, which, in turn, are necessary to support human life. This, of course, is a gross oversimplification of the way in which medieval thinkers viewed the problem of explanation. Not all scientific explanation was teleological and not all teleological explanation was, or need be, as crude as the example given above. Nevertheless, this characterizes the basic way in which the medieval mind, even the philosophic mind, viewed the world, and the world, so viewed, was certainly a place in which man felt at home.

The conception of nature that finally emerged in the seventeenth century, after a long process of development, and that we associate primarily with such names as Kepler, Galileo, Descartes, and Newton differs in almost every respect from its predecessor. Whereas the older universe was finite, teleologically and hierarchically ordered, with each kind of substance obeying its own unique set of laws, the modern universe is infinite, mechanically ordered, and governed by a single set of universal laws that apply to all phenomena, celestial and terrestrial alike. The key to this new conception is the role given to mathematics in scientific explanation. In the famous and oft-quoted words of Galileo:

> Philosophy is written in that great book which ever lies before our eyes—I mean the universe—but we cannot understand it if we do not first learn the language and grasp the symbols, in which it is written. This book is written in the mathematical language, and the symbols are triangles, circles, and other geometrical figures, without whose help it is impossible to comprehend a single word of it; without which one wanders in vain through a dark labyrinth.[3]

The universe of Galileo and the new science is thus fundamentally geometrical in character. Geometrical reasoning had already led Copernicus to abandon the geocentric hypothesis and Kepler to conclude that the orbits of the planets about the sun are elliptical rather than circular (the supposedly perfect motion). Similarly, the telescope had revealed spots on the sun and thus corruption in the allegedly incorruptible heavenly bodies. The privileged status of these heavenly bodies, as well as the central position of the earth, had therefore to be abandoned, and the closed cosmos of medieval thought gave way to the infinite, geometrically ordered universe of modern science. The denizens of this universe are not unique substances with their natural places, functions, and purposes, but rather, phenomena completely describable in mathematical terms. Moreover, it was the assumption that all salient relations between phenomena could be expressed in such terms that underlay the quest for universal laws of nature.

It is also important to realize, however, that for Galileo and the other great founders of modern physical science, the mathematical structure of reality was not merely a convenient hypothesis that proved useful for scientific description and prediction. This, after all, was what the dispute between Galileo and the Church was all about. Rather, this mathematical structure was viewed as the truth about the nature of things. The "real world" was quite simply the geometrical, quantitative world of the mathematical physicist. It consisted solely of bodies moving in space and interacting with each other according to precise, mathematically expressible laws. Not only was teleological explanation thus rejected as "unscientific," but final causes were themselves banished from nature and placed in either the inscrutable will of God or the imagination of man.

As a direct result of this changed perspective, the whole world of ordinary human experience, with its colors, sounds, and odors and its striking, inexplicable happenings, was at best granted a kind of secondary status and at worst relegated to the realm of illusion. This "scientific" outlook is perfectly exemplified in the widely held distinction between primary and secondary qualities. The primary qualities of a body, on this view, were such features as shape, size, mass, and motion, all of which can be measured and dealt with quantitatively. It was of these qualities that the body was really composed. Secondary qualities, on the other hand, which include the above-mentioned colors, sounds, and odors, were regarded as subjective, or in the mind. Galileo himself characterized these secondary qualities as "mere names" having no place in nature; for him, as for many others, perceptual experience of these qualities was understood to be the result of an interaction between the real physical object, composed solely of primary qualities, and the sentient organism.[4]

This changed conception of nature obviously brought with it a whole host of philosophical problems. What, for instance, is the relationship between this conception and the biblical view of God, man, and nature? Does the truth of science imply the falsity of divine revelation? Also, what is the place of human beings in nature so conceived? Are they completely subject to its mathematical laws, and, if so, what becomes of the freedom of the will, by virtue of which one earns either salvation or damnation? Finally, there is the problem of knowledge, which here arises in a distinctively modern form: how can the human mind, whose only access to reality is through sense experience, ever acquire knowledge of this nonsensible, abstract world of mathematical physics? The very truth that physicists claim about the world seems to entail a hopeless skepticism, since it renders the "real" world inaccessible to the human mind. Since Galileo himself was a physicist, not a philosopher, he did not attempt to deal in a systematic fashion with these crucial issues. This task was left to Spinoza's great predecessor Descartes, who for that very reason is generally regarded as the father of modern philosophy.

Descartes came to philosophy as both a scientist and a Christian, or, at least, a professed Christian. As a scientist, he was motivated by the dream of a "universal mathematics," an all-embracing science of order and proportion through which all fields of knowledge could be integrated into a single whole and mastered by a single method, that of mathematics. The greatest fruit of this endeavor toward a unified science was analytic geometry, in which Descartes showed that one and the same set of relations or proportions could be expressed either algebraically or geometrically. The attempt to apply this method to nature resulted in a purely geometrical physics, which proved to be not nearly as successful. As a professed Christian, Descartes conceived of human beings as possessing a free will and an immortal soul. He also tended to resolve any conflicts between faith and science or philosophy by assigning them to different realms and claiming that the sacred truths of the former are beyond the capacity of human reason, or the "natural light."

As a philosopher, Descartes developed the split between mind and nature that was implicit in Galileo into a full-fledged metaphysical dualism. The key to this dualism is the concept of substance, a concept that likewise plays a crucial role in Spinoza's philosophy. Substance is defined by Descartes in the *Principles of Philosophy* as "that which so exists that it needs no other thing in order to exist."[5] Strictly speaking, only God fits the definition: for only God is totally independent, and all created things depend on God for their creation and conservation. Nevertheless, since the realm of nature, or matter, and the realm of thought are independent of one another, in the sense that each can be conceived without the other, they are classified as created substances. The former is called corporeal, material, or extended substance (*res extensa*); the latter, mind, or thinking substance (*res cogitans*). Each kind of substance has one principal property, or attribute, that constitutes its essence. The essence of the former is extension in length, breadth, and depth. Thus, all its properties can be expressed geometrically, whence Descartes arrived at his idea of a geometrical physics. The essence of the latter is simply thought, and all other specifically mental functions—for example, imagining, willing, and feeling—are merely diverse forms of thinking. The perfect symmetry of this scheme is vitiated somewhat, however, by the fact that, whereas there is only one extended substance of which all physical bodies are merely modifications, each individual mind is conscious of itself and of its independence from all things save God (which is the basis for the belief in its immortality) and thus constitutes a distinct thinking substance.

Having split the worlds of mind and matter (which includes the human body) in so uncompromising a fashion, Descartes was obviously faced with the problem of explaining their relationship. This problem is itself complex, however, and arises in at least two distinct forms. The first, the epistemological form, requires an explanation of how a thinking substance, which has immediate access only to its own thoughts, can ever attain to a certain knowledge of matter, or extended substance. This is equivalent to asking how the science of physics is possible. The second, the metaphysical form, concerns the interaction between two distinct substances. How can events in nature affect the mind, and how can thoughts and free volitions have any effect in the corporeal world—for example, how can my decision to raise my arm lead to the physical act? This issue has come to be known as the "mind-body problem."

Descartes's solution to the epistemological problem, as presented in his *Meditations on First Philosophy*, is certainly the best-known aspect of his philosophy. Its most characteristic and controversial feature is the attempt to overcome skepticism from within by doubting everything until one arrives at something that simply cannot be doubted. This indubitable truth would then be able to stand firm against any skeptical attack and serve as the "Archimedean point" on which Descartes can confidently proceed to erect the edifice of scientific knowledge. The first beliefs to be sacrificed to this procedure of methodical doubt are those based on sensory evidence, including the belief in the existence of one's own body and the external physical world. After all, it is at least conceivable that all life is a consistent dream, and, in any event, the senses themselves do not furnish any sure criterion for distinguishing between waking and dreaming. But far-reaching as it already is, this doubt does not stop here. By means of the ingenious hypothesis of a deceiving God, Descartes finds it possible even to cast doubts (albeit feeble ones) on the basic truths of mathematics. However, just when it appears that the victory of skepticism is going to be complete, Descartes arrives at his indubitable truth. This concerns one's own existence while thinking. Even if one is being systematically deceived, one must still exist in order to be deceived. Thus: "I am, I exist is necessarily true each time that I pronounce it, or that I mentally conceive it."[6]

This does not take us very far, however, and in order to progress to other truths, which have been temporarily abandoned by the process of methodical doubt, we must see just what it is about this truth that exempts it from doubt. Descartes's more or less technical answer is that we "clearly and distinctly perceive" it to be true. Now to clearly and distinctly perceive a proposition to be true really amounts in the end, for Descartes, to either grasping it immediately through intuition as self-evident or seeing that it can be deduced from self-evident truths (intuition and deduction thus being the two sources of rational knowledge). The crucial problem of Cartesian epistemology is, then, whether everything we perceive in this manner can be safely regarded as true. Descartes tries to answer this affirmatively by demonstrating that God exists, and that he is no deceiver, which suffices to remove all grounds for doubting such propositions. God, in other words, functions for Descartes as the guarantor of our clear and distinct perceptions. This does not guarantee the truth of all our propositions or beliefs, of course, but it does guarantee those that deal with our geometrical conceptions of extension. We can, therefore, be sure that extended substance (the external world) exists and has the characteristics assigned to it by the science of physics.

Descartes's attempt at a solution to the mind-body problem is much less systematic. It basically amounts to an admission that the problem is insoluble, at least in terms of the appeal to clear and distinct perceptions, which is the standard of scientific evidence. Since it was this appeal that led Descartes to the separation of mind and body in the first place, it can hardly enable him to explain the union between the two radically disparate substances. Instead, Descartes simply appeals to experience, a procedure he likewise follows in his defense of the freedom of the will: "Everyone feels that he is a single person with both body and thought so related by nature that the thought can move the body and feel the things which happen to it."[7] The relationship must, therefore, be accepted as a brute fact, even though it cannot be explained adequately. Yet Descartes did not abandon all efforts to explain how mind and body interact, and he even tried to provide a physiological account of their interaction. This account is based on the hypothesis, later ridiculed by Spinoza, that the pineal gland in the brain is the "seat of the soul," and that it serves as the point of union between the immaterial thoughts, passions, and volitions of the mind and the "animal spirits," which are the small particles of matter by which messages are allegedly relayed from the brain to the rest of the body, and vice versa.[8] Through this rather fanciful explanation, Descartes evidently hoped to unite his completely mechanistic physiology (the conception of the human body as a machine) with his conception of an immaterial, independent, and immortal soul, or thinking substance.

Such was the first great attempt to construct a philosophy based on the mathematical conception of nature and to resolve the problems concerning man and his place in nature that inevitably arose as a result of this conception. It can be seen as an effort, to use Spinoza's significant phrase, to understand "the union that the mind has with the whole of nature," where "nature" is construed as the infinite, extended realm of mathematical physics. As such, it clearly failed, however, and the dream of a unified science, which would include a science of man in one universally applicable system of explanation, which was already at least suggested by Descartes's idea of a universal mathematics, remained unfulfilled. In part because of Descartes's basically Christian starting point and in part because of some of his metaphysical assumptions—for example, the concept of substance—Cartesian man was never really integrated into nature. With his free will and immaterial and immortal soul, he remained an alien being, whose very knowledge of nature could be assured only by a question-begging appeal to divine veracity, and whose actual interaction with it was an inexplicable fact and a manifest exception to universal lawfulness.

II Some Central Themes in Spinoza's Philosophy

In his editorial preface to Descartes' "Principles of Philosophy," Meyer, speaking for Spinoza, notes several areas in which his philosophy differs from that of Descartes. These include the conception of the will and its alleged freedom and the notion that the human mind constitutes a distinct thinking substance. Special attention is given, however, to the Cartesian notion "that this or that surpasses the human understanding." As Meyer points out in reference to Spinoza: "He judges that all those things, and even many others more sublime and subtle, can not only be conceived clearly and distinctly, but also explained very satisfactorily—provided only that the human Intellect is guided in the search for truth and knowledge of things along a different path from that which Descartes opened up and made smooth."9 Thus, in opposition to the Cartesian appeal to the limits of knowledge, an appeal that was undoubtedly motivated by theological considerations, Spinoza affirms an absolute rationalism. Given the proper method, reality as a whole is intelligible to the human mind, and Spinoza claims in his Ethics to have done nothing less than demonstrate this truth.10

Above and beyond this, however, the greatest single difference between the philosophies of Descartes and Spinoza and the root of most of the others lies in the fact that the main thrust of Spinoza's philosophy is ethical. He is before everything else a moralist, concerned, like the great Greek thinkers, with determining the true good for humanity. This is not at all to suggest that Descartes was unconcerned with ethical issues, only to point out that they were never central to his thought as they were to Spinoza's. Thus, although questions about the nature and limits of human knowledge, the nature and existence of God, and the relationship between the human mind and body are given considerable attention in the *Ethics* and will hence occupy us to a large extent in our analysis of Spinoza's philosophy, it must never be forgotten that Spinoza's treatment of these issues is based on, and often colored by, his ethical concerns.

Speaking in general terms, Spinoza's moral philosophy can be placed within the intellectualistic tradition, which goes back to the classical Greek moralists, Socrates, Plato, and Aristotle. Common to all these thinkers is the identification of virtue, or in the case of Aristotle the highest virtue, with knowledge. Otherwise expressed, the highest virtues are intellectual, whereas the so-called "moral virtues," or virtues of character, such as self-control, courage, and benevolence, are seen as either effects of intellectual virtue or preparatory stages necessary for its realization. Spinoza accepts this doctrine in an unqualified form and contends that it is only through knowledge that one can overcome the bondage to the passions that constitutes the essence of human misery. He is therefore willing to affirm the hard doctrine that only the wise can be truly happy and truly free.

In at least verbal agreement with Maimonides and other representatives of medieval Jewish, Christian, and Islamic religious traditions, Spinoza regards God as the prime object of knowledge. The attainment of a genuine knowledge of God is therefore viewed as the ultimate goal of human life and the key to the achievement of blessedness. Moreover, not only does Spinoza see human existence as culminating in a knowledge of God, but he also claims, again in agreement with the religious tradition, that this knowledge necessarily leads to love. Thus, the entire argument of the *Ethics* culminates in the "intellectual love of God" (*amor intellectualis Dei*) through which the human mind is allegedly able to transcend its finitude and be united with the eternal. This conception constitutes Spinoza's purely philosophical alternative to the beatific vision and provides much of the religious, perhaps even mystical, tone some have found in his philosophy.

The ground of this conception lies, however, in Spinoza's uncompromising rationalism rather than his religious sensitivity. Although much of his language is reminiscent of the religious tradition, his overall point of view is diametrically opposed to that of this tradition. The God who functions as the first principle of knowledge and who is the object of a purely intellectual love, has very little in common with the God of Abraham, Isaac, and Jacob. The latter is a personal being who created humanity in his own image and manifests a providential concern for each individual, as well as for the race as a whole. By contrast, Spinoza's God is defined as "a being absolutely infinite, i.e., a substance consisting of an infinity of attributes, of which each one expresses an eternal and infinite essence" (ID6). As we shall see in the next chapter, there can only be one such substance; so this conception leads to the replacement of Cartesian pluralism by a monistic metaphysic in which thought and extension, the two created substances of Cartesian thought, are conceived as attributes of God, the unique, infinite substance.

In the meantime, it is important to realize that Spinoza identifies God not only with substance, but also with nature. This identification is not with nature considered as the sum total of particular things, however; it is rather with nature considered as an infinite (in the sense of all-inclusive) and necessary system of universal laws, in which all things have their determinate and necessary place and with reference to which they must be understood. The "divinity" of nature, so conceived, thus consists in its infinity and necessity. As truly infinite, or, in Spinoza's technical language, "absolutely infinite," there is nothing beyond it on which it depends—that is, no "creator" God, nor any purpose that it embodies. As a necessary system of universal laws, nothing in it is contingent, and nothing could possibly be other than it is. Moreover, knowledge of such a God is obviously equivalent to knowledge of the infinite and necessary order, in which human beings, like everything else in nature, have their determinate place, and the intellectual love that supposedly springs from this knowledge is the joyful acceptance and affirmation of the very same order.

This complex activity of knowledge, acceptance, and affirmation, constitutes, for Spinoza, our highest destiny and chief good. It is not a means to happiness, but happiness itself, in its most authentic and lasting form. Similarly, virtue, so conceived, is its own reward and not, as the religious tradition so often affirms, merely a means for acquiring future rewards or avoiding future punishments. Finally, Spinoza tells us that this very same activity is the source of human freedom. But freedom is not to be conceived, as Descartes and others have conceived it, as some mysterious power that in some inexplicable way exempts man from the laws and power of nature. Rather, it consists entirely in the apprehension of the necessity of these very laws. Spinoza's point is essentially the claim that was later brought home so forcefully by Freud. We gain control of our emotions and achieve freedom only by acquiring knowledge of these emotions and their causes.[11]

This view, which we have attempted to sketch in only its broadest outlines, can be seen as the most fully developed defense of the ideal of scientific objectivity as a life task that is to be found in the history of Western thought. The maxim "Know thyself," which for Socrates expressed the sum and substance of human wisdom, but which led to the ironic conclusion that the only thing one can know about oneself is that one knows nothing, became for Spinoza the demand to become aware of one's place in the infinite and necessary scheme of things. This demand is grounded in the conviction that things are, indeed, necessary and determined; that through the proper use of intellect, one is capable of comprehending this necessity; that the course of infinite nature is completely indifferent to human purposes; and, consequently, that moral and religious categories such as good and evil or sin and grace have no basis in reality but are merely products of human thought and desire. It is also based on Spinoza's firm conviction, however, that the recognition of these facts is the source of peace and satisfaction; not the "peace that passeth understanding" of religious ecstasy, but the true and lasting peace that does not so much derive from, as actually consist in, understanding.

Spinoza provided the clearest statement of his basic standpoint in the critique of final causes that he appended to the first part of the

Ethics. Final causes there stand for almost everything that Spinoza opposes. Not only does he reject any appeal to them on the grounds that it would constitute an inadequate, unscientific mode of explanation, an attitude he shares with all proponents of the new science, but he treats this conception as an important expression of the theistic, pluralistic world view that stands in the way of achieving the desired understanding of ourselves and our place in nature.

According to Spinoza's analysis: "All the prejudices I here undertake to expose depend on this one: that men commonly suppose that all natural things act, as men do, on account of an end" (I, Appendix). When combined, as it has been since the Middle Ages, with the Judeo-Christian conception of God, this notion leads to the familiar belief that God created all things for the benefit of man. But such a belief is the result of viewing things through the imagination, rather than the intellect, which alone grasps things through their true causes. Given human nature, however, such a procedure is inevitable; for everyone ought to be willing to admit "that all men are born ignorant of the causes of things, and that they all want to seek their own advantage, and are conscious of this appetite." From this it follows that all human beings think themselves free and act with an end in view (what they take to be useful). Moreover, being ignorant of true causes, they tend to judge other natures by their own, and when they find many things in nature that prove useful to them, for example, "eyes for seeing, teeth for chewing, plants and animals for food, the sun for light, the sea for supporting fish, etc. . . . they consider all natural things as means for their own advantage." Now being aware that they did not create all these great conveniences themselves, they were naturally led by their imagination to the belief that "there was a ruler, or number of rulers of nature, endowed with human freedom, who had taken care of all things for them and made all things for their use." Thus arises the belief in the gods, and with it, as we can clearly see—although Spinoza does not here make it explicit—the superstitious idea that human virtue consists in doing what is pleasing to these gods, so that they will continue to confer their benefits on us. Yet one soon realizes that these benefits are not distributed equitably, that "conveniences and inconveniences happen indiscriminately to the pious and the impious alike." This gives rise to what has come to be known as the "problem of evil"—namely, the problem of reconciling the apparent evil in the world with the goodness of God. This problem, in turn, is generally resolved by an appeal to ignorance in the form of the pious claim that "the judgments of the Gods far surpass man's grasp." As Spinoza knew well from personal experience, this appeal can lead to the grossest superstition and the most irrational acts, for it serves as the great justification for religious oppression in all its forms. Furthermore, he reflects: "This alone . . . would have caused the truth to be hidden from the human race to eternity, if Mathematics, which is concerned not with ends, but only with the essences and properties of figures, had not shown men another standard of truth."

With this total repudiation of final causes, Spinoza is, in effect, advocating the universalization of the method of mathematics—that is, the method whereby things are understood in terms of their logical, lawful relationships to each other, not in terms of their imaginative, contingent relationships to our needs and desires. In the preface to part 3 of the *Ethics* he insists that, just as the laws of nature are everywhere the same, "*so the way of understanding the nature of anything, of whatever kind, must also be the same, viz. through the universal laws and rules of nature.*" The central point here is that the mental and emotional life of human beings is no exception to this principle. Spinoza emphasizes this by proclaiming that he will "consider human actions and appetites just as if it were a question of lines, planes, and bodies." Not only is such a mode of explanation alone scientific, but even more important for Spinoza, it is the way in which we have to regard our own actions and desires, as well as those of others, if we are ever to achieve virtue, happiness, and freedom.

III The Geometrical Method

We cannot complete our brief overview of Spinoza's philosophy without taking at least some note of the geometrical form in which he cast it. The geometrical order, or method of demonstration, is modeled on that of Euclid's *Elements*. It normally begins with the presentation of a set of definitions, axioms, and postulates and proceeds, on the basis of these, to demonstrate a number of theorems or propositions. This is equivalent to what Descartes called the "synthetic method of demonstration," which he contrasted to the analytic method of discovery. Descartes made use of this method, at the request of some of his critics, for the presentation of some of the basic principles of his philosophy.[12] Moreover, such an endeavor was not unique to Descartes but was rather very much in the spirit of the seventeenth century, with its emphasis on mathematics as the standard of intelligibility and scientific explanation.[13] But, although Spinoza was neither the first nor the last to employ this method, he was the first to do so on such a large scale, and it must have cost him a great deal of effort. Each of the five parts of the *Ethics* begins with a set of definitions and axioms, and the argument is presented as in Euclid, in a series of propositions, each with its own demonstration. These propositions, in turn, are interspersed with frequent scholia, in which Spinoza abandons the formal manner of presentation and adds significant illustrative material and occasional criticism of opposing views. Finally, a number of the parts have prefaces and appendixes which introduce and supplement the argument in important ways.

Like much else in Spinoza, the significance of the geometrical method of demonstration has been the subject of considerable dispute. The basic issue is quite simply whether this method of demonstration is really required by the content, or whether the connection between the two is more external, with the choice of a geometrical form being motivated purely by extrinsic factors, such as its pedagogical value. Moreover, as is unfortunately so often the case with Spinoza, he has left us with no real evidence regarding his own views on the matter, so that the question must be resolved by more indirect means.

Although one can point to a number of distinguished scholars on either side of the argument,[14] it would seem that, if we are to take Spinoza seriously as a philosopher, we must also take his method seriously. Perhaps the best way to begin is through a consideration of the way in which Spinoza viewed his definitions and the role he gave to them in his argument. This information is not provided by the *Ethics*, which does not attempt to justify or even explain its own mode of procedure, but is to be found in Spinoza's correspondence and in the *Treatise on the Emendation of the Intellect.*

The modern reader, especially the philosophically trained reader, has a good deal of trouble with Spinoza's definitions, of which the already cited definition of God can serve as an example. Such a reader is often left with the impression that Spinoza simply and arbitrarily defines his key terms in such a way as to arrive at his desired conclusions. The argument of the *Ethics* is thus viewed as an impressive and intricate chain of reasoning that nowhere touches reality. Now, regardless of how we may ultimately come to view this judgment, we must at least realize that Spinoza himself was keenly aware of the problem. In a letter to his young friend Simon De Vries, he distinguishes between two kinds of definitions in a way that parallels the traditional distinction between nominal and real definitions. The former kind stipulates what is meant by a word, or what is thought in a given concept. Such a definition can be conceivable or inconceivable, clear or obscure, helpful or unhelpful, but since it is arbitrarily concocted by the human mind, it cannot, strictly speaking, be called either true or false. The latter kind of definition (real definition), which in Spinoza's terms "explains a thing as it exists outside of the understanding," defines a thing, rather than a name. It therefore can be either true or false; it is, in fact, a proposition, differing from an axiom only in its specificity.[15]

At first glance the definitions we find in the *Ethics* seem to be of the former variety. They are introduced by expressions such as "by . . . I mean that," or "a thing is called . . . ," which suggest that we are merely being told how the term in question is being used, and it is just this feature of Spinoza's definitions that gives rise to the above-mentioned objections. The actual course of the argument makes it clear, however, that Spinoza intends his definitions to be considerably more than that; for merely nominal definitions cannot provide us with any information about reality.[16] Like the definitions of geometrical figures found in Euclid, Spinoza's definitions are designed to describe not only the names used, but also the objects named. They, therefore, are presented as true propositions describing the essence of things. Thus, just as the mathematician can deduce the properties of a figure from his real definition, so Spinoza, the metaphysician, proposes to deduce the basic properties of reality, or nature, from his fundamental real definitions.[17]

But then the obvious question arises: How does Spinoza know that he has arrived at a true definition, one that, in his own terms, provides us with an adequate, or clear and distinct, idea of the object in question? Here, perhaps more than in any other area, we can discern the influence of the geometrical way of thinking on Spinoza, and especially the approach of the analytic geometry developed by Descartes. What Spinoza does, in effect, is to ask how the mathematician knows that he has arrived at a real definition of a figure. This is found to be the case when he is able to construct it. His definition is thus a rule for the construction of a figure—what is often called a "genetic definition"—and from such a definition alone, all the properties of the figure can be deduced. To cite Spinoza's own example, the nominal definition of a circle as "a figure in which the lines drawn from the center to the circumference are equal" is rejected in favor of the genetic definition as "the figure that is described by any line of which one end is fixed and the other movable."[18] This definition tells us how such a figure can be constructed, and from the rule for construction, we can deduce all its properties.

Spinoza's central point is that the same principles apply to our knowledge of nature, or reality, as to our knowledge of abstract entities such as mathematical objects. Thus, we have a real definition, an adequate, true, or clear and distinct idea of a thing (all these terms, as we shall see later, being more or less interchangeable) insofar as we know its "proximate cause" and can see how its properties necessarily follow from this cause. "For really," Spinoza writes, "knowledge of the effect is nothing but acquiring a more perfect knowledge of its course."[19] Moreover, in such instances there is no room for doubt of the kind envisaged by Descartes. When the mind has a true idea, it immediately knows it to be true, since it grasps the logical necessity with which the properties of the object follow from the idea. The metaphysician, as well as the mathematician, can therefore arrive at genetic definitions of things, and it is through such definitions that one acquires rationally grounded knowledge.[20]

If, however, knowledge of a thing is equivalent to knowledge of its cause, which Spinoza identifies with its logical ground, or the principle in terms of which it is understood, then either we find ourselves involved in an infinite regress, which, in turn, would lead to a hopeless skepticism, or the whole cognitive enterprise must be grounded in a single first principle. Furthermore, this first principle in terms of which everything is to be explained obviously cannot itself be explained in terms of anything else. It must, therefore, have the reason or ground of its existence in itself, or, in the language of the schools, which Spinoza adopts, be *causa sui* (self-caused). The first principle, of course, is the concept of God,[21] and we can thus see how Spinoza's method leads necessarily to his concept of God. As Spinoza himself clearly tells us: "As for order, to unite and order all our perceptions, it is required, and reason demands, that we ask, as soon as possible, whether there is a certain being, and at the same time, what sort of being it is, which is the cause of all things, so that its objective essence may also be the cause of all our ideas, and then our mind will ... reproduce Nature as much as possible. For it will have Nature's essence, order, and unity objectively."[22]

How then do we know that our thoughts are arranged in the proper logical order, that they "have Nature's essence, order, and unity objectively"? Spinoza's answer is that we know this in precisely the same way in which the mathematician knows that he has arrived at the correct idea of a circle. In both instances, the properties follow with strict logical necessity from the cause, and the mind is able to see that nothing is undetermined, nothing left unexplained. The argument of the *Ethics* is intended to lead us to understand reality as a whole in just this way. We must come to see "that from God's supreme power, *or* infinite nature, infinitely many things in infinitely many modes, i.e., all things, have necessarily flowed, or always follow, by the same necessity and in the same way as from the nature of a triangle it follows, from eternity and to eternity, that its three angles are equal to two right angles" (IP17S). The necessity with which the truth about the interior angles of a triangle follows from the nature of the triangle is strictly logical, and it is based on the real definition of the triangle. But if, as Spinoza claims, things follow from God with *precisely the same necessity* and in *precisely the same manner*, then it would seem to be highly appropriate, to say the least, for the method of demonstration to be the same in the one case as in the other.

We can, therefore, conclude that the geometrical form of Spinoza's philosophy is intimately related to, if not actually inseparable from, its content; and we shall have to keep this constantly in mind throughout our investigation of the argument of the *Ethics*. This is not to suggest that the geometrical form of presentation is "demanded" or "required" by the philosophy in the strong sense that its basic conclusions cannot even be accurately expressed apart from it. No philosopher, with the possible exceptions of Plato, Hegel, and Kierkegaard, has ever achieved such an interpenetration of form and content. Furthermore, as has already been noted, the geometrical method is a method of demonstration, not of discovery, so that it would be nonsensical to try to argue that Spinoza actually arrived at his philosophy by beginning with certain definitions and axioms and proceeding from these to deduce his conclusions. As he affirms explicitly, method presupposes a certain body of knowledge and serves only to put it into the best possible logical order.[23] Nevertheless, given the assumptions about the nature of knowledge that we have just touched on and shall examine in more detail later, the geometrical method is the most adequate vehicle for presenting this philosophy. Not only does it allow Spinoza to deduce, or at least attempt to deduce, all his conclusions from a single first principle—namely, the concept of God—and to illustrate the absolute necessity governing all things, but, for these very reasons, it presents his view of the universe in the form in which, according to his theory of knowledge, it can be adequately grasped by the intellect. Such a form is therefore, from Spinoza's point of view, necessary for the realization of his practical goal.

CHAPTER 3

God

The first part of the *Ethics*, entitled "Concerning God," is devoted to an analysis of the nature of God and to the delineation of the main outlines of the relationship between God and the world. It contains Spinoza's analysis of the basic structure of reality (his metaphysics) and his criticisms of the Judeo-Christian conception of God. The discussion falls roughly into three parts, which determine the three divisions of this chapter. The first (P1–P15) offers an exposition of the nature, or essence, of God—that is, an account of what God is—together with a set of demonstrations that God, so conceived, exists necessarily. Here Spinoza introduces his fundamental category of substance, in light of which he develops his conception of God as "a being absolutely infinite, i.e., a substance consisting of an infinity of attributes, of which each one expresses an eternal and infinite essence" (D6). The second section (P16–P30) is concerned with the divine power, or causality, which is equivalent to the infinite power of nature. This naturally leads to an analysis of the relationship between God and the world; and within the context of this analysis, Spinoza presents a first characterization of particular things in nature as finite modes. The last section (P30–P36) makes explicit many of the results that have already been established and uses them as the basis of a polemic against the whole Judeo-Christian religious tradition. This polemic culminates in the appendix dealing with final causes which we have already considered.

I God as Substance

By developing his doctrine of God in light of his concept of substance, Spinoza makes a rather original use of one of the most important
44

concepts in the history of Western philosophy. The concept arose with the Greeks, in connection with their attempt to resolve a fundamental problem regarding the universe—namely, the problem of change. Explanation of change seems to require recognition of something permanent or abiding that underlies change, and in relation to which it can be understood. The concept of substance serves this function. It was introduced to refer to the permanent element, or elements, in the universe, the abiding substratum, whereas the changing features of experience were viewed as its states, or qualities. Thus, Aristotle, who provided the first systematic treatment of the concept of substance, states that "the most distinctive mark of substance appears to be that, while remaining numerically one and the same, it is capable of admitting contrary qualities."[1] But Aristotle not only claimed that substances are the substrata of change, he also insisted that they are the subjects of predication.[2] Intelligible talk about the world seems to require expressions both for qualities and for things, or subjects, that have these qualities. Moreover, since we can conceive of a thing, or subject, without at least some of its qualities, which are therefore called "accidents," but cannot conceive of a quality except in relation to a thing, or subject, it follows that the latter are more fundamental. The various subjects of predication—that is, the particular things in nature, such as human beings, horses, and trees—were thus viewed by Aristotle as substances in the primary sense, the basic elements in the universe in terms of which everything else is to be understood.

By the time of Descartes, the concept of substance had changed considerably, and in a way that accords with the development of the mathematical science of nature. Descartes, it will be recalled, defined substance primarily in terms of independent existence, as "a thing which so exists that it needs no other thing in order to exist."[3] Each substance, so conceived, has one fundamental attribute, or property, that constitutes its nature or essence and through which it is known. As we have seen, the essence, or essential property, of corporeal substance is extension, and it is on the basis of this conception that Descartes argued for the possibility of a completely geometrical science of nature. Like Aristotle, Descartes used the concept of substance to refer to what is fundamental in nature, that in terms of which everything else is to be explained (this is accomplished by defining it in terms of independent existence); but in accordance with his radically different view of scientific explanation, he conceived of what is "substantial" in a very different manner. Nevertheless, there is a residue of Aristotelianism in Descartes's theory, for in addition to the well-known account that we have just considered, he gives another account in which substance is defined as "everything in which there resides immediately, as in a subject, or by means of which there exists anything that we perceive, i.e., any property, quality, or attribute, of which we have a real idea."[4] He thus conceived of substance as a subject of predication, as a *thing* that has *properties* and is, in fact, only known in terms of these properties. Moreover, it is in light of this conception that he used the words *attribute*, to designate the principal, or essential, property through which each substance is known,[5] and *mode*, to refer to the nonessential properties, which cannot be conceived without substance, but without which substance or its principal attribute can be conceived.[6]

Spinoza's definitions, as opposed to the conclusions that he derives from them, are often thought to involve only relatively minor variations on those of Descartes. *Substance* is defined as "what is in itself and is conceived through itself, i.e., that whose concept does not require the concept of another thing, from which it must be formed" (D3). So defined, it is then distinguished both from *attribute*, by which Spinoza means "what the intellect perceives of a substance as constituting its essence" (D4), and from *modes*, by which he understands "the affections of substance *or* that which is in another through which it is also conceived" (D5). Leaving aside for the moment the definition of *attribute*, the most striking way in which this conception of substance differs from the Cartesian account is that Spinoza includes conceptual, as well as ontological, independence, or self-sufficiency, in his characterization. Thus, a substance must not only "exist in itself," but must also be "conceived through itself." Correlatively, the modifications of substance are dependent in both senses.

This difference turns out to be much more significant than it initially appears to be, particularly if, as seems reasonable, one construes conceptual independence to mean explanatory self-sufficiency. For, by including such independence in his definition of substance, Spinoza, in effect, denies that Cartesian substances are really substances. (They are conceived through their attribute, not through themselves.) Further, ontological and conceptual independence are not contingently conjoined characteristics of substance for Spinoza. On the contrary, only that which can also be conceived—that is, explained— through itself can also exist in itself, and vice versa. Thus, since Cartesian substances are not conceived through themselves, it follows that they do not exist in themselves either; that is, they do not have the ontological independence claimed for them by the Cartesian theory.[7]

Although Spinoza never explicitly develops such an argument, one can easily be constructed on his principles. Its starting point is the axiom that "what cannot be conceived through another, must be conceived through itself" (A2), which amounts to the claim that everything is explicable. Given this axiom, together with the principle that whatever exists in itself—that is, is ontologically independent— cannot be conceived through or explained in terms of something else, it follows that whatever truly exists in itself must also be conceived through itself. Correlatively, whatever can be conceived through itself must also exist in itself. Since, according to Spinoza, "the knowledge of an effect depends on and involves, the knowledge of its cause" (A4), if something existed in something else—that is, if it were causally dependent on something else—then it would likewise have to be conceived in terms of this cause, which contradicts the original assumption. But (by A2) if it does not exist in another, it must exist in itself.

Most important, by making conceptual independence or explanatory self-sufficiency a criterion of substance, Spinoza makes it possible for substance to fulfill the function that it is intended to, but does not actually, fulfill in the Cartesian scheme—namely, that of providing an ultimate ground of explanation, a source of the intelligibility of things. Spinoza's basic assumption, which we will consider in more detail in connection with our analysis of his demonstration of the existence of God, is that only that which is conceived through itself can fulfill this function, because nothing else is capable of providing a resting place for thought, a place where the explanatory buck stops, as it were. For the present it must suffice to note that Cartesian extended substance cannot fulfill this function because of its dependence on God, a dependence that, for Descartes at least, leads ultimately to the grounding of the basic laws of nature in the will of God.[8]

Moreover, if the above account is correct, it appears that Spinoza has abandoned the last vestige of Aristotelianism in the Cartesian conception—namely, the conception of substance as the subject of predication, or the bearer of properties.[9] Any such subject must be conceived either as a bare substratum, a completely indeterminate "something I know not what" (to use Locke's famous phrase),[10] in which case its explanatory power is nil, or as having a determinate nature in terms of which its properties, or states, can be understood (like Aristotle's primary substances), in which case this nature itself requires explanation. The point can be expressed in the language of traditional ontology by saying that Spinoza replaced the conception of substance as *a being* with the conception of it as *Being itself*. Nevertheless, it seems more in accord with the rationalistic-scientific thrust of his thinking to identify substance (and ultimately God) with the logically necessary, and hence self-explanatory, order of nature. As we shall see in more detail later, however, it is the order of nature conceived as the source, or ground, of things and their intelligibility (*natura naturans*), not as the system of individual things that depend on and are conceived through this order (*natura naturata*). Correlatively, although causally and conceptually dependent on it, these things are not properties, predicates, or states of substance.[11]

Finally, this puts us in a position to deal with the thorny problem of the Spinozistic conception of an attribute. At the center of the difficulty is the phrase "that which the intellect perceives as [*tanquam*] constituting." Some scholars, emphasizing the simplicity of substance, which entails that there can be no real distinction between attributes, have interpreted this in a subjectivist manner. On this view, the notion that substance contains a number of distinct attributes is merely a consequence of the way in which the finite intellect perceives substance and does not express a truth about substance as it is in itself. Others contend, to the contrary, that the diversity of attributes reflects a real, or "objective," diversity in the nature of substance.[12] Although we can hardly go into the details of this seemingly endless controversy here, it does seem clear that the bulk of the evidence supports the objectivist interpretation. Spinoza's God is, after all, "a substance *consisting of* an infinity of attributes" (my emphasis). Moreover, as we have already seen, his whole philosophy culminates in a knowledge of God, who functions as the very principle of intelligibility. Now, as the definition makes clear, it is through these attributes that the intellect understands God, or substance: it would seem to follow from this, therefore, that if this knowledge is to be adequate—and Spinoza claims that it is—then said attributes must really pertain to the nature of God. To deny this would lead one to the rather paradoxical and un-Spinozistic conclusion that the source of the intelligibility of things is itself unintelligible.

But if attributes are not subjective interpretations foisted on sub-stance by the perceiving intellect, what are they? The natural response is that they are essential properties of substance—that is, properties through which it is conceived. This is the Cartesian position, and those who interpret Spinoza's conception of substance through Cartesian spectacles maintain that it is also his. Such an interpretation, which is fairly standard in the literature, is not without its strengths. For one thing, it certainly accounts for the "objectivity" of attributes; for another, it also explains why Spinoza frequently identifies substance and attribute, and treats the attributes as if they were themselves substances.[13] But it runs into trouble with the claim that a single substance can have more than one attribute. As we shall see shortly, this contention is sheer nonsense to the Cartesian; yet it is an essential feature of the Spinozistic conception of substance.

The problem disappears, however, if one construes Spinoza's sub-stance as a necessary and universal order of things, rather than a thing in which properties inhere. Attributes, which the intellect perceives as constituting the essence of substance, can then be understood as the different forms in which this order is expressed or, perhaps better, the different perspectives from which it can be viewed. Many analogies suggest themselves at this point, none of which is satisfactory ultimately. One is to conceive the substance-attribute relationship as analogous to the relationship between a proposition and its expressions in different languages.[14] Another, somewhat closer to the mathematical spirit of Spinoza, is to think of it in terms of the model of Cartesian analytic geometry, which affirms an identity between a geometrical curve and its algebraic equation.[15] More generally, this geometry presented Spinoza with a science in which one and the same rational order is expressed in two distinct, yet logically equivalent, ways.

Although these analogies are helpful, they fail to do much justice to the inclusion of the phrase "what the intellect perceives" in Spinoza's definition. This suggests a quite different analogy, one drawn from visual perception, which also takes seriously the notion of perspective. Following this suggestion, we note that it is sometimes claimed that every physical object is necessarily perceived from a certain point of view. Thus, we never simply perceive a table, but always see it from the front, behind, above, and so on. The "real table" would be fully revealed only through the sum of all possible perspectives. Nevertheless, each distinct perspective acquaints us not just with a property or separable part of the table, but rather with the table as a whole—that is, as a distinct, unified entity, even if it is perceived from a particular, limited point of view. Now, much the same can be said abut Spinoza's attributes. Each of them *is* substance, albeit substance as grasped from a particular point of view. Nature, after all, *is* extension in the sense that the physicist can give a coherent account of it in physical terms, without bringing in any nonphysical propositions, such as final causes. But nature, so conceived, is also an object of thought; so it would seem to be equally possible to view substance as a system of thought.[16]

Like any analogy, the present one cannot be pressed too far. Indeed, it falls short in at least two essential respects. First, each attribute of substance, unlike each visual perspective of a thing, is self-contained and does not refer to other attributes. Second, no attribute is in any way privileged. Each provides us with an equally adequate expression of substance. Even allowing for these differences, however, the point remains that, although the finite intellect necessarily interprets nature from a particular perspective, it is able to comprehend the true nature or essence of substance, not merely some of its properties. Leibniz was later to express a similar thought with his contention that each monad (finite substance) represents, or perceives, the universe from a particular point of view; and both Spinoza and Leibniz drew from this thought the rather significant consequence that human knowledge is similar in kind, if not in scope, to God's knowledge.

So far we have been concerned mainly with Spinoza's definitions. We must now turn to the arguments based on them. His first goal, to which the opening propositions of the *Ethics* are addressed, is to prove that there can be in the universe only one substance (God or nature), that it possesses an infinity of attributes, and that it exists necessarily. Although these conclusions are positive, the bulk of the argument takes the form of a critique of possible pluralistic alternatives. This critique falls into two parts, since there are basically two types of substantial pluralism to be considered. According to the first type, there is a plurality of substances of the same nature or attribute. The Aristotelian conception of individual substances, falling under various natural kinds and the Cartesian conception of distinct thinking substances are the main examples of such a position. Spinoza's critique of this type of pluralism culminates in the sweeping claim: "*In nature there cannot be two or more substances of the same nature or attribute*" (P5).

Because it not only undermines directly a traditional conception of substance, but also plays a crucial role in the demonstration of subsequent propositions, this proposition is clearly one of the most important in the first part of the *Ethics*. Not surprisingly, then, it is also one of the most controversial. The initial premise that "*two or more distinct things are distinguished from one another, either by a difference in the attributes of the substances or by a difference in their affections*" (P4) is certainly reasonable enough, given Spinoza's definitions. Problems begin, however, with the second premise, which asserts that if two or more substances were distinguished from one another only on the basis of their attributes, then there could not be more than one with the same attribute. Leibniz had already objected to this on the grounds that two substances might have some attributes in common and others that were distinctive. For example, substance *A* might have attributes *x* and *y*; and substance *B*, attributes *y* and *z*.[17] A possible response is to suggest that, at this stage of the argument for monism, Spinoza is assuming a Cartesian framework, which means that he is considering only substances with one attribute.[18] For such substances it is clear that, if we consider only their attributes and if these are assumed to be identical, then there could be no basis for distinguishing the substances. From this it seems reasonable to conclude that the substances themselves must be numerically identical (one, not two). This is a straightforward application of what Leibniz termed the principle of the "identity of indiscernibles." Although it does seem to be the case that Spinoza is here considering only substances with one attribute, the attempt to build one's whole defense on this fact seems only to postpone the day of reckoning. The problem is that Spinoza appeals again to this principle at a later, crucial stage in the argument for monism (P14), when it is clear that it must apply to substances with more than one attribute.[19] Consequently, if the overall argument for monism is to be rescued, it is important to provide an interpretation of the present argument that does not turn on the assumption that it is limited to substances with only one attribute.

The key to such an interpretation lies in the correct understanding of what Spinoza means by *attribute* and of what it might mean to claim that two attributes belonging to, or "constituting," two distinct substances are identical. (In contemporary philosophical jargon, this is the question of the "identity-conditions" of attributes.) Let us recall that, for Spinoza, attributes are expressions of the essence, or nature, of substance. This allows him to claim that each attribute *is* substance, considered from a certain point of view or taken under a certain description, which, in turn, explains why he sometimes identifies substance and attribute. But if this is so, then it follows that attribute *y* of substance A is identical to attribute y of substance B, just in case they express the same nature or essence—that is, are descriptions of the same thing. Yet this contradicts the objector's assumption that A and B are distinct substances. Consequently, it turns out on analysis that if the two attributes are really identical, then they cannot express the nature of two distinct substances. Conversely, if they do express the natures of two distinct substances, then the attributes cannot be identical.

Unfortunately, even this does not settle matters completely. There is also a problem with the third premise, in which Spinoza considers the possibility that substances sharing the same attribute and thus not distinguishable on that basis might nonetheless be distinguished with regard to their affections. Against this possibility, which clearly allows for a plurality of substances with the same attribute, Spinoza remarks cryptically, "since a substance is prior in nature to its affections (by P1), if the affections are put to one side and [the substance] is considered in itself, i.e. (by D3 and A6), considered truly, one cannot be conceived to be distinguished from another, i.e. (by P4), there cannot be many, but only one [of the same nature or attribute], q.e.d." The problem here is that it seems to be begging the question for Spinoza to assert that there would be no distinction between the two substances if one were to set the affections aside. It may be true, but why *should* one set the affections aside? Certainly, a Cartesian would deny the appropriateness of such a procedure, for example, two Cartesian thinking substances would supposedly be distinguished by their respective thoughts, which are distinct affections of the two substances. The text is not clear on this point, but a plausible reading of the argument has been suggested by Bertrand Russell in the context of a discussion of Leibniz.[20]

According to Russell, the argument seems to be that, on the assumption currently under consideration, the substances must be indistinguishable prior to the assignment of predicates (affections); however, the assignment of predicates cannot provide a basis for distinguishing otherwise indiscernible substances unless it is presupposed that they are numerically distinct to begin with. In other words, although we could certainly distinguish between the two Cartesian substances by referring to their distinct affections, we take this to mark a distinction between substances only because we have already assumed that the distinct affections must belong to numerically distinct substances. After all, the same thinking substance could certainly have two distinct affections, even simultaneously. Consequently, Spinoza could claim that it is really the Cartesian, not he, who is begging the question by refusing to set the affections aside.

Having thus eliminated the possibility of a plurality of substances with the same attribute or nature, Spinoza must consider the possibility of a plurality of substances with different attributes, or natures. This possibility is particularly important for Spinoza, because it is reflected both in Descartes's distinction between extended and thinking substances (which, apart from their dependence on God, have nothing in common) and in the Judeo-Christian conception of created substance. Spinoza's critique of this alternative is in two parts. In the first (P6–P8), he attempts to show that no substance can be finite, in the second (P9–P10), that it must be infinite in the absolute, or eminent, sense—that is, that it must consist of "an infinity of attributes, each of which expresses an eternal and infinite essence" (D4). This, of itself, entails merely that only God, as defined by Spinoza, could count as substance. Nevertheless, it allows Spinoza to make his positive case for monism by arguing that God, or substance, so defined, exists necessarily (P11), and that no other substance can either be or be conceived (P14).

First, since "*two substances having different attributes have nothing in common with one another*" (P2), and since "*if things have nothing in common with one another, one of them cannot be the cause of the other*" (P3), which is itself based on the principle that "things that have nothing in common with one another also cannot be understood through one another, *or* the concept of the one does not involve the concept of the other" (A5), it follows that "*one substance cannot be produced by another substance*" (P6). With this concise line of reasoning, Spinoza rejects the notion of created substance common to Cartesian rationalism and the Judeo-Christian tradition.

The next step is to show that "*it pertains to the nature of a substance to exist*" (P7), or, equivalently, that "its essence necessarily involves existence." According to Spinoza's extremely cryptic argument, the unique relationship between the essence of a substance and its existence is a direct consequence of the fact that has just been established that it cannot be produced or caused by anything external to itself. Since a substance cannot be produced, he argues that "it will be the cause of itself," and this (by D1) means that "its essence necessarily involves existence *or* it pertains to its nature to exist."

This argument rests on what has been called, at least since Leibniz, "the principle of sufficient reason"—that is, the principle that everything must have a ground, reason, or cause (these terms being generally used synonymously) that determines its existence. Spinoza, like most rationalists before Kant, seems simply to have assumed this. In fact, he even argues that a cause, or reason, must be assigned not only for the existence, but also for the nonexistence of anything (P11, second proof). Nothing, in other words, can simply exist or not exist; either way, there must be a rational ground, or cause, through which its existence or nonexistence can be understood. In light of this principle, he reasons that, since substance cannot have the cause, or reason, for its existence in anything external to itself, for then it would not be substance, it must have it in itself. Substance, therefore, is self-caused, or self-sufficient, being. Moreover, as such, existence belongs to its very nature. As he goes on to add, however (in a scholium that is attached to the next proposition for some reason), this proof is really unnecessary. For, if people kept in mind the true nature of substance (that which is in itself and conceived through itself), the proposition would be viewed as "a universal axiom and accounted a truism (P8S2). Spinoza's point here is that this manner of existence follows logically from the very definition of substance—as indeed it must if the definition is to function in the required manner in his arguments.

This, in turn, provides the basis for the claim that "*every substance is necessarily infinite*" (P8). Starting with the premise just established that existence pertains to the nature of substance, Spinoza reasons that it must exist as either finite or infinite. The conclusion that it must exist as infinite is arrived at by rejection of the alternative. To assume that substance is finite is to assume that it is limited by something of the same nature, which presumably would also have to exist necessarily. But this contradicts the principle that there cannot be more than one substance with the same nature or attribute. Consequently, substance must exist as infinite.

At first glance it might seem that by showing that existence pertains to the nature of substance and that substance is infinite, Spinoza has already succeeded in identifying substance with God and thus in establishing the basic principle of his monism. But this is not the case. Like many philosophers of his time, Spinoza distinguished between a number of different senses of the word *infinite*.[21] In particular, he distinguished (see D6) between something being "infinite in its own kind"—that is, nonfinite or unlimited—and something being "absolutely infinite"—that is, all-inclusive or, as Spinoza puts it, involving infinite attributes. The former sense pertains to individual attributes and, as we shall see, to certain modes. Although unlimited, things that are infinite in this sense leave room as it were, for realities existing outside themselves. Descartes's extended substance (which for Spinoza becomes the attribute of extension) is a case in point. Although not limited by anything (for example, empty space), it does not constitute all reality, because it does not include within itself the realm of thought.[22]

Given these preliminaries, it should be clear that, up to now, the argument has shown only that substance is infinite in the first sense; what still needs to be done is to prove that it is infinite in the second, or absolute, sense. Until this has been accomplished, we are left with the possibility that there are a plurality of distinct substances with nothing in common. To put the same point somewhat differently, it must be proved that all such putatively distinct substances are attributes of a single, all-inclusive substance. Since such a proof is directed explicitly at the Cartesians, it must also deal with the basic Cartesian dogma that a substance cannot have more than one attribute.

The basis for this new argument is the claim that "*the more reality or being each thing has the more attributes belong to it*" (P9).

Unfortunately, in support of this important proposition, Spinoza does nothing more than refer the reader back to his definition of *attribute*! Nevertheless, it is possible to understand what he is getting at if we keep in mind the interpretation of Spinozistic attributes as expressions of substance, perspectives from which it can be considered, or, in more contemporary terms, descriptions under which it can be taken. On this intepretation, the claim that something possesses more reality than something else is equivalent to the claim that there are more perspectives from which it must be viewed, or more descriptions under which it must be taken, if it is to be conceived adequately. For example, consider a simple human action, the raising of an arm, say. Presumably, one could give a complete neurophysiological account of such an action in terms of impulses sent to and from the brain, the contraction of muscles, and so forth. No matter how detailed one made the description, however, one could never exhaust the reality of the action; indeed, one could never even come to understand it as an action (as opposed to a mere bodily movement). For to understand it as such requires, or at least is generally thought to require, a psychological description in terms of the beliefs, intentions, desires, and so on of an agent. In that sense there is "more reality" to an action than is given by a purely neurophysiological account, no matter how complete. Moreover, this "greater reality" can be understood in terms of the possession of a greater number of attributes.[23]

Continuing this line of argument, it follows that a being that possessed all reality (the *ens realissimum* of the tradition) could be described from every conceivable perspective, each of which, in Spinoza's language, would yield an expression of its "eternal and infinite essence." Consequently, although Spinoza does not argue explicitly this way, he could claim at this point that the Cartesian must either admit that a single substance can possess more than one attribute or deny the possibility of an ens realissimum. The orthodox Cartesian could not opt for the latter alternative, since this would amount to atheism; but nothing said so far seems to preclude the possibility that a more radical champion of the one substance–one attribute dogma might deny God's existence in this way.[24] In order to block this possibility, Spinoza must establish the existence of an ens realissimum and prove that it is the only substance.

Before turning to this, however, it is necessary to say a word about the controversial topic of the infinite attributes. Although many scholars have rejected the notion of an infinity of attributes as an anachronism, incompatible with the main thrust of Spinoza's metaphysics, much recent work recognizes the central role that the notion plays in the argument for monism and attempts to give it a reasonable sense. Its significance in this regard stems from its function in the rejection of the possibility of a plurality of substances with different attributes, or natures. Put simply, since a substance with an infinity of attributes possesses *all* the attributes there are, none are left for any other conceivable substance. Combining this with the proposition already examined that no two substances can share an attribute, it would seem to follow that the possibility of any other substance (apart from the ens realissimum) has been eliminated. This is the explicit argument of proposition 14.

For our present purpose, the important point is that this analysis indicates that *infinite* must here be taken as equivalent to *all*, and not, as one might suppose, to *infinitely many*.[25] Thus, it is perfectly compatible with the possibility that there are only two attributes— namely, thought and extension.[26] Since Spinoza admits that these are the only two with which we are acquainted, and since the assumption that there are others creates major difficulties further down the line for his epistemology and theory of mind, one might wish that he had explicitly acknowledged the point. Unfortunately, however, he did not. In fact, there is considerable textual evidence showing that Spinoza clearly believed that there were more than two attributes.[27] Moreover, this belief is perfectly in accord with the seventeenth-century cast of mind, which was so enthralled with the infinity of nature. A typical representative of this attitude is Spinoza's contemporary Malebranche, who warned explicitly against jumping to the conclusion that thought and extension exhaust the infinite reality of nature.[28]

In any event, Spinoza's next task is to establish the existence of an ens realissimum. This is attempted in proposition 11, which states simply that "*God or a substance consisting of infinite attributes, each of which expresses eternal and infinite essence, necessarily exists.*" In support of this claim, Spinoza provides three proofs modeled after arguments for the existence of God found in Descartes and other philosophers. We shall see, however, that, given the unorthodox nature of Spinoza's God, these arguments are put to a rather different purpose.

Although we have space here only to discuss the first of these proofs, a consideration of it in connection with the parallel proofs of his predecessors should suffice to reveal the radical thrust of his thought, as well as the nature of his response to one who might deny an ens realissimum. The first proof is Spinoza's unique version of the ontological argument, which was first developed by St. Anselm and later reformulated by Descartes. The characteristic feature of this famous argument is its attempt to derive the necessity of the divine existence from the mere concept of God. One of the many difficulties with this argument in its various formulations is that it is often not clear whether what is being claimed is merely that it is necessarily true that God exists (*de dicto* necessity), or that God exists in a unique way—namely, necessarily (*de re* necessity). Descartes's version seems to invite the first reading. He maintains that it is necessary that God exist on the grounds that "existence can no more be separated from the essence of God than can its having three angles equal to two right angles be separated from the essence of a triangle, or the idea of a mountain from the idea of a valley."[29] This contention is based on the definition of God as an all-perfect being and the assumption, which has often been challenged, that existence is a perfection. If existence is a perfection and God (by definition) possesses all perfections, we cannot, without contradicting ourselves, deny his existence; which is equivalent to saying that it is necessarily the case that God exists.

Spinoza's version of this argument makes reference to neither the notion of perfection, which he later equates with reality, nor the definition of God. Instead, it simply draws the logical consequence of the already established principle that "existence belongs to the nature of substance" and applies it to God, who is identified with substance in the very formulation of the proposition "God or substance ... necessarily exists." This argument consists of two stages, which really do little more than provide two equivalent expressions of the above principle. We are told first that this principle implies that we cannot conceive of God, or substance, as not existing, and then, as in Descartes's argument, that this means that God necessarily exists.

On the face of it, this argument, like Descartes's, might seem to be an attempt to prove that it is necessarily the case that God exists. But this is difficult to reconcile with the Spinozistic conception of God/substance. Radical skepticism aside, not only is Spinoza's God/substance not the sort of being about whose existence one can have any doubts, it is, strictly speaking, not *a being* at all. Nor is it the sum, or aggregate, of particular things. As already indicated, it is best construed as the universal order of nature, which is expressed in all conceivable ways and to which all things belong. Hence, what Spinoza must be trying to prove here is not simply that it is necessarily true that this order exists—although he would certainly regard this as an eternal truth—but also and primarily that it possesses necessary existence—that is, that it is a necessary order. Moreover, since necessary existence means independent existence, or being self-caused, and since this is applied to substance, or reality, as a whole, rather than to a transcendent deity, Spinoza's argument has the effect of denying the very creator God whose existence Descartes endeavored to establish. His argument is then, in a very real sense, a demonstration of the nonexistence of God—at least of the God of the Judeo-Christian tradition.[30]

Nevertheless, it should not be inferred from this that the result of Spinoza's argument is purely negative, and certainly not that he ends up denying the existence of an ens realisimum. On the contrary, his goal is to establish that the universal and necessary order of nature *is* the ens realissimum, constituted by an infinity of attributes and possessing ontological and conceptual independence. Moreover, this project is closely related to both Spinoza's rationalistic method and his ethical concerns. As already noted, a basic assumption of this method is that thought must find a resting place in a single first principle, which not only serves to explain everything else, but which is itself perfectly intelligible in its own right. Moreover, since a first principle cannot, by definition, be explained in terms of anything prior, it must somehow be self-explicating or self-justifying. Anything less would fail to satisfy the demands of thought, for it would provide us with a principle of explanation that itself stands in need of explanation, and this would obviously lead to an infinite regress and be cause for hopeless skepticism. But explanation, for Spinoza, is in terms of causes: "The knowledge of an effect depends on, and involves, the knowledge of its cause" (A4). To understand something or, equivalently, to have an adequate idea of it involves seeing how its existence and nature follow necessarily from its cause. When dealing with a first principle, however, which is intelligible in itself or, in Spinoza's terms, is "conceived through itself," we cannot look for a prior or external cause. Its existence must therefore follow from its own nature, or it must be self-caused; both of which entail having necessary existence. The conclusion that God, or substance, exists necessarily thus seems to be demanded by Spinoza's method, as it alone serves to ensure the ultimate rationality of the whole order of nature.

Admittedly, such a mode of argumentation can be subjected to severe criticism. For instance, one can claim, with some justification, that it is simply a mistake to look for the kind of explanation that Spinoza attempts to provide. It may be perfectly proper to assume that everything in nature has a cause in terms of which it may be understood and from which it necessarily follows, but one cannot say the same thing of nature as a whole. To attempt to do so is to treat the whole of nature as if it were another particular thing, and this, in the technical language of contemporary philosophy, is to commit a "category mistake." Moreover, one could argue that this basic mistake generates, in turn, the misguided need to make use of contradictory expressions such as "self-caused" and "necessary existence."

Yet, even if the force of this line of objection is acknowledged—and it raises profound issues that cannot be dealt with adequately here—it must at least be recognized that Spinoza's argument answers a deep metaphysical need, and that his philosophy as a whole contains one of the most forceful expressions of this need in the history of Western thought. This is the need for reason to reach an ultimate that is truly self-contained, in reference to which one cannot meaningfully ask the question "Why?" Most philosophers in the Judeo-Christian tradition have found such an ultimate in God the creator. But although Spinoza repudiated this ultimate as a figment of the imagination, neither his rationalistic method nor his concern for a true and lasting good allowed him to stop there. It was not enough for him to show that nature, conceived under the category of substance, cannot possibly depend on a transcendent God. He likewise could not accept the view, expressed by some twentieth-century existentialists, that reality is simply there, a brute, inexplicable, and ultimately absurd fact; for this would in effect introduce sheer contingency at the very heart of things, which would not only render nature unintelligible, but would also undermine any possibility of human beings achieving a lasting good.

But if nature is not just there, so to speak; if its order, from which all things necessarily follow, is a necessary order, then it must be the only conceivable order. When reason recognizes this, all questions cease; for to see that no alternative is even conceivable, that the matter could not possibly have been otherwise, is to understand in the fullest possible sense. Consequently, we should not be surprised to find Spinoza claiming, after two propositions dealing with the indivisibility of substance, that "*except God, no substance can be or be conceived*" (P14). The importance of this proposition in the argument for monism and its reliance on a proper interpretation of proposition 5 has already been noted. In the present context, the emphasis is on the addendum that another substance cannot be conceived. If we keep in mind what we have already learned about substance in Spinoza, we can see that he is here providing us with the strongest possible affirmation of the rationality and necessity of the order of nature. The only remaining question concerns the all-inclusiveness of this order—that is, whether there may be things or events (presumably not substances) that somehow stand outside it and are not subject to its laws. Spinoza answers this question in the last proposition of this section, where he asserts that "*whatever is, is in God, and nothing can be or be conceived without God*" (P15). Given the argument up to this point, this claim does not seem to involve any further difficulties.

II Divine Causality and the Modal System

With the above proposition we arrive at the decisive expression of Spinoza's monism. Nothing exists or can be conceived apart from this one, self-contained system, which can be characterized as God, substance, or nature. Nevertheless, the very formulation of this thesis involves a dualism of sorts. In giving up the distinction between God *and* nature, we are forced to distinguish between two aspects of God *or* nature—that is, between God, or nature, as the self-sufficient source of things and their intelligibility and the same God, or nature, as the system of particular things that are dependent on and conceived through this source. Moreover, it is through the formulation of this distinction that Spinoza later identifies God with nature, just as he had previously identified substance with God.[31] The first of the two aspects is termed *natura naturans* (active, or generating, nature), and the second *natura naturata* (passive, or generated, nature). The former refers to God as conceived through himself—that is, as substance with an infinity of attributes—and the latter to God as the modal system, which is conceived through these attributes (P29S).[32] Furthermore, this distinction within God or nature entails a similar distinction with regard to divine causality. In his treatment of this subject, Spinoza first considers this causality as it is in itself—that is, in its inherent nature, as *natura naturans* (P16–P20)—and then as it is expressed in the modal system, as *natura naturata* (P21–P29).[33]

Spinoza establishes the essential features of his theory of divine causality at the very beginning of his analysis. "From the necessity of the divine nature," he asserts, "there must follow infinitely many things in infinitely many modes, i.e., everything which can fall under an infinite intellect" (P16). He thereby determines the *nature* of the divine causality, or power, affirming that it operates through the "necessity of the divine nature," and the *extent* of this power, maintaining not only that it produces "infinitely many things in infinitely many modes"—that is, an infinite number of things, each of which is reflected in each of the infinite attributes—but also that it includes "everything which can fall under an infinite intellect"—that is, everything conceivable.

By locating the causality, or power, of God in the very "necessity of the divine nature," Spinoza is not only rejecting any appeal to the "will of God" as a causal force or to final causes in any form, he is also conceiving of the causal relationship between God and the world in terms of the model of the logical relationship between ground and consequent. God functions in Spinoza as the logical ground of things. The latter follow from his nature in precisely the same way as the conclusion of a valid deductive argument follows from its premises. Such a conception of causality is not only consistent with, but is actually required by, Spinoza's deductive model of explanation. If genuine knowledge involves the realization of the necessary consequences of our adequate ideas, and if these ideas are themselves ultimately grounded in the idea of God, then it follows that these same ideas are derivable from the idea of God as conclusions from a premise. Furthermore, if this whole logical chain of reasoning is to be something more than a consistent dream, if it is to yield truth, as Spinoza certainly believes it does, then it must reflect the structure of reality. "A true idea," he affirms, "must agree with its object" (A6). The logical order of our adequate ideas is thus the expression in the attribute of thought of the necessary causal order of reality. As we shall see in more detail in our consideration of Spinoza's theory of knowledge, we have genuine knowledge precisely to the extent to which the order of our ideas reflects this necessary order.

In light of the above considerations, it is both significant and understandable that Spinoza bases his demonstration of the infinite extent of the divine causality on his theory of definition. From the proper definition of a thing, Spinoza reasons, it should be possible to infer several properties of that thing. Moreover, the more reality the essence of the thing defined involves, the more properties can be derived from its definition. This contention was sharply criticized by Tschirnhaus, who claimed, on the basis of geometrical examples, that from the definition of a thing taken alone, only one property can be deduced.[34] Spinoza responded by granting that this may be true with regard to "the most simple things" or to "things of reason" (including geometrical figures), but that it does not apply to "real things." As an example, he cites the possibility of deriving several properties—such as necessary existence, immutability, infinity, uniqueness—from the very definition of God as a "Being to whose essence belongs existence."[35] Spinoza is here invoking the same conception of degrees of reality that he utilizes in his argument for an infinity of attributes. Given this conception, which identifies a thing's degree of reality with the number of attributes it possesses, it follows that the more reality a thing has, the greater the number of consequences that can be derived from its definition. Now, since it has already been established that God has an infinity of attributes, Spinoza concludes that an infinite number of things must necessarily follow from the divine nature.

We must keep in mind, however, that Spinoza asserts not only that an infinite number of things follow necessarily in infinite ways from the very nature of God, but also that this includes everything "which can fall under an infinite intellect." This addition is not without its importance. An infinite intellect, which Spinoza later describes as an eternal and infinite mode of thought, is one that possesses the complete comprehension of everything conceivable. Since the conceivable defines the limits of the possible, it follows that anything not falling within the scope of such an intellect is impossible. Moreover, since God allegedly produces everything that falls within such an intellect's scope, it follows that God produces everything possible, or, equivalently, that whatever God does not produce is impossible.

The subsequent propositions in this section specify more precisely the nature of divine causality. The first point to be made is that "*God acts from the laws of his nature alone, and is compelled by no one*" (P17). As the demonstration indicates, the assertion that God acts from the laws of his nature means precisely the same as the claim just established that things follow from the necessity of the divine nature. The further qualification, that God acts only in this manner and is compelled by no one, follows from the proposition that there is nothing outside God. Thus, Spinoza concludes that nothing can possibly move God to act "except the perfection of his own nature" (P17C1); and that "God alone is a free cause" (P17C2). The latter point reflects Spinoza's own definition of *free* as what is self-determined, not undetermined (D7). We shall see that in his moral philosophy Spinoza holds that, to a limited extent, human beings have the capacity to become free in this sense. In the last analysis, however, freedom in the full sense is attributable only to God, who is absolutely self-determined.

Continuing his analysis of divine causality, Spinoza makes use of some scholastic distinctions that were apparently current in contemporary textbooks and affirms that "*God is the immanent, not the transitive, cause of all things*" (P18). A transitive, or transient, cause is one that is separable from its effects, whereas an immanent cause is inseparable. Accordingly, by characterizing the divine causality in this manner, Spinoza is merely underscoring his already established doctrine that God is not a being apart from the world, but the immanent ground of its intelligibility. But God is not immanent in the sense that he is "in the world"; rather, the world is in him in the manner in which a consequent is "in" its logical ground.[36]

A traditional theological doctrine that Spinoza does retain, albeit in a manner consistent with his own views, is that of the eternity of God and of all the attributes (P19). The crux of the demonstration is the definition of eternity as "existence itself, insofar as it is conceived to follow necessarily from the definitions alone of the eternal thing" (D8). As he goes on to add in his explanation of this key definition, *eternity* here means essentially necessary existence, so that the existence of something eternal is itself an "eternal truth"—that is, a logically necessary truth.[37] Moreover, eternity, so construed, is absolutely opposed to time or duration, even though this duration may "be conceived without a beginning or end." The eternity of God is thus to be conceived as a logical consequence of—or, better, as identical with—his necessary existence, and not construed imaginatively as endless duration, as existing "for ever and ever." Furthermore, since the attributes express the "essence of the divine substance," they likewise are eternal in precisely the same sense.

On the basis of the above proposition, Spinoza concludes his analysis of natura naturans with the assertion that *"God's existence and his essence are one and the same"* (P20). This is another traditional theological formula. Spinoza uses it to make the point that God does not just happen to exist. Not only does existence follow from his nature, but his very nature—that is, essence—is to exist. For Spinoza, this is really nothing more than another expression of the eternity of God, but he draws two consequences from it: first, that the existence of God is an eternal truth—that is, a logically necessary truth (P20C1)—and, second, that "God *or* all of God's attributes, are immutable" (P20C2). Any change in God's mode of existence, in light of the above proposition, would be at the same time a change in the divine nature. But if God could change in this manner, it would mean that he was no longer God, which is absurd. Traditionally, this doctrine has been used to prove that God does not change his mind, that the divine decrees are inviolable. But for Spinoza, for whom God is identical with the order of nature and the "decrees of God" are equivalent to the laws of nature, the unchangeableness of God really means nothing more than the unchangeableness and necessity of these laws.[38]

This doctrine of the eternity and immutability of God both completes the discussion of natura naturans and serves as a transition to natura naturata, the modal system that exists in, and is conceived through, God. Spinoza's treatment of this theme seems to have been explicitly modeled on the theory of emanation, which was developed by Neoplatonic philosophers and their medieval followers in the Jewish, Christian, and Islamic traditions.[39] Expressed in its simplest terms, this theory held that the unviverse "flowed," or followed, from God in a series of necessary stages, beginning with immaterial beings such as the "intelligences," and ending with the material world. This notion of the progression, or emanation, of things, and especially of the material world, from God was intended to provide an alternative to both the orthodox theory of creation, according to which the material world was created by God *ex nihilo*, and the kind of dualism advocated by the Gnostics, which allowed for a preexisting matter out of which the world was fashioned. The problem with the first view is that it does not explain how something finite and allegedly "imperfect" (matter) can be produced by an infinite and perfect deity. The difficulty with the second view is that it grants to matter an existence independent of God (thereby denying divine omnipotence). By making matter ultimately dependent on God, yet conceiving of this dependence as mediated by several stages, and thus as indirect, the emanationists hoped to overcome the difficulties of both alternatives.

Spinoza, as we have seen, likewise rejected the doctrine of creation, as well as any view that would grant either matter or the material world an existence independent of God. Moreover, he can be said to have viewed the relationship between natura naturans and natura naturata in terms of emanation, albeit with the quasi-mythical notion of "flowing" replaced by the strictly logical relationship of ground and consequent. This view is expressed in his highly complex and often obscure theory of modes. Unlike the emanationists, however, Spinoza does not use his doctrine as a device to connect an infinite God with a world of finite things. He does not do so because he never viewed them as apart; by making extension an attribute of God, he effectively dismissed the whole problem of deriving a material world from an immaterial deity. Instead, Spinoza's theory of modes offers both an explanation of the relationship between the basic principles and categories of scientific explanation and the order of nature (as expressed in the attributes of thought and extension) and an account of how finite things express and are related to this order.

Modes, it will be recalled, were defined by Spinoza as "affections of a substance, *or* that which is in another through which it is also conceived." A mode is therefore, by definition, a dependent being, and what it depends on is God, or substance. But not all modes relate to God in the same way or have the same status. Spinoza's first concern is to establish the eternity and infinity of modes that follow directly from God. To this end he writes: "*All the things which follow from the absolute nature of any of God's attributes have always had to exist and be infinite, or are, through the same attribute, eternal and infinite*" (P21). The basic point is simply that whatever follows directly from God, or substance, partakes to some extent of the nature of that from which it follows. Such modes must, therefore, like substance or, rather, the relevant attribute, be eternal and infinite. Yet they obviously cannot be eternal and infinite in precisely the same way as substance and its attributes; for this would mean that they were themselves substances. Spinoza indicates this difference by asserting that they are eternal and infinite through an attribute—that is, in virtue of their cause. Moreover, he goes on to maintain that this holds not only for modes that follow immediately from some attribute of God, but also for modes that follow directly from these—that is, which are "modified by a modification, which, through the same attribute, exists necessarily and is infinite" (P22). We thus find a distinction between "immediate" and "mediate" eternal and infinite modes, with the former derived directly from an attribute, the latter directly from the former (P23).

Unfortunately, Spinoza gives us precious little information about these modes. The only one explicitly referred to in the *Ethics* is "God's idea," or the "idea of God" (*idea Dei*) (P21), which is presumably equivalent to the previously mentioned infinite intellect.[40] In the *Short Treatise* Spinoza mentions two: "motion" in the attribute of extension and "intellect" in the attribute of thought.[41] Finally, in response to a query on this point by his friend Schuller, Spinoza is a bit more expansive. He distinguishes between the immediate and the mediate eternal and infinite modes. As examples of immediate modes, he gives "motion and rest" in the attribute of extension and "absolutely infinite intellect" in the attribute of thought. The only example he gives of a mediate mode is the "face of the whole universe" (*facies totius Universi*), which pertains to extension, and of which he states that "although it varies in infinite modes, yet remains always the same."[42]

Of somewhat greater help for an understanding of Spinoza's doctrine is his account in the *Treatise on the Emendation of the Intellect* of the "fixed and eternal things," which are generally regarded as equivalent to the eternal and infinite modes of the *Ethics*.[43] Spinoza's concern there is with the proper ordering of our ideas; and his main point is that they must be deduced from "true causes," or "real beings," as opposed to abstract universals—for example, the genera

and species of Aristotelian science. He is careful to point out, however, that by "real things" he does not mean the objects of ordinary
experience—"the series of singular changeable things"—but rather,
"the series of fixed and eternal things." An empirical approach,
which would attempt to ground knowledge in the former, is rejected as
both impossible and unnecessary: impossible, because this series is
infinite, both in extent and complexity, and consequently, the human
intellect could never arrive at adequate knowledge of any particular
thing by tracing its causal ancestry; and unnecessary, because the
essence, or true nature, of these things is accessible in a different
manner. According to Spinoza: "That essence is to be sought only
from the fixed and eternal things, and at the same time from the laws
inscribed in these things, as in their true codes, according to which all
singular things come to be, and are ordered. Indeed, these singular,
changeable things depend so intimately, and (so to speak) essentially,
on the fixed things that they can neither be nor be conceived without
them."[44]

As this passage makes clear, Spinoza's doctrine is that we can only
arrive at adequate knowledge of particular things through, and in
terms of, the series of fixed and eternal things. His highly metaphorical characterization of these things as "codes" in which the laws
of nature are inscribed calls attention to their status as ultimate
principles, or categories, of scientific explanation. It is somewhat
strange, of course, that Spinoza should here characterize these principles as "things" and later, in the *Ethics*, as "modes," but presumably
he did this to underscore their difference from Aristotelian class
concepts. The latter, as we shall see in our discussion of Spinoza's
epistemology, are viewed as mere products of the imagination, without adequate basis in the nature of things. The fixed and eternal things,
by contrast, are more real than the particular things, since they are the
source of the very essences of these things—that is, they are that in
terms of which their natures are to be understood. As such, they are
rather like what Hegel later called "concrete universals"—that is,
universals which, as unique wholes, contain the particulars within
themselves. At least, Spinoza suggests as much when he writes: "So

although these fixed and eternal things are singular, nevertheless, because of their presence everywhere, and most extensive power, they will be to us like universals, *or* genera of the definitions of singular, changeable things, and the proximate causes of all things.[45]

This extremely schematic account is made more intelligible by a consideration of the designated eternal and infinite modes of extension. As Spinoza makes clear in his account of the elements of corporeal nature in the *Ethics*, each particular body is conceived of in terms of its proportion of motion and rest.[46] This, in turn, is tantamount to claiming that "motion and rest" functions as a basic category of scientific explanation, which is perfectly in accord with Galilean-Cartesian physics. Furthermore, by giving motion and rest the status of an eternal and infinite mode, Spinoza endeavors to overcome a basic difficulty in Descartes's physics. Having identified matter with extension, Descartes concluded that it could not contain a principle of motion (force) and hence of individuation within itself. Consequently, he found it necessary to introduce the action of God in order to explain the origin of motion and the division of matter into distinct bodies. Such a view was completely unacceptable to Spinoza, as we have seen, and his doctrine that motion and rest is derived directly from the attribute of extension (which follows from its status as an eternal and infinite mode) can be understood as his attempt to correct this aspect of Cartesian physics.[47]

The "face of the whole universe" can be understood in a similar manner. As a mediate eternal and infinite mode of extension, it must follow directly from motion and rest. Now, like all eternal and infinite modes, motion and rest is immutable; but, since the proportion of motion and rest in particular regions of corporeal nature is constantly changing, the immutability can hold only of corporeal nature as a whole. The face of the whole universe is identical, however, with corporeal nature as a whole. Consequently, it is in terms of it that Spinoza endeavors to "deduce" the principle of the conservation of motion, which is a basic principle of Cartesian physics.[48] Furthermore, in the portion of the *Ethics* to which Spinoza refers Schuller with regard to this conception, he argues that, precisely because it maintains a constant proportion of motion and rest, corporeal nature as a whole can be regarded as a distinct individual "whose parts, i.e., all bodies, vary in infinite ways, without any change of the whole Individual."[49] Since it is identical with corporeal nature as a whole, the same can be said of the face of the whole universe. Consequently, it, like the other fixed and eternal things, must be conceived as a "universal individual," or a concrete universal, that includes its particulars within itself and in terms of which these particulars must be understood.

The doctrine of eternal and infinite modes, which, as we have just seen, is constructed on the basis of a few hints scattered throughout a variety of texts, raises problems enough in its own right. Certainly, many (but not all) contemporary philosophers would have difficulty with the idea that the fundamental laws of nature have the kind of necessity Spinoza seems to ascribe to them by linking them directly to the attributes of God. The most pressing problem, however, concerns his attempt to connect this general framework with the particular things, processes, and events in nature—that is, the series of finite modes. The basic problem can be formulated in either metaphysical or scientific terms. Speaking metaphysically, it seems clear that particulars, or finite modes, cannot be derived directly from either the attributes or the eternal and infinite modes, because then they would themselves be eternal and infinite. Speaking scientifically, it is equally clear that particular occurrences cannot be deduced solely from a set of universal principles and laws. Consequently, Spinoza must explain how, in spite of this, particulars do, nonetheless, depend on God and in some sense participate in the divine necessity.

Spinoza begins his attempt to deal with this problem by noting that *"the essence of things produced by God does not involve existence"* (P24), and that *"God is the efficient cause, not only of the existence of things, but also of their essence"* (P25). The first of these propositions follows from the analysis of what it means to claim that the essence of something involves existence—namely, that it is self-caused (D1). Given this, it is self-contradictory to say of something both that it is produced by God and that its essence involves existence. The second proposition is equally clear. Its negation entails that the essences of things could be conceived apart from God, which contradicts the theorem that *"whatever is, is in God, and nothing can be or be conceived without God"* (P15). Moreover, from the second claim, Spinoza infers that "particular things are nothing but affections of God's attributes, or modes by which God's attributes are expressed in a certain determinate way" (P25C). This is the first explicit reference to particular things, or finite modes, in the argument. Unfortunately, its significance is not immediately apparent, because instead of developing his account of such modes, Spinoza continues with his general account of the divine causality. Thus, he argues that everything that has been determined to act in a certain way must have been so determined by God, and that anything that has not been so determined cannot determine itself (P26). Correlatively, once determined, a being cannot render itself undetermined (P27). Only after completing the outlines of his general account of the dependence of all things on God does Spinoza return to the problem of the specific nature of the dependence of particulars, of finite modes. He writes:

> *Every singular thing, or any thing which is finite and has a determinate existence, can neither exist nor be determined to produce an effect unless it is determined to exist and produce an effect by another cause, which is also finite and has a determinate existence; and again, this cause also can neither exist nor be determined to produce an effect unless it is determined to exist and produce an effect by another, which is also finite and has a determinate existence, and so on, to infinity.* [P28]

At first glance, this picture of an infinite causal chain of individual things, which never gets back to God as its starting point, seems to contradict the doctrine of the dependence of all things on God. The contradiction, however, is only apparent. First, since each of these things is a finite mode, in depending on other finite modes, it is still depending on God, albeit on God *qua* modified in a determinate way. Second, since each individual thing, as a "modification of a modification," is an instantiation of a general law, or principle (an eternal and infinite mode), it is also the case that each is governed by these general laws, or principles, and therefore, ultimately by God.

The upshot of the matter is that, within the arcane metaphysical framework in which Spinoza presents his doctrine of divine causality, there is at least the outline of a thoroughly modern conception of scientific explanation.[50] According to this conception, every particular occurrence in nature must be understood in terms of two intersecting lines of explanation. On the one hand, there must be a set of general laws, which for Spinoza at least, are logically necessary (since they are derived from the attributes and eternal and infinite modes of God); on the other hand, there must be a chain of antecedent conditions, which instantiate these laws and serve as the causes of subsequent occurrences. Both are necessary in order to explain a given occurrence. In order to explain the phenomenon of thunder, for example, we must appeal to the laws of physics.[51] By means of these laws alone, however, one could never deduce or explain the occurrence of a particular clap of thunder at a particular time. This requires that we refer also to the antecedent state of the atmosphere. Nevertheless, given the appropriate atmospheric state at t_1 (as specified by the laws of physics), the clap of thunder follows necessarily at t_2. Certainly, the universality of this deterministic scheme is at least part of what Spinoza means when he claims that "*in nature there is nothing contingent, but all things have been determined by the necessity of the divine nature to exist and produce an effect in a certain way*" (P29).

The really interesting question, however, is whether this is *all* Spinoza means by his denial of contingency. Certainly, claims such as that "*things could have been produced by God in no other way and in no other order than they have been produced*" (P33) suggest a stronger doctrine to the effect that things could not have been otherwise, that the actual order of nature is the only conceivable (logically possible) order, or, as it is usually put, that the actual world is the only possible world. Traditionally, Spinoza has been read as advocating the latter position; but this has been called into question in recent literature.[52]

In order to grasp just what is at stake here, it is important to realize that the deterministic scheme attributed to Spinoza so far does not entail that things could not have been otherwise. On the contrary, it maintains that particular occurrences are necessary only in relation to their cause, not that they are absolutely, or unconditionally, necessary. To return to the previous example, the necessity of a thunder clap at t_2 is a function of the laws of nature (themselves unconditionally necessary in Spinoza's view) and the occurrence of the appropriate atmospheric conditions at t_1. Without the latter, there would be no thunder. To be sure, the occurrence of the appropriate atmospheric conditions is itself a necessary consequence of prior conditions, and so on ad infinitum; thus, no matter how far we proceed along the infinite chain of finite modes, we can never encounter one that is not relatively necessary—that is, necessary, given its cause. At no point, however, would we come across one that is unconditionally necessary. But if no member of the chain is unconditionally necessary, then, since a change in one member would entail a change in the entire series, it would seem to be at least conceivable that the order of finite modes could have been other than it is.

In addition, it is sometimes claimed not only that the stronger doctrine (usually called "necessitarianism") does not follow from the weaker (usually called "determinism"), but that it is incompatible with the basic principles of Spinoza's thought. The contention is that necessitarianism entails that the essence of finite things involves their existence, which is to say that their existence, like that of God, is unconditionally, or absolutely, necessary. But this explicitly contradicts proposition 24 and undermines the contrast between natura naturans and natura naturata. Thus, in order to save Spinoza from himself, there is a strong temptation to argue that Spinoza is committed only to determinism.

Although the issues are far too complex and technical to be dealt with adequately here, something can be said regarding Spinoza's position and a possible Spinozistic response to the kind of criticism of necessitarianism sketched above. The first thing to note here is that Spinoza himself explicitly distinguishes two grounds on the basis of which things can be deemed necessary. Thus, in his discussion of contingency (understood as the opposite of necessity), he remarks that "a thing is called necessary either by reason of its essence or by reason of its cause" (P33S1).[53] Given this, the key question is whether

Spinoza's distinction between different grounds for affirming necessity is compatible with the necessitarian claim that there is a single kind of necessity (absolute or logical) pertaining to all things. Spinoza's critics and those who wish to save him from himself assume that it is not, because they tend to identify the contrast between logical, or absolute, and relative necessity with Spinoza's contrast between being necessary by reason of essence and being necessary by reason of cause. This may seem to be a natural thing to do, but there are good Spinozistic reasons for not doing it. For one thing, as has just been emphasized, Spinoza's distinction is not between kinds of necessity, but rather between grounds for claiming that something is necessary. For another, Spinoza is committed to the proposition that something can be both absolutely, or logically, necessary and "necessary by reason of its cause," rather than "by reason of its essence."[54]

In order to clarify what is meant by this and to show its relevance to our present concerns, we need a further distinction: namely, that between a consideration of finite modes or a finite subset of such modes taken individually and a consideration of the infinite series of such modes as a totality. From what we have already seen, it is clear that the former kind of consideration can never eliminate contingency; any particular finite mode or finite subset of such modes, considered in abstraction from the whole order of nature, can easily be thought (or imagined) to have been otherwise. In that sense, then, it is contingent. It does not follow from this, however, that the infinite totality of finite modes, the order of nature considered as a whole, can itself be viewed as contingent. Indeed, how this totality is to be characterized is precisely what is at issue.

One possible way of dealing with this question is to dismiss it out of hand as illegitimate, on the grounds that it rests on a category mistake, the misconstrual of the sum total of things as itself a kind of higher order "super-thing." This is precisely how Kant, in his account of "The Antinomy of Pure Reason," dealt with similar questions about the totality of things. Such a move is not open to Spinoza, however. Not only does he regard the whole order of nature as an individual of a higher order; he is required to do so by virtue of his understanding of the principle of sufficient reason. In other words, he cannot reject the "why" question with respect to either a particular individual or the totality of individuals.[55]

Similar considerations prevent Spinoza from acquiescing to another reasonable response to the totality question: namely, that of stipulating that this totality—that is, the whole order of nature—is simply a brute fact. The reason for this should be clear from the previous discussion of the ontological argument, the goal of which, it will be recalled, was not to prove that substance exists, but rather that it possesses necessary, as opposed to contingent, or *de facto*, existence. Once again, to allow sheer contingency at this or, indeed, any level is to deny the ultimate intelligibility of things and thus to undermine the deepest commitment of Spinoza's philosophy.

We thus see that, for Spinoza at least, intelligibility requires necessity. To understand why something is the case is to understand that, in some sense, it had to be. In dealing with the order of nature considered as a whole, however, the necessity required cannot be of the merely relative variety applicable to a particular item or set of items within this order. This is because there can be nothing contingent outside this order, on which it could depend. To assume the contrary is, in effect, to ground this order in the will of God. But not only does this reintroduce contingency at the heart of things; it also involves the very creationism that Spinoza takes such great pains to repudiate.

Given all this, it seems clear that Spinoza's extreme rationalism commits him to the doctrine of the absolute, or logical, necessity of the whole order of nature. In a word, Spinoza is a necessitarian, not simply a determinist. The actual world is the only possible world. But this does not mean that this order is necessary because of its essence, rather than its cause. Its cause is God; and God acts from the necessity of his nature (P17C2), not from free will. Consequently, a different order is inconceivable. This is not because the thought of a different order (another possible world) is self-contradictory, however; it is rather because it entails that God, the cause, or logical ground, of this order would be different. As we shall see in more detail in the next section, it is this latter thought that is self-contradictory. Admittedly, major objections can and have been raised against this position, particularly insofar as it relies so heavily on a strong form of the principle of sufficient reason. But these are objections to the position that Spinoza held, not to the claim that he held it.

III Some Theological Implications

The traditional conception of God as a person endowed with intellect and free will and the associated doctrine of the creation of the world have been left far behind by the relentless progress of Spinoza's argument. Nevertheless, apart from a brief aside (P17S), in which Spinoza affirms that he will show later that "neither intellect nor will pertain to God's nature," his repudiation of the traditional doctrine of God, as well as some of the other doctrines that we have already touched on, has remained more or less implicit and beneath the surface. The main function of the final section of the first part of the *Ethics* (P30–P36 and the appendix dealing with final causes that we have discussed already) is to make all this perfectly explicit and to underline the radical distinction between the God of the *Ethica ordine geometrico demonstrata* and the God of the religious tradition.

The first target is the notion of the divine intellect, which has traditionally been viewed as archetypal—that is, as the source of the plan in accordance with which the world was created by an act of divine will. This is contrasted with the ectypal human, or finite, intellect, which derives its ideas from preexisting objects. Now Spinoza, as we have already seen, does not completely reject the whole notion of a divine, or infinite, intellect. He does deny it any creative or archetypal function, however, and he carefully interprets it so as to avoid any anthropomorphic implications.

The former of these tasks is accomplished through the proposition that "*an actual intellect, whether finite or infinite, must comprehand God's attributes, and God's affections, and nothing else*" (P30). This innocent-sounding assertion is based on the truism that "a true idea must agree with its object" (A6), and the contention already established that there are literally no other objects for any mind to consider except the attributes of God and their modifications. The significance of this lies in the fact that it effectively undermines any attempt to establish a qualitative difference, or difference in kind, between a human, or finite, and a divine, or infinite, intellect. Any intellect, whether finite or infinite, must relate to its objects in precisely the same way. Thus, to the extent to which it possesses adequate ideas, the human intellect apprehends its objects in precisely the same manner as an infinite intellect. Moreover, for Spinoza, far from being an archetypal or creative intellect, the infinite intellect is not really an actual intellect at all. It is rather the mere idea of the sum total of possible knowledge, or the knowledge of the whole order of nature, as expressed in and through each of the infinite attributes. Nevertheless, because it refers to the complete knowledge of a unique whole (nature), Spinoza attributes to it a certain specificity and concreteness and hence views it, like other fixed and eternal things, as a kind of universal individual that has a reality above and beyond that of the items of which it is composed.[56]

This already presupposes that the infinite understanding is a mode, belonging to natura naturata rather than natura naturans, and Spinoza proceeds to make this explicit: *"The actual intellect, whether finite or infinite, like will, desire, love, etc., must be referred to Natura naturata, not to Natura naturans"* (P31). The point of this, of course, is that one cannot meaningfully apply the notion of intellect to God and affirm, in the manner of the religious tradition, that "God has an intellect." Yet, given the fact that Spinoza regards thought as a genuine attribute of God, the exclusion of intellect from the divine nature might seem to be a bit strange. The actual argument turns on the very distinction between thought as an attribute, or "absolute thought," and intellect. As Spinoza affirms in the scholium, by *intellect* is meant "intellect itself"—that is, the act of understanding—and not some mysterious capacity or potentiality—for example, the "potential intellect" of Aristotle. But this act, as well as other modes of thought, such as volitions and desires, depends on, and can only be conceived through, thought itself. Spinoza thus seems to view the act of intellection or understanding as the affirmation of a particular, determinate portion of the total realm of thought, which, therefore, presupposes this realm as a pregiven totality, precisely in the manner in which a particular body presupposes the whole of extension for Descartes. The limitation to a particular affirmation applies only to a finite intellect, but since Spinoza has just shown that the infinite intellect does not differ in kind from the finite variety, but rather affirms, in precisely the same manner, the whole realm of adequate ideas, it too can be said to presuppose the attribute of thought and thus to be a mere mode.

As the formulation of the above proposition makes clear, this conclusion holds not only for intellect, but for other modes of thought, including will. Nevertheless, Spinoza proceeds to argue that *"the will cannot be called a free cause, but only a necessary one"* (P32). The point here is to show that even if one wished to attribute will to God or to talk about an infinite will, one could not conclude that God acts from freedom of the will. God, to be sure, has been defined as a "free cause," and this has been shown to be equivalent to being self-determined; but what we now see is that God is not such a cause by virtue of a free will. This follows from the very definition of will as "only a certain mode of thinking." The point here is that, as a mode, will, whether finite or infinite, requires a cause that conditions it to act. Consequently (by D7), it cannot be called a free cause, but only a necessary, or constrained, one.

But, if things follow necessarily from the nature of God, rather than from an act of free will, then it certainly holds that *"things could have been produced by God in no other way, and in no other order than they have been produced"* (P33). We have already discussed this proposition, in conjunction with proposition 29, in our consideration of Spinoza's necessitarianism. In that context, it has considerable systematic importance. Like the other propositions discussed in this section, however, it also has significance for the understanding of Spinoza's opposition to traditional theology.

Perhaps no belief is more integral to the Western religious tradition, which includes Judaism, Christianity and Islam, than that God created the world through an act of free choice, and that, if he had so desired, he could have created either a different world or no world at all. Only such a God, it is commonly believed, can be considered in any meaningful sense to be a person to whom one can appropriately attribute moral qualities such as goodness and mercy, and only such a God can be a suitable object of worship. After all, if God had no choice in the matter, how can we possibly call creation good or God a perfect being? Indeed, what is the difference between a God who functions without free choice and blind fate? Spinoza had previously touched on this problem in passing; but now he confronts it head on and attempts to show that, even on the basis of their own assumptions, theologians must accept his conclusions.

First, assuming for the sake of argument that God acts out of freedom of will, a God who could change his desires or decree other than what he has would necessarily have a different intellect and will. But since, as the proponents of this theory assume, God's intellect and will pertain to his nature, this implies that God's very nature would be different. Yet these same theologians also assume that God's actual nature is supremely perfect. Consequently, they are forced to conclude that if God had in fact decreed other than he did, he would be less than perfect. Against this it might be objected that there is no intrinsic perfection or imperfection in things, and that what is perfect or imperfect depends solely on the will of God, "and so, if God had willed, He could have brought it about that what is now perfection would have been the greatest imperfection, and conversely" (P33S2). This is the view of Calvin and Descartes, in fact, and Spinoza is easily able to show that it succumbs to precisely the same dialectic. Since God necessarily understands what he wills, Spinoza reasons, this view amounts to the claim that God might understand things differently from the way in which He does understand them, which leads to the same absurdity as before. God's will, after all, cannot be different from God's perfection, and, therefore, on the theologians' own assumption, things cannot be different. But although Spinoza totally repudiates the theory which "subjects all things to a certain indifferent will of God, and makes all things depend on his good pleasure," he nevertheless suggests that it is nearer to the truth than the theory which holds that "God does all things for the sake of the good" (P33S2). This doctrine, which is at least as old as Plato's *Euthyphro* and which was later developed by Leibniz, is dismissed with the utmost contempt. By conceiving of God as acting for the sake of some preestablished goal (the good), it submits God to a kind of external control, and, therefore, like the other view, undermines his divinity.

Even granting that God could not have created a less than perfect world, however, and that only one such world is conceivable,[57] it still does not follow that God had to create any world at all. Perhaps, then, in the sheer contingency and unfathomable mystery of the decision to create, we can locate the cherished element of divine choice. To such a claim Spinoza has a ready answer: "*God's power is his essence itself*" (P34). This conclusion is derived from the principle that things follow from the very nature or essence of God. Its clear implication is that the suggestion that God might not have exercised his power—that is, that he might not have created at all—is once again equivalent to the absurd claim that God has the power not to be God. Spinoza thus concludes against the theologians that "*whatever we conceive to be in God's power, necessarily exists*" (P35), which amounts to an explicit denial of the suggestion that the world might not have come into existence. The final proposition, "*There is no cause from whose nature some effect does not follow*" (P36), does not seem to fall within this line of argument, but it does reflect Spinoza's view that every particular thing participates in or expresses the infinite power of God, or nature, in a conditioned manner.[58] It also serves, perhaps, as a transition to the discussion of final causes, which are in fact regarded by Spinoza as causes from which no effects follow.

Despite his diametrically opposed point of view, Spinoza had no qualms about meeting theologians on their own ground and showing either that their views could be reduced to absurdity or that they entailed his own. In so doing, he completed his project of replacing the traditional conception of God as a superhuman person with the scientifically inspired conception of nature as an infinite, necessary, self-contained, and, above all, thoroughly intelligible system. It is important to realize, however, that Spinoza did not merely wish to keep the word *God* while emptying it of all significance. Rather, his intent was to show that, properly understood, it referred to nature, and to nature alone. This nature does not possess an intellect or a will, and thus it does not act for the benefit of humanity. Yet, although it is not *intelligent*, it is *intelligible*, which the God of the theologians is not. Moreover, since there is literally no power apart from it that can in any way limit it, this nature is in the fullest sense of the word *omnipotent*. Thus, no matter what one may think of Spinoza's logic, there can be no doubt about his sincerity and the depth of the conviction with which he identified God and nature. For Spinoza, as for other thinkers of a similar persuasion such as Goethe, who have no use for the traditional conception of God, the features of nature mentioned above are more than enough to qualify it as divine.

CHAPTER 4

The Human Mind

I n his brief preface to part 2 of the *Ethics*, entitled "On the Nature and Origin of the Mind," Spinoza writes: *"I pass now to explaining those things which must necessarily follow from the essence of God, or the infinite and eternal Being—not, indeed, all of them, for we have demonstrated (IP16) that infinitely many things must follow from it in infinitely many modes, but only those that can lead us, by the hand, as it were, to the knowledge of the human Mind, and its highest blessedness."*

This sets the agenda, not only for the second part, but for the remainder of the *Ethics* as a whole. It also provides a clear indication of the ultimately practical orientation of Spinoza's thought. The elaborate metaphysical analysis of part 1 was not presented as an end in itself, but rather as a necessary first step in the acquisition of knowledge regarding the nature of the human mind. Thus, in accordance with his deductive method, Spinoza's account of the mind will involve an application of general metaphysical principles. Even this project, however, which is the specific concern of part 2, is not undertaken as an end in itself, but as a necessary prelude to the determination of the nature of human blessedness and the means to attain it.

The argument of part 2 can be divided into three parts: an analysis of the nature of the mind and its relation to the body (P1–P15); an analysis of the intellect and of the nature and extent of human knowledge (P16–P47); and an analysis of the will, its alleged freedom, and its relation to the intellect (P48–P49). Unlike most contemporary philosophers, and even to some extent Descartes, Spinoza does not treat these topics in isolation. In each case his analysis is based on the same general principles; moreover, his treatment of the mind-body problem serves as the point of departure for his treatment of the other two. For the purpose of exposition, however, it is convenient to divide Spinoza's analysis in this manner, and the present chapter is structured accordingly.

I The Mind and Its Relation to the Body

In spite of its extreme crypticness, which has generated wildly different interpretations, Spinoza's account of the mind and its relation to the body is one of the most intriguing aspects of his philosophy. Moreover, far from being a historical curiosity, it has proved to be of considerable relevance to contemporary discussions of the topic.[1] Spinoza's theory is designed primarily to account for the unity of human nature and to show that the mind, as well as the body, is part of universal nature and, therefore, subject to its necessary laws. As such, this theory contrasts sharply with Cartesian dualism, with its conception of mind and body as two distinct, yet interacting, substances. It is equally opposed, however, to a materialistic theory, such as that of his contemporary Thomas Hobbes, which allows only for bodies and motion in the universe and therefore identifies thought with a physical process.[2] Although many aspects of Spinoza's psychological theory undoubtedly owe a great deal to Hobbes,[3] Spinoza staunchly resisted any attempt to reduce thought to its physical correlate or to explain ideas in terms of anything in the realm of extension.[4]

Spinoza endeavors to avoid both Cartesian ontological dualism and Hobbesian reductive materialism by appealing to his doctrine of attributes. This allows him to affirm the autonomous, self-contained nature of thought, without making mind into a distinct substance. As two of the infinite attributes of the one substance, thought and extension are not separate entities, but distinct expressions of the same reality. Moreover, since the human mind and the human body are both finite modifications of these attributes, the same can be said of them. The general principle is that, just as "the thinking substance and the · extended substance are one and the same substance, which is now comprehended under this attribute, now under that . . . a mode of extension and the idea of that mode are one and the same thing, but expressed in two ways" (P75). Later, after having characterized the human mind as the idea of the body (P13), Spinoza remarks in passing that "the Mind and the Body are one and the same Individual, which is conceived now under the attribute of Thought, now under the attribute of Extension" (P21S). He thus advocates a kind of mind-body identity theory, albeit one that differs from the usual materialistic versions of such a theory in its insistence on giving equal weight to the mental.

As already indicated, Spinoza's argument for his identity thesis moves deductively from general principles concerning the attributes of thought and extension to specific conclusions concerning the mind and body as finite modifications of these attributes or, better, as finite expressions of substance conceived under the attributes of thought and extension respectively. The first thing to be established is that thought and extension are two of the infinite number of attributes of God (P1 and P2). From this Spinoza deduces several basic claims. To begin with, since thought is an attribute of God and hence an expression of his infinite essence, *"in God there is necessarily an idea, both of his essence and of everything that necessarily follows from his essence"* (P3). This proposition serves a twofold function. First, it underscores the all-inclusiveness of the attribute of thought and of its immediate eternal and infinite mode, the infinite intellect. Such an intellect, as we have seen already, stands for the realization of all possible knowledge, the complete description of the universe. Consequently, it encompasses everything that follows from the nature of God, which, given Spinoza's necessitarianism, means everything conceivable. Second, it entails that there is an idea, or modification, in the attribute of thought corresponding to the modifications of substance in each of the infinite attributes. This, as will become apparent later, is a crucial ingredient in Spinoza's account of the mind-body relationship, but it also raises questions about the overall coherence of his position, questions that were pressed by Tschirnhaus in his correspondence with Spinoza.[5]

The next thing to be established is the self-containedness of the attribute of thought. This is already implicit in the claim that, since

God is one, the idea of God—that is, the infinite intellect—is one (P4). It is made fully explicit, however, in the next proposition: "*The formal being of ideas admits God as a cause only insofar as he is considered as a thinking thing and not insofar as he is explained by any other attribute. I.e., ideas, both of God's attributes and of singular things, admit not the objects themselves, or the things perceived as their efficient cause, but God himself, insofar as he is a thinking thing*" (P5). Since God, insofar as he is a thinking thing, is equivalent to thought viewed as an attribute, Spinoza's point is simply that each idea must be caused by another idea, and that this is what makes the realm of thought a self-contained whole. But, as he proceeds to remind the reader, this by no means reflects any special privilege for thought; on the contrary, it holds for all the attributes, each of which can be conceived as a self-determined, self-contained whole (P6).

Having established the all-inclusiveness and self-containedness of the attribute of thought, Spinoza's next task is to spell out the implications of these characteristics for the understanding of the relationship between thought and the only other attribute known to us, extension. More specifically, what he must show is that "*the order and connection of ideas is the same as the order and connection of things*" (P7). Although this would seem to be a fairly obvious consequence of previously established principles, it turns out to be one of the most perplexing, as well as one of the most important, propositions in the entire *Ethics*. Certainly, it is a key to Spinoza's account of the nature of the human mind and its relation to the body.

The perplexing nature of this proposition stems in part from the very different senses in which this deceptively simple formula can be taken and in part from the peculiar way in which Spinoza attempts to demonstrate it. The first-mentioned source of perplexity, however, is itself a direct consequence of the ambiguities inherent in Spinoza's conception of an idea. Thus, if we are to understand this proposition, or even why it is so perplexing, we must digress a bit in order to consider briefly Spinoza's account of ideas. Since this account is central not only to his views on the mind-body relation, but also to his treatment of knowledge and will, our consideration should prove helpful for understanding part 2 of the *Ethics* as a whole.

According to Spinoza's official definition, an idea is a "concept of the Mind that the Mind forms because it is a thinking thing" (D3). By distinguishing between conception (*conceptum*) and perception (*perceptionem*) in his explanation of this definition, Spinoza emphasizes the activity of the mind. Insofar as the mind has ideas, it does not passively perceive, but actively conceives, it object. Moreover, since we shall see that to conceive of something is to form a belief about it, ideas can be equated with beliefs.[6] In other words, to have an idea of something is to have a belief about it, not simply to have a mental picture or description of it. Although further discussion of this topic must await the consideration of Spinoza's actual arguments, we can see already how this conception of an idea makes it possible for him to identify the mind with ideas (strictly speaking, with a single complex idea). Insofar as ideas are essentially acts of conceiving, or believing, this identification amounts to the claim that the mind is nothing above and beyond its activity, that its unity and individuality are the unity and individuality of this activity. We will also see that this conception has its precise parallel in Spinoza's conception of body.

Unfortunately, things do not remain quite so simple once one takes into consideration some of the other things that Spinoza says about ideas. At times, particularly when he is referring to ideas "in God," Spinoza seems to equate ideas with propositions—that is, with the content of beliefs—rather than with actual acts of belief. Carried to its extreme, this results in what has been called the "logicising" of the attribute of thought, by which is meant the reduction of this attribute to the sum total of true propositions.[7] At other times, however, particularly when he is considering the mind as the idea of the body, he seems to treat ideas as if they were (or could be) nothing more than mental correlates of physical occurrences or states, without any propositional content whatsoever. Moreover, insofar as ideas are considered in the latter manner, their "object" is identified with their physical counterpart (in the case of the human mind, this is the human body); whereas, insofar as they are considered as beliefs, it is assumed that they can refer to any number of objects. Not surprisingly, then, Spinoza has frequently been accused of a gross confusion or equivocation in his account of ideas.[8]

This problem, in its various forms, will be with us throughout this chapter and the next, but we can begin our consideration of it by noting the contrast made by Spinoza between the "formal" and the "objective" reality of ideas. This is a traditional scholastic distinction, which is also found in Descartes and which Spinoza adapts to his own purposes. In brief, the formal reality of an idea is its reality as a mental episode, or occurrence; whereas its objective reality is its reality as a representation with a propositional content.[9] Thus, construing ideas as beliefs, every idea can be described as both a mental episode with its own psychological reality (a believing) and a propositional content that is affirmed in such an episode (what is believed). Construed as mental episodes, ideas have causes, which, according to Spinoza, are always other ideas (P5). Construed as beliefs, they have grounds, or premises, which again must always be other ideas. At least part of the confusion surrounding Spinoza's account of ideas can be removed simply by keeping this distinction in mind.

Of more immediate relevance is the fact that this distinction enables us to see just what is so perplexing in Spinoza's claim that *the order and connection of ideas is the same as the order and connection of things*. One wants to know whether this applies to ideas considered formally or objectively or both. A consideration of the uses to which the proposition is put in the subsequent argument makes it clear that it is intended to apply to ideas taken in both ways. In other words, it is to be taken both as a psychological claim about the causal sequence of mental occurrences, or episodes (the formal reality of ideas), and as a logical claim about the inferential ordering of our conceptions or beliefs (the objective reality of ideas). Now, there seems to be relatively little difficulty with this claim insofar as it applies to the objective reality of ideas. Since this reality is its conceptual content, and since this is equivalent to the reality of the object of which it is an idea *qua* grasped in thought, the order and connection of ideas, so construed, is identical to the order and connection of things. At least this is the case insofar as we are considering "true ideas"—that is, the order of ideas as contained in the infinite intellect of God. It is by no means obvious, however, that the same can be said about the formal reality of ideas. There would seem to be no reason why the causal sequence of ideas considered as mental occurrences should have to mirror the causal sequence of the "things" of which they are ideas.

The problem is only compounded by the proof offered by Spinoza on behalf of this proposition. Although, as we have seen, the first six propositions of part 2 seem to pave the way for it, Spinoza contends that it is evident simply from axiom 4 of part 1, which he here takes as the principle that "the idea of each thing caused depends on the knowledge [*cognitione*] of the cause of which it is an effect."[10] Once again, while this axiom can be taken to support the logical reading of the proposition, which doesn't really need it, it hardly seems to support the psychological reading. Why, after all, should a claim about the dependence of the knowledge, or cognition, of an effect on the knowledge, or cognition, of a cause have anything to do with the causal order of ideas considered as mental occurrences?[11]

This is one of many places in the *Ethics* where it is difficult for an interpreter to be confident about any proposed solution. Nevertheless, the basis for a possible explanation lies in the recognition of the fact that Spinoza is here talking specifically about the ordering of ideas in the infinite intellect of God—that is, the logically correct ordering of ideas. As we shall see in the next section, insofar as it has adequate ideas, the human mind also conceives things in this manner. But this means that, in such cases at least, the ideal logical order is also an actual psychological order. Consequently, since the logical order of ideas mirrors the causal order of things (IA4), and since (in this situation at least) the psychological order is identical with the logical order, the psychological order of ideas must likewise mirror the causal order of things. The point, in other words, is that, insofar as the intellect conceives things adequately, its ideas not only causally condition one another—for example, belief that A, or the act of believing A at t_1, is the cause of belief that B, or the act of believing B at t_2 (by P5)—but the causal order is also a logically correct order of inference—for example, the belief that A provides "adequate" (logically compelling) grounds for the belief that B. If this, or something like it, is Spinoza's view, then one can see why he could take proposition 7 to apply to ideas considered as formal, as well as objective, realities and even why he might appeal to the fourth axiom of part 1 in support of this claim.

Admittedly, the situation is considerably more problematic in the case of inadequate ideas, for which, by definition, the ordering is not logical—that is, where the belief that A precedes and causes but does not provide adequate grounds for the belief that B. That the parallelism doctrine is supposed to apply here too is evident from Spinoza's account of our inadequate imaginative and perceptual knowledge (which will be considered in the next section). Spinoza will claim that the causal order of our imaginative or perceptual ideas (considered with respect to their formal reality as mental episodes) mirrors the causal order of the states of our own body, which is itself determined by the order in which the body is affected by external bodies. Given its centrality to Spinoza's whole account of the human condition (our status as finite modes), it is not difficult to see why he would want to claim this. What *is* difficult to see is just how the above axiom is relevant to such a claim. One can make it relevant, of course, by taking it to entail the desired result; but then the "axiom" would stand as much in need of justification as the proposition it is supposed to support.

Fortunately, things are not quite as desperate as they appear to be, for this aspect of proposition 7 can be shown to follow from Spinoza's conception of substance, as developed in part 1, together with the earlier propositions of part 2, quite independently of any appeal to the axiom. The reasoning goes roughly like this. If thought is an attribute of God (P1)—that is, if it is one of many expressions of the necessary and universal order of nature; and if there must be an idea or mode of thought corresponding to the modes expressed in each of the other attributes (including extension) (P3);[12] and if these ideas, or modes of thought, considered with respect to their formal reality constitute a self-contained causal order (P5), then this causal order must correspond to the causal order as it is expressed under the attribute of extension (or any other attribute for that matter). The key to the argument is the move from the claim that there is a one-to-one mapping of modes as expressed in thought to modes as expressed in each of the other attributes to the claim that there is a similar mapping of the causal order of these modes as expressed in the various attributes. Although it is not easy to cite specific definitions, axioms, or propositions that license this move, which is perhaps why Spinoza felt compelled to press the axiom into service, it is likewise not easy to see how it could be denied without denying the unity of substance.

Even granting the main claims of proposition 7, however, more work must be done before Spinoza will be in a position to develop his conception of the human mind. One point to be considered, which might at first seem irrelevant to the main task, is the problem of ideas of nonexistent, or what other philosophers might call "potential," things. As infinite, the idea of God, or the infinite intellect, must include the ideas of all possible—that is, conceivable—things, not only ideas of things that happen to exist at a particular moment. This seems to conflict with the claim that *the order and connection of ideas is the same as the order and connection of things*. But the problem is solved by distinguishing between two senses in which a thing (mode of extension) can be said to exist. It can exist either in the sense that it can be deduced from the attribute of extension or in the sense that it follows from a given condition and actually exists, which for Spinoza means that it has a certain duration. Given the identity between the two orders, it follows that ideas must likewise exist in this twofold sense (P8). In other words, Spinoza uses the very principle that seems to give rise to the problem to resolve it.

In the scholium to this proposition he attempts to illustrate his thesis by means of a mathematical analogy. The nature of a circle, he points out, is such that if any number of straight lines intersect within it, the resulting rectangles will be equal to one another. None of these possible rectangles can be said to actually exist unless the circle exists. Nevertheless, given the circle, an infinite number of rectangles possibly exist in the sense that they can be constructed in the circle. Moreover, since each of these possible rectangles can be conceived, and thus *is* conceived by the infinite intellect, the same can be said in regard to the ideas of these rectangles. If, however, we suppose that of these infinite rectangles two actually exist, or are actually constructed, then, Spinoza concludes "their ideas also exist now not only insofar as they are only comprehended in the idea of the circle, but also insofar as they involve the existence of those rectangles. By this they are distinguished from the other ideas of the other rectangles" (P8S).

The significance of this analogy, which Spinoza admits is imperfect, becomes apparent as soon as one realizes that Spinoza will claim that the human mind is itself just an idea of an actually existing thing. As such, it must likewise exist in a twofold sense. As an idea in God, it subsists as a kind of eternal possibility; and as the idea of something actually existing, it has both an objective reality, which consists in the affirmation of the actual existence of its object (the human body), and a formal reality, which endures for as long as its object endures. We shall see that this is crucial for an understanding both of Spinoza's account of the nature of the mind in the remainder of part 2 and of his highly obscure remarks about the mind's eternity in part 5.

Our present concern, however, is still with the general metaphysical principles from which Spinoza will derive the nature of the mind. In order to follow this derivation, we need to learn a bit more about the ideas of actually existing things. Spinoza points out that such ideas do not follow directly from God *insofar as he is infinite*, but rather, from God "*insofar as he is considered to be affected by another idea of a singular thing which actually exists; and of this* [idea] *God is also the cause, insofar as he is affected by another third* [idea], *and so on, to infinity*" (P9). Since this is a direct consequence of the modal status of these ideas, it is not surprising. Of considerably more interest is the corollary, which states that "whatever happens in the singular object of an idea, there is knowledge of it in God, only insofar as he has the idea of the same object" (P9C). This likewise sounds innocent enough on the face of it; but since to be in God just means to be in the corresponding finite mode, this entails that whatever is in the object is reflected in its corresponding idea and nowhere else. The significance of this will soon become apparent.

The next step is to establish the connection between the mind and the idea of an actually existing thing. Since a human being is not a substance (P10), and since it is an undeniable fact that "man thinks" (A2), it follows that the essence of a human being must be constituted in part by certain modifications of the attribute of thought. But since for Spinoza, as for Descartes, ideas are the fundamental modifications of thought, in the sense that other modifications—for example, desires and volitions—presuppose ideas of their objects, it also follows that the basic modification constituting the mind must be an idea. Finally, since it is clear that human beings actually exist, it must be the idea of an actually existing thing. Combining all these points, Spinoza concludes that "*the first thing that constitutes the actual being of a human Mind is nothing but the idea of a singular thing which actually exists*" (P11).

On the basis of this contention, Spinoza adds, in a significant corollary, that the human mind is "part of the infinite intellect of God." We have already seen enough to realize that this mystical-sounding claim, which is central to Spinoza's epistemological and moral theories, is merely his way of making the point that the human mind is a member of, and participates in, the absolute, or total, system of thought. It is a finite, limited member, however, and Spinoza expresses this point by noting that statements of the form "The human mind perceives this or that" are equivalent to metaphysical statements of the form "God has this or that idea, not in so far as he is infinite, but in so far as he is displayed through the nature of the human mind" (P11C). This, again, is Spinoza's rather elaborate way of saying that perception follows from the particular nature of the perceiving mind and not from the absolute system of thought. We should note, however, that the word *perception* is used here, as elsewhere, in a very broad sense, to refer to all mental events, of which conscious apprehension is merely one particular manifestation.

This broad sense of perception, together with the principle of the identity of the order and connection of ideas with the order and connection of things, forms the basis of Spinoza's contention that "*whatever happens in the object of the idea constituting the human Mind must be perceived by the human Mind, or there will necessarily be an idea of that thing in the Mind; i.e., if the object of the idea constituting a human Mind is a body, nothing can happen in that body which is not perceived by the Mind"* (P12). This is one of the more paradoxical-sounding propositions in the *Ethics*, since it seems to commit Spinoza to the absurdity that the mind must be consciously aware of everything that occurs in the body (down to the sub-microscopic level). Fortunately, there is no need to read Spinoza in this way. His point is rather that the mind reflects the state of the body as a whole. Consequently, given the identity of the two orders, it follows that the state of the idea constituting a human mind must be a function of the state of the entire body. In other words, the mind varies in accordance with variations in the physical organism, and nothing occurs in the organism that does not have its mental correlate. It is in this sense, and in this sense alone, that the mind can be said to "perceive" everything that occurs in the body.[13]

One might still ask, however, how this can be reconciled with the characterization of ideas as beliefs. Certainly, it is just as paradoxical to claim that the mind has a belief about everything that occurs in the body as it is to contend that it perceives everything that occurs in it. One possible way to overcome the difficulty is to saddle Spinoza with the rather problematic notion of unconscious belief, which would commit him to the claim that there are an indefinite number of unconscious beliefs regarding various bodily occurrences. Another, more promising, way is to take the proposition to imply merely that the beliefs which the mind has (all of which are consciously held) reflect the state of the entire body. This would commit Spinoza only to the doctrine that everything that occurs in our body has its ideational counterpart, which, to some degree at least, influences our beliefs, not to the doctrine that we actually have beliefs (conscious or otherwise) *about* everything that occurs in the body. As we shall see in the next section, this is perfectly in accord with Spinoza's account of knowledge.

The nature of the connection between the mind and the body becomes fully explicit in the next proposition, in which Spinoza finally asserts that *"the object of the idea constituting the human Mind is the body, or a certain mode of extension which actually exists, and nothing else"* (P13). Although the demonstration of this proposition, which turns on the distinction between ideas being in God *qua* constituting our mind and *qua* constituting some other mind is highly obscure, the basic point seems clear enough: namely, that the human mind has an immediate, sensitive awareness of its own body and of its own body alone (I feel my own pain and not someone else's). Thus the object of the idea constituting my mind must be my body.

Far more problematic is the notorious scholium attached to this proposition. Presumably referring to the entire argument up to this point, Spinoza remarks: "For the things we have shown so far are completely general and do not pertain more to man than to other Individuals, all of which, though in different degrees, are nevertheless animate. For of each thing there is necessarily an idea in God, of which God is the cause in the same way as he is of the idea of the human Body. And so, whatever we have said of the idea of the human Body must also be said of the idea of any thing" (P13S).

The refusal to exempt human beings from the universal order of nature is characteristic of Spinoza. It is also readily understandable, given his overall approach. What is perplexing is the claim that all things, or at least all "Individuals,"[14] are animate (*animata*). Since the Latin adjective *animatus* is cognate with the French *âme* (soul), as well as the English *animate*, it would seem that Spinoza is attributing not merely life (which would be paradoxical enough), but also a soul in some sense analogous to a human mind (*mens*) to all things.[15] In short, it appears that Spinoza was led by his reasonable concern not to exempt human beings from the universal order of nature to affirm a wildly implausible panpsychism.

An initially attractive way of dealing with this problem is to rid Spinoza's claim of its paradoxical character by maintaining that all he means by it is that for every thing, or individual, x, there is in God, or in some Platonic heaven, an idea in the sense of a set of true propositions about x. This solution amounts to the previously mentioned logicizing of the attribute of thought. It seems attractive at this point because Spinoza indeed holds that for every x there must be some such set of true propositions, and he does identify this set with the idea of x

in God. The difficulty with it, construed as a complete account of what Spinoza means by the attribution of a "soul" to a thing, is that it effectively eliminates the mental from the Spinozistic universe.[16] If the claim that x has a soul, or mind, means merely that there is a set of true propositions about x, then the claim that human beings have minds reduces to the claim that there is a set of true propositions about their individual bodies. This, to be sure, is a consequence with which a materialist would be quite content; but, for the reasons already given, it does not seem plausible to attribute such a view to Spinoza.

A far more plausible alternative is to take the claim that all things are animated to mean simply that there is a sense in which all things are alive.[17] Although such panvitalism might seem to be almost as outrageous as the panpsychism it is intended to replace, it is actually in accord with the main thrust of Spinoza's thought. Thus, in his Appendix to *Descartes' "Principles of Philosophy,"* where he is presumably speaking in his own voice, Spinoza defines life as "*the force through which things persevere in their being.*"[18] Moreover, later in the *Ethics*, he states that "*each thing, as far as it can by its own power, strives to persevere in its being*" (IIIP6). Given the above definition, this entails that everything is "alive"; and from this it is but a short way to the conclusion that everything has a "soul" in the sense of a principle of animation. The implications of this will become clearer in the next chapter, in which we will consider Spinoza's doctrine of *conatus*. For the present it must suffice to note that, although on this interpretation minds, or souls, are certainly attributable to far more things than rational beings (the Cartesian position), it does not commit Spinoza to the doctrine that everything has a mental life that is even remotely analogous to that enjoyed by the human mind.

Be that as it may, Spinoza still has the problem of explaining the superiority of the human mind over the "minds" of things lower down in the order of nature. He has a ready and ingenious solution to this problem, however. It turns on the distinction between different degrees of animation, or levels of mind, the precise degree, or level, being a function of the nature and capacity of the body. As he puts it in the same scholium: "In proportion as a Body is more capable than others of doing more things at once, or being acted on in many ways at once, so its Mind is more capable than others of perceiving many things at once. And in proportion as the actions of a body depend more on itself alone, and as other bodies concur with it less in acting, so its mind is more capable of understanding distinctly."

In spite of his arcane terminology and a priori deductive method, Spinoza here arrives once again at a thoroughly modern view— namely, that mind is a function of organic complexity. The more a body is able to interact with its environment, both to affect it and be affected by it, the greater the power of mind to perceive this environment. On this view, then, conscious awareness and rational insight are located on a continuum of "mental" powers, rather than being regarded as properties of a distinct thinking substance, as in the Cartesian view.

Although such a conception has many interesting implications, Spinoza largely ignores them in order to concentrate on the primary object of his concern, the human mind. As his functional approach makes clear, however, in order to understand the human mind, we must first acquire a more accurate knowledge of the nature of the human body. But, given Spinoza's deductive method, any such knowledge must be based on general considerations concerning the nature of all physical bodies. Consequently, Spinoza found it necessary to interrupt his analysis of the human mind and its cognitive capacities in order to make a brief foray into the realms of physics and biology. This occurs in a series of lemmata, axioms, and postulates that immediately follow proposition 13.

The analysis is divided into three parts. The first deals with the properties of the most simple bodies; the second is concerned with complex, organic bodies, or "individuals"; and the third consists of a series of postulates dealing specifically with the human body. As one might expect, the basic principle of the whole analysis is that all bodies are combinations of motion and rest. Accordingly, "*bodies are distinguished from one another by reason of motion and rest, speed and slowness, and not by reason of substance*" (L1). It follows from this that all bodies must agree in certain respects—that is, all bodies are conceived in terms of the same attribute and its principal modification (L2). Moreover, since every body is a finite mode, "*a body which moves or is at rest must be determined to motion or rest by another body, which has also been determined to motion or rest by another, and that again by another, and so on, to infinity*" (L3). From this, Spinoza is able to derive one of the basic principles of physics, the law of inertia: "A body in motion moves until it is determined by another body to rest; and . . . a body at rest also remains at rest until it is determined to motion by another" (L3C).

The discussion then shifts to complex bodies, which are compounded from the simple bodies, and it is in this context that Spinoza deals with the notions of individuality and life. The first question to be considered is the problem of identity. More specifically, in light of what principle can one claim that a number of distinct, simple bodies constitute a single individual? Spinoza's answer, which is based on the preceding analysis, is in terms of contact and preservation of the same proportion of motion and rest. Insofar as any given group of bodies is compelled by other bodies to remain in contact with one another, or insofar as they move in such a way as to communicate their motions to each other "*in a certain fixed manner,*" Spinoza contends, "*they all together compose one body or Individual, which is distinguished from others by this union of bodies.*"[19] A complex body, or individual, can thus retain its identity throughout a change in its component parts; and this principle provides the basis for Spinoza's schematic account of organic unity.

As Spinoza proceeds to suggest in the following lemmata (L4–L7), which deal, in terms of motion and rest, with the basic biological functions of metabolism, growth, motion of the limbs, and locomotion, the very essence of such unity—that is, the unity of a living being—consists in its ability to remain identical not only in spite of, but actually by means of, a constant change in its component parts (cells) and an ongoing interaction with its environment. Unfortunately, we cannot here consider this topic in any more detail. Nevertheless, it is worthy of note that, within the confines of a very brief space, Spinoza succeeds in developing the outlines of a speculative theory of organism that goes much further and gives promise of dealing with the nature of life in a far more adequate manner than Descartes's purely mechanistic account of the body.[20]

The discussion concludes with a series of postulates that, as already noted, apply these principles to the human body. We are told that this body is an individual of a very high degree of complexity, composed of a number of parts which are themselves complex individuals (P1). Some of these parts are fluid, some soft, and some hard (P2), but each of them, and consequently the body itself, is affected in a number of distinct ways by external factors (P3). Not only is the human body so affected, it also requires for its preservation "a great many other bodies, by which it is, as it were, continually regenerated" (P4). Finally, since it contains soft and fluid parts, it is capable of forming and retaining impressions when affected by external bodies (P5), while at the same time it can also affect external bodies in a variety of ways (P6). In short—and this is the whole point of Spinoza's analysis—since the human body is an extremely complex individual, which stands in a complex and reciprocal relationship with its environment, it turns out to be a suitable correlate for the human mind.

This is explicitly affirmed in the next two propositions, which conclude the discussion of the mind-body problem and prepare the ground for the analysis of human knowledge. Spinoza here points out that, since the human body is capable of affecting and being affected by a large number of bodies in a variety of ways, the human mind, as the idea of that body, "*is capable of perceiving a great many things, and is the more capable, the more its body can be disposed in a great many ways*" (P14). The perceptual power of the mind is thus a function of the sensitivity of the body. Finally, just as the human body is a complex individual composed of a great number of bodies, so, Spinoza concludes, "*the idea that constitutes the formal being of the human Mind is not simple; but composed of a great many ideas*" (P15).

II Human Knowledge

Although the view has been challenged recently, it is generally thought that epistemological questions play a decidedly subordinate role in Spinoza's philosophy.[21] According to the usual interpretation, Spinoza is, on the one hand, a dogmatic metaphysician who starts with God and works his way down to human beings and, on the other hand, a moralist concerned with the true good for human beings. Epistemological claims, to the extent that they enter at all into Spinoza's program, are deduced from metaphysical first principles and are formulated with an eye to their practical implications. In this respect, Spinoza is thought to differ markedly from Descartes, the empiricists, and Kant, all of whom regarded epistemological questions as primary.

The traditional reading is certainly correct in that, in the *Ethics* at least, Spinoza does not begin with a consideration of what we can know and how knowledge claims can be justified against a possible skeptical attack.[22] Instead, as we have seen, he begins with claims about substance, God, and so on, which seem to presuppose that the human mind possesses a significant body of metaphysical knowledge that is somehow immune to skeptical doubt. But Spinoza was hardly oblivious of the need to justify these metaphysical claims. Accordingly, in the second part of the *Ethics*, he attempts not only to show how we can have a genuine knowledge of nature, but also to demonstrate the apparently audacious claim that *"the human Mind has an adequate knowledge of God's eternal and infinite essence"* (P47). At the same time, Spinoza also desires to demonstrate that such knowledge comes from reason, and that insofar as the mind operates with ideas based on sense perception, it cannot arrive at any adequate knowledge at all. Consequently, his analysis of knowledge is divided into two parts, with the account of sense perception preceding that of reason, the positive power of the intellect.

One of the keys to Spinoza's analysis is the notion of adequacy, and in particular the conception of an adequate idea, which we have already touched on in passing. As Spinoza tells us at the beginning of the second part of the *Ethics*, "By adequate idea I understand an idea which, insofar as it is considered in itself, without relation to an object, has all the properties or intrinsic denominations of a true idea" (D4). In the explanation that follows this definition, he further notes, *"I say intrinsic to exclude what is extrinsic, viz. the agreement of the idea with its object."* Much the same point is made in response to

Tschirnhaus's query concerning the relationship between truth and adequacy, where Spinoza writes: "I recognize no other difference between a true and an adequate idea than that the word true refers only to the agreement of the idea with its *ideatum*, while the word adequate refers to the nature of the idea in itself; so that there is really no difference between a true and adequate idea except this extrinsic relation."[23]

These statements indicate that truth and adequacy are reciprocal notions. All true ideas are adequate, and vice versa. They differ only in that truth is defined in terms of the agreement of the idea with its object, or ideatum (these terms are equivalent). Because of this definition, Spinoza is usually regarded as advocating a version of the correspondence theory of truth—that is, the view that construes truth as the correspondence with, or agreement between, beliefs or propositions and states of affairs or facts.[24] A major difference between Spinoza's view and the correspondence theory as traditionally construed is that for him, idea and ideatum are not regarded as distinct entities, but as one and the same thing expressed in two ways. In part for this reason and in part because of his conception of the attribute of thought as a self-contained system which, as such, does not involve reference to any extrinsic reality, Spinoza is sometimes thought to hold a coherence theory of truth.[25] Reduced to its simplest terms, this theory maintains that the truth of a belief or proposition is a function of its place within the total system of true beliefs or propositions. Such a conception is generally associated with certain forms of idealism, wherein it is maintained that in some sense the structure of reality reflects the structure of thought (rather than vice versa). However, just as Spinoza's view differs from the correspondence theory as commonly understood in that he regards idea and ideatum as one and the same thing, so too, it differs from the coherence theory in that he maintains that the order of true thoughts (the content of infinite intellect) reflects the order of reality (as expressed in extension and the other attributes).

In light of this, it seems more fruitful to approach Spinoza's account of truth by way of his conception of adequacy. As the passages cited above suggest, adequacy is an inner characteristic of an idea by virtue of which it is judged to be true. This can also be expressed by saying that adequacy functions as the criterion of truth. The basic feature of an adequate idea, however, is its completeness. As we saw in our preliminary discussion of Spinoza's method, an adequate idea is simply one from which the properties of its ideatum can be deduced. For example, the mathematician's idea of a triangle is adequate because all the mathematically relevant properties of the figure can be derived from it. Correlatively, the conception of a triangle possessed by someone ignorant of geometry is inadequate precisely because this cannot be done. Such a person may have a vague idea of a triangle, which includes an awareness that it is a figure with three sides; but since he does not know what follows from this, he does not possess the true concept, or adequate idea, of a triangle.

The conception of adequacy and its function as the criterion of truth provide the basis for Spinoza's response to the specter of radical skepticism produced by Descartes's methodical doubt. It will be recalled that, for Descartes, grounding our knowledge requires, first of all, proving that God exists and that he is no deceiver. Until this is accomplished, the possibility remains that we may somehow be deceived by a malignant genius, even with regard to what seems most evident—for example, the truths of mathematics. Against this, it has frequently been objected (beginning with Descartes's own contemporaries) that such a procedure for refuting skepticism is circular, since, in order to prove that God exists and is not a deceiver, it is necessary to assume the truth of our clear and distinct ideas. Among those not content with the Cartesian account was Spinoza, who discusses the issue in both *Descartes' "Principles of Philosophy"* and the *Treatise on the Emendation of the Intellect*.[26] His basic point is that just as we can have a clear and distinct—that is, adequate—idea of a triangle without knowing whether we are being systematically deceived by a Cartesian demon, so too, we can have such an idea of God. Once we have such an idea of God, however, there can no longer be any rational basis for doubt regarding God's nature—it is simply self-evident that God is not a deceiver. This, in turn, undermines the Cartesian basis for doubt regarding any of our clear and distinct, or adequate, ideas. Finally, since the truth of such ideas is apparent from reflection on the nature of the ideas themselves (adequacy functions as the criterion of truth), Spinoza concludes that we are entitled to regard such ideas as true.

The earlier analyses also underlie Spinoza's typically cryptic account in the *Ethics*, where, presumably in response to the Cartesian skeptic, he states that "*he who has a true idea at the same time knows that he has a true idea, and cannot doubt the truth of the thing*" (P43). As he explains in the attached scholium, this is because "to have a true idea means nothing other than knowing a thing perfectly *or* in the best way." We have already seen that knowing a thing in this manner involves seeing how all its properties follow necessarily from its nature or definition. In such cases, nothing remains ambiguous; nothing is left unexplained, undetermined, or uncertain. Consequently, there is no need to appeal to God, or, indeed, to anything outside the ideas themselves, in order to guarantee their truth. To cite Spinoza's appropriate and uncharacteristically elegant metaphor: "As the light makes both itself and the darkness plain, so truth is the standard both of itself and of the false" (P43S).

The reference to falsity in this context is likewise extremely significant, for it shows that the very same conception of adequacy that serves as criterion of truth also provides the basis for determining the nature of error or falsity. At first glance, error would seem to be a major problem for Spinoza. Since the order and connection of ideas is the same as the order and connection of things, and since an idea and its object are not two distinct things between which disagreement or lack of correspondence is possible, but merely one and the same thing expressed in two manners, one might be tempted to ask how an idea can ever fail to agree with its object or, correlatively, how, on the basis of Spinoza's metaphysical assumptions, such a thing as error or falsity is even conceivable.

Spinoza begins his brief, yet significant, account of this topic in the *Ethics* by acknowledging that there is a sense in which all ideas are true. Specifically, "*all ideas, insofar as they are related to God, are true*" (P32). As the proof of this proposition makes clear, this follows from the identification of the order and connection of ideas with the order and connection of things. But this still leaves us with the question of what it means to say that ideas are related to God. Presumably, this is intended to contrast with a situation in which these ideas are related to a human or some other mind and to suggest that in the former, but not the latter, case they necessarily agree perfectly with their object. In other words, the proposition seems to reduce to the not very informative claim that all ideas which agree with, or adequately express, their objects are true.

Nevertheless, this proposition is not quite as empty as it first appears; for from the fact that an idea in its inherent nature, as a modification of the attribute of thought, must necessarily agree with its object, we can infer that "*there is nothing positive in ideas on account of which they are called false*" (P33). Furthermore, since falsity is not a positive characteristic of any idea, which means that there simply are no ideas which do not agree with their objects, error can be due only to the way in which an idea is in, or grasped by, a particular mind. Any given mind can possess or conceive a particular idea either completely or in part only, as in our earlier example in which the mathematician possesses the complete, and hence adequate, idea of a triangle, whereas the person ignorant of mathematics does not. Thus, whereas any idea that is conceived adequately—that is, completely—by the human mind is true and is, in fact, conceived in precisely the same way as an infinite intellect would conceive it (P34), obviously not very many ideas are conceived by the human mind in this manner. Those that are not are conceived inadequately, so that "*falsity consists in the privation of knowledge, which inadequate, or mutilated and confused ideas involve*" (P35). Falsity, in other words, is really partial truth that is mistakenly taken as the complete truth about a state of affairs. This typically occurs when the mind perceives the idea of an effect without considering the idea of its cause. In such cases our ideas are said to be "like conclusions without premises" (P28).

Spinoza illustrates his conception of error with two examples that help to clarify his meaning. The first is his favorite bête noire, the notion of freedom of the will. Belief in such freedom, he points out, arises simply because people are ignorant of the true causes of their actions. This ignorance is due to the fact that their inadequate ideas of their actions do not include ideas of their determining causes. Consequently, they tend to explain these actions in terms of a mysterious faculty of will, "but these are only words for which they have no idea." The second example is even more revealing, and Spinoza's analysis is worth quoting in full:

> Similarly, when we look at the sun, we imagine it as about 200 feet away from us, an error that does not consist simply in this imagining, but in the fact that while we imagine it in this way, we are ignorant of its true distance and of the cause of this imagining. For even if we later come to know that it is more than 600 diameters of the earth away from us, we nevertheless imagine it as near. For we imagine the sun so near not because we do not know its true distance, but because an affection of our body involves the essence of the sun insofar as our body is affected by the sun. [P35S]

Spinoza here underscores the fact that our imaginative idea of the sun as a disk in the sky located about two hundred feet from the earth is not intrinsically false, since it contains an accurate description of how the sun actually *appears* under certain conditions, or, in Spinoza's language, how it is perceived by virtue of its affection of the body. Presumably, it still appears this way to someone who has an adequate—that is, scientific—idea of it. But the adequate idea includes within it an explanation (in accordance with the laws of optics) of just why the sun appears as it does under given perceptual conditions. This is lacking in the inadequate, imaginative idea, which, accordingly, involves a confusion between how the sun appears and how it really is. This confusion, which could be remedied by a causal account of why the sun appears as it does, is the error. Spinoza's claim, which is never really worked out, is that all cases of error, or inadequate ideas, can be explained in a similar fashion.

Although Spinoza's treatment of error follows it in the text, it is in fact presupposed by his account of sense perception and its significance for human knowledge. Spinoza characterizes such perception and the thought based on it as perception "according to the common order of nature." This is the order in which the mind actually receives its ideas in experience. Given the parallelism doctrine, this corresponds precisely to the order in which the body is affected by the objects of these ideas. Spinoza contends that the mind is necessarily passive when it perceives in this manner, and this contention constitutes one of the bases for his theory of the passions. For the present, however, the important point is that perceptual ideas reflect the condition of the organism in its interplay with the environment (which is their actual "object," or correlate), rather than the true nature of some independent reality. Thus, insofar as the mind takes such ideas to represent some external thing as it is in itself, rather than the manner in which that thing affects its own sensory apparatus, it inevitably falls into error. Correlatively, error is avoided insofar as our thought follows the "order of the intellect." The latter is the order of logical dependence "by which the Mind perceives things through their first causes." Since this order, unlike the former, depends on the activity of the mind, rather than external causes (which vary from situation to situation), Spinoza contends that it is "the same in all men" (P18S).

At the root of Spinoza's account of perception and, indeed, of his whole analysis of knowledge is the principle that "*the idea of any mode in which the human Body is affected by external bodies must involve the nature of the human Body and at the same time the nature of the external body*" (P16). This follows from the status of the body as a finite mode, which, as such, is determined by its network of relations with external bodies, and from the conception of the mind as the idea of the body, which reflects in the realm of thought everything that occurs in the world of extension. The key implication of this principle is that the human body provides the focal point from and through which alone the human mind can perceive its world.

This, in turn, has two consequences, one positive and one negative, which Spinoza presents in the form of corollaries. The first is that "the human Mind perceives the nature of a great many bodies together with the nature of its own body." From this we can conclude that sense perception *does* provide an awareness of external bodies. This is crucial, because it makes clear that Spinoza does not want his claim that the body is the "object" of the idea constituting the human mind to be taken as implying that the only object which a human mind can represent is its own body. The point is rather that the mind represents other things on the basis of their relationship to its object, the body.[27] The second corollary is that "the ideas which we have of external bodies indicate the condition of our own body more than the nature of external bodies." This is precisely the principle underlying the account of error. Since the perceptual awareness of external bodies is a function of the state of one's own body or, more precisely, of one's sensory apparatus, this awareness provides information only concerning how a body appears, and this, strictly speaking, is a fact more about the constitution of one's own body than about the nature of the external body.

Moreover, since the ideas in the mind reflect the nature both of one's own body and of external bodies, and since the order and connection of ideas is identical with the order and connection of things, it follows that the laws determining the relations of ideas in the mind must reflect the laws determining the relations of bodies conceived under the attribute of extension. Consequently, a foundation is laid for a quasi-mechanistic psychology, which formulates universal laws concerning the relations of ideas. This provides the key to his account of imagination and memory and, as we shall see in the next chapter, to his theory of the passions.

Spinoza often uses the term *imagination* in a very broad sense to denote all thought, including sense perception, in which the order of ideas in the mind reflects the order of affections of the body. Ultimately, this encompasses all thought that is according to the "common order of nature." The reason for using *imagination* in this way seems to be that the bodily affections are themselves characterized as "the images of things," and their corresponding ideas the "imaginations of the mind" (P17S).[28] In the present context, however, Spinoza's concern is mainly with imagination in the more limited and usual sense of the mind's propensity to form ideas of absent objects.

Depending on circumstances and the conclusions drawn, this propensity can be viewed as either a power or a defect of the mind.[29] In either case it is perfectly natural and is explicable in terms of a general principle which constitutes a psychological version of the law of inertia: "*If the human Body is affected with a mode that involves the nature of an external body, the human Mind will regard the same external body as actually existing, or as present to it, until the Body is affected by an affection that excludes the existence or presence of that body*" (P17).

The same line of thought is applied to memory, understood as the mind's ability to recall the idea of a past object on the basis of a present image or impression. The principle at work here, which is a consequence of the law governing the operation of the imagination, is that "*if the human Body has once been affected by two or more bodies at the same time, then when the Mind subsequently imagines one of them, it will immediately recollect the others also*" (P18). As Spinoza noted in the scholium, memory, so construed, is really association, and the law that he presents here regarding the operation of memory is basically equivalent to what has subsequently been called "the law of the association of ideas." For Spinoza, as for the later "associationists," the importance of this law stems from the fact that it provides an explanation of how the mind moves from the thought of one thing to the thought of another that stands in no logical connection with the first. The basis is habit, which is itself the product of past associations in experience. To cite Spinoza's own examples, a soldier, on seeing the tracks of a horse, will tend to think of a horseman and then of war, whereas a farmer, seeing the same tracks, will naturally proceed to the thought of a plough and a field. In neither case is the transition logical, and thus it does not lead to genuine knowledge. Nevertheless, in both cases it is natural and predictable, for, as Spinoza concludes, "each one, according as he has been accustomed to join and connect the images of things in this or that way, will pass from one thought to another" (P18S).

Having articulated the basic principle underlying sense perception and described two of the fundamental operations of the mind with

regard to its sensible ideas, Spinoza is ready to proceed to his treatment of perceptual knowledge per se. First he points out, on the basis
of the preceding analysis, that the mind's knowledge of the body
depends on the body's having been affected by external bodies (P19),
or, in more modern terms, that one's awareness of one's own body
depends on external stimuli. But since the mind is the idea, or mental
correlate, of the body, what holds of one holds of the other (they are
both in God in the same manner) (P20). Given this, Spinoza contends,
albeit somewhat incongruously in light of his theory of attributes, that
"*the idea of the Mind is united to the Mind in the same way as the Mind
is united to the Body*" (P21). Hence, just as the mind is aware of the
body, so it is also aware of itself—that is, "*the human Mind perceives
not only the affections of the Body, but also the ideas of these affections*" (P22).

The doctrine of ideas of ideas, which stand to the original ideas in
precisely the same way as those ideas stand to their ideata, is another
of the more perplexing and controversial aspects of the *Ethics*. It is
tempting to read Spinoza as here offering the basis for a theory of
conscious awareness. The need for such a theory is already apparent
from Spinoza's claims that the human mind somehow perceives everything that occurs in its object (the body), and that there is a sense in
which all things are animated. One way of making sense of these
claims is to hold that they do not entail conscious awareness, and that
the latter occurs only when there is also an idea of an idea in the same
mind.[30] Unfortunately, there seems to be a fatal difficulty to such a
reading in that Spinoza is committed by his doctrine of parallelism to
the principle that there must be in God an idea of every idea, just as
there is an idea corresponding to the modes expressed in all the
attributes. Consequently, if Spinoza is claiming that wherever there is
an idea of an idea, there is conscious awareness, then he would seem to
be committed to the twin absurdities that we have conscious awareness
of everything that occurs in our bodies, and that all things possess
some form of conscious awareness.[31]

It is clear that, within the framework of Spinoza's metaphysics, the
best way to avoid these consequences is to make self-awareness, like

intelligence, or "mindedness," a function of organic complexity. Moreover, although Spinoza hardly develops this point, there is at least a hint of it in the next proposition, in which he claims that "*the human Mind does not know itself, except insofar as it perceives the ideas of the affections of the Body*" (P23). The significance of this proposition and its demonstration lies in the implication that external stimuli are needed for the mind's awareness of itself, as well as for its awareness of its own body (by P19 and P20). Now, since (by P13S) in order for the body to be receptive to stimuli from other bodies that affect it in various ways, it must have a corresponding sensitivity— that is, a capacity to receive and process sensory data like that possessed by the human brain—it follows that such a capacity is also necessary for self-awareness. Admittedly, all this is vague and speculative, since Spinoza himself never really attempts to provide an explicit account of self-awareness. Nevertheless, the considerations outlined above suggest the possibility of constructing such an account along Spinozistic lines.[32]

Be that as it may, it is clear that the ideas correlated with the "images" received by the human body as a result of its being afffected by other bodies do not provide the mind with adequate ideas either of the parts of its own body or of the nature of the affecting bodies (P24 and P25). That the former is true is because one's awareness of the parts of one's own body reflects the way in which this body is affected by external bodies (the sensory input); that the latter is true is because we perceive these bodies only insofar as they "appear" to us—that is, by virtue of the manner in which they affect us, not as they are in themselves. At the same time, it is also the case that it is only by means of such ideas that the human mind can form the idea of the actual existence of external objects (P26). Such knowledge, in other words, requires sensory input, or experience.

These considerations, in turn, lead to some initially unsettling conclusions. Since the idea of one's own body depends on the ideas of external bodies, and since it has been established that the latter are inadequate, it follows that the same holds for the idea of one's own body (P27), and hence that the knowledge of one's own body possessed in this manner is similarly confused (P28). But the difficulty does not stop here: since what holds for the idea of the body applies equally to the idea of the idea, which has already been shown to be equivalent to the mind's idea of itself, it can also be concluded that such ideas do not provide adequate knowledge of the human mind (P29). The outcome of the initial stage of Spinoza's analysis of knowledge thus seems to be a radical skepticism, which is further extended to include knowledge of the duration of one's own body and that of external bodies (P30–P31). The human mind, as a finite mode, seems able to apprehend the world and itself only through the distorting perspective of its own body and to be totally unable to perceive things in the manner of an infinite intellect.

No sooner does Spinoza arrive at this seemingly hopeless skeptical conclusion, however, than he begins to qualify it. These consequences follow, he notes, only insofar as the mind "perceives things from the common order of nature, i.e., so long as it is determined externally, from fortuitous encounters with things . . . and not so long as it is determined internally, from the fact that it regards a number of things at once, to understand their agreements, differences, and oppositions. For so often as it is disposed internally, in this or another way, then it regards things clearly and distinctly, as I shall show below" (P29S). Since it is precisely in terms of being "determined internally," or self-determined, that Spinoza conceives freedom, we can see immediately that the epistemological problem of the possession of adequate knowledge is intimately connected with, if not identical to, the practical problem of the attainment of freedom. Nevertheless, it would seem that it is precisely this possibility, whether expressed in its epistemological or its practical form, that is precluded by Spinoza's conception of the mind as a finite mode. Spinoza's present concern, therefore, is to demonstrate that, despite appearances, this is not the case, at least not completely.

With reference to thinking, being determined internally can only mean that the mind is guided by its own thoughts, which are ordered inferentially as premises to a conclusion (the order of the intellect), rather than in the manner in which they occur in the mind as the result of the body's being affected by external bodies (the common order of nature). The immediate problem, therefore, is to explain how the mind, as the idea of the body, whose every modification must correspond to a modification of this body, can ever be in a position to do this. The basis of Spinoza's answer lies in the claim that there are certain ideas that the human mind possesses completely and hence can conceive adequately, because, unlike the ideas derived from ordinary sense experience, they do not "involve" or logically depend on, ideas of particular modifications of the body. These ideas fall into two classes, corresponding to two levels of generality. Spinoza calls them respectively "common notions" and "adequate ideas of the common properties of things."

These two classes correspond to the innate ideas advocated by other philosophers, which were, in fact, sometimes called "common notions." Both Descartes and Leibniz appealed to the ancient theory of innate ideas in order to explain the foundations of our rational knowledge. Their basic claim was that our knowledge of necessary and universal truths, adequate knowledge in Spinoza's sense, cannot be derived from experience. On the contrary, it was thought that the sources of such knowledge must lie in the mind and reflect its very structure, and that only this can account for its necessity and universality. This theory was not construed in a naive psychological sense, however; that is, it was not maintained, as some critics of the theory seemed to think, that either the infant or the untutored savage, who were favorites of the philosophical literature of the time, were actually conscious of the "true concept of God" or the basic principles of mathematics.[33] Rather, innate ideas were viewed as dispositions that pertain universally to the human mind, but of which any given individual is not necessarily conscious. As Descartes expressed the matter in response to a critic:

> For I never wrote or concluded that the mind required innate ideas which were in some sort different from its faculty of thinking, but when I observed the existence in me of certain thoughts which proceeded, not from extraneous objects nor from the determination of my will, but solely from the faculty of thinking which is within me, then, that I might distinguish the ideas or notions (which are the forms of these

thoughts) from other thoughts *adventitious* or *factitious*, I termed the
former *"innate."* In the same sense we say that in some families
generosity is innate, in others certain diseases like gout or gravel, not
that on this account the babes of these families suffer from these
diseases in their mother's womb, but because they are born with a
certain disposition or propensity for contracting them.[34]

Spinoza's conception of the mind as the idea of the body does not
allow him to distinguish, in the manner of Descartes, between innate
and adventitious ideas—that is, between those that come from the
mind and those that come from experience. To him, all ideas are
equally innate, since they are all modifications of the attribute of
thought, and none is "caused" by anything in the realm of extension.
Correlatively, all are equally adventitious, since each must have its
physical correlate. Nevertheless, this conception of mind does allow
Spinoza to make an analogous distinction, which leads to much the
same result. This is the distinction between ideas that are correlated
with specific features of particular bodies and those whose correlates
are common to all bodies or a large class therof. Things that are
common to all bodies and are *"equally in the part and in the whole,"*
Spinoza notes, do not *"constitute the essence of any singular thing"*
(P37). It follows from this that the common notions, the ideas that
correspond to these things, do not arise in the mind in connection with
the experience of any particular object. Thus, on the basis of the
preceding analysis, Spinoza can contend that the mind possesses them
in their totality and understands them adequately (P38). Finally, since
these ideas correspond to what is common to all bodies, they, like the
innate ideas of Descartes and Leibniz, are common to all minds (P38C).

We have already seen that all bodies are particular modifications of
the attribute of extension and are constituted by a certain proportion of
motion and rest. The latter, therefore, are certainly common to all
bodies and are present equally in the part and in the whole. Thus, the
ideas corresponding to them, which would seem to include the axioms
of geometry and the first principles of physics, must certainly be
included among the common notions. Furthermore, if we extend this
line of reasoning to the attribute of thought and point to thoughts that

are present equally in a part and in the whole—that is, in all thoughts—we arrive at the laws of logic, the first principles of thought, which must likewise be regarded as common notions.[35] This brings us to the second category of adequate ideas, those of the common properties of things. These have a lesser degree of generality than the common notions and refer only to properties shared by certain bodies. Specifically, they refer to properties that are common and peculiar to the human body *"and certain external bodies by which the human Body is usually affected, and is equally in the part and in the whole of each of them"* (P39). Although it is far from clear just what Spinoza has in mind here, the implication once again is that the commonality of these ideas enables the mind to grasp them completely and, hence, adequately. Thus, in spite of the extreme sketchiness of the account, which Spinoza intended to remedy in a future work dealing with epistemology,[36] the basic point emerges with sufficient clarity. It is simply that, insofar as the human mind possesses such ideas and deduces other ideas from them, it will know things truly or in an adequate manner (P40).

But one detail could not be left to the projected future work. In order to avoid complete misunderstanding, Spinoza felt it necessary to distinguish between his common notions and adequate ideas of the common properties of things, the very foundations of scientific reasoning, and the universals, or general terms, of the scholastics. The latter are of two kinds. The first are the so-called "transcendentals" such as "Being, Thing, Something," which are the most general concepts of all, applicable to all genera. The second are the various genera and species into which all substances in nature fall. As already noted, Aristotelian science proceeded largely by classifying substances in terms of such universals, and Spinoza's basic contention is that not only do such concepts not yield adequate knowledge of the nature of things, but they reflect the limits of the imagination, rather than the power of the intellect. The mind, Spinoza points out, is only capable of imagining distinctly a limited number of things simultaneously—specifically, only as many as its body can form images of simultaneously. When these images become confused, the mind tends to form general ideas answering to these confused images. Thus, the transcendentals are the most confused ideas of all, since they reflect the intellect's inability to make distinctions. What, after all, is emptier than the concept of a mere "something"? Moreover, the situation is similar in the case of class concepts, such as "man," "horse," "dog," and so on. These merely reflect the inability of the imagination to capture the small differences between individuals and can hardly serve as vehicles for adequate—that is, scientific—knowledge. In short, these general ideas do not answer to the essence of things, as Aristotelians claim, but merely reflect what a particular individual happens to regard as important, which, in turn, is a function of the condition of that individual's body. To cite Spinoza's own example: "Those who have more often regarded men's stature with wonder will understand by the word *man* an animal of erect stature. But those who have been accustomed to consider something else, will form another common image of man—e.g., that man is an animal capable of laughter, or a featherless biped, or a rational animal" (P40S1).

Spinoza then uses the contrast between the two radically different types of general notions (Aristotelian and Spinozistic) to distinguish between two kinds of knowledge. Those of Aristotelian science yield what Spinoza calls "knowledge of the first kind, opinion or imagination." This, in turn, is subdivided into two species, corresponding to two distinct ways in which such notions can be formed: namely, either from the confused perception of particular things as they are encountered in experience (called "knowledge from random experience"), or from signs, which includes both sensory and memory images. By contrast, Spinoza's common notions and adequate ideas of the common properties of things yield "knowledge of the second kind" or "reason" (*ratio*). They differ in that the former (in both species) involves only inadequate, and the latter only adequate, ideas.

At this point Spinoza abruptly and unexpectedly introduces the possibility of a third kind of knowledge, termed "intuitive knowledge" (*Scientia Intuitiva*). Although he adds that the actual existence of this kind of knowledge will not be established until later, he does

note that it "proceeds from an adequate idea of the formal essence of
certain attributes of God to the adequate knowledge of the essence of
things." Moreover, he proceeds to illustrate all three kinds of knowledge by a single example:

> Suppose there are three numbers, and the problem is to find a fourth
> which is to the third as the second is to the first. Merchants do not
> hesitate to multiply the second by the third, and divide the product by
> the first, because they have not yet forgotten what they heard from their
> teacher without any demonstration, or because they have often found
> this in the simplest numbers, or from the force of the Demonstration of
> P7 in Bk. VII of Euclid, viz. from the common property of propor-
> tionals. But in the simplest numbers none of this is necessary. Given the
> numbers 1, 2, and 3, no one fails to see that the fourth proportional
> number is 6—and we see this much more clearly because we infer the
> fourth number from the ratio which, in one glance, we see the first
> number to have to the second (P40S2).

As the example suggests, the basic difference between the second
and third kinds of knowledge is that the former deduces its conclusions from previously given general principles, whereas the latter
grasps the truth in an immediate manner, without having to appeal to
any such principles. In contradistinction to the first kind of knowledge
(illustrated in Spinoza's example by the procedure of the merchants
who rely on memory), both reason and intuition, Spinoza maintains,
are sources of adequate knowledge. Nevertheless, he recognizes two
respects in which intuition is superior. First, as the description,
although not the example, suggests, intuition, unlike reason, is able to
arrive at knowledge of the essence of individuals. Whereas the
province of reason is general truths—for example, axioms— which
hold universally and do not pertain to any individuals in particular,
intuition achieves "adequate knowledge of the essence of things."
Consequently, it is concrete and particular, whereas reason is abstract
and general. This is not of any immediate significance to the argument; but it does become crucial in the last part of the *Ethics*, where
Spinoza attempts to demonstrate the preeminent role of intuition in the
attainment of human blessedness. Second, knowledge from general

principles alone remains ungrounded ultimately. As in Spinoza's example, the conclusion is inferred correctly from the principle, but the status of the principle itself remains a mystery. Within the framework of Spinoza's metaphysics, this mystery can be removed only by grounding the principle in the nature of God. This grounding, both of principles and their consequences, is achieved by the third kind of knowledge.

Before we can descend by intuition from the eternal and infinite essence of God, however, we must first understand how reason can ascend to a knowledge of this essence. Thus, Spinoza must demonstrate that the human mind does, in fact, possess an adequate idea of this essence. His argument follows the already discussed refutation of skepticism by means of the appeal to the conception of a true idea as its own standard. He begins by pointing out that "*it is of the nature of Reason to regard things as necessary, not as contingent*" (P44). Things, after all, *are* necessary; hence any adequate knowledge of them must reflect this fact. It is only insofar as we are misled by our imagination that we come to believe in the contingency of things (P44C1). Moreover, to regard things as necessary is to regard them without any relation to time, which, in turn, is to regard them as eternal. Thus, Spinoza concludes, "it is of the nature of Reason to perceive things under a certain form of eternity" (*sub quadem aeternitatis specie*) (P44C2).

But to conceive things in this way is to conceive them in relation to God. Consequently, Spinoza affirms that "*every idea of each body, or of each singular thing which actually exists, necessarily involves an eternal and infinite essence of God*" (P45). Although this sounds paradoxical, it is an obvious consequence of Spinoza's metaphysical principles. Since all things depend on God, both for their essence and for the very fact of their existence, or "the force by which each one perseveres in existing" (which he is careful to distinguish from the duration of their existence), the idea of each thing that actually exists must necessarily involve the idea of God. Furthermore, since the idea of God, like the common notions, is involved in the idea of everything and can be apprehended either in the whole or in the part, Spinoza concludes by the same line of reasoning that he used in connection with the common notions that "*the knowledge of God's eternal and infinite essence which each idea involves is adequate and perfect*" (P46). Finally, since every finite thing is part of that infinite system (*natura naturata*) that is grounded in God (*natura naturans*), it follows that, in the last analysis, the adequate idea of anything involves the idea of the whole, or of God. We thus return once again to that central tenet of Spinoza's thought, that the knowledge of anything in nature depends ultimately on the knowledge of God. This is simply a consequence of the principle that "the knowledge of an effect depends upon and involves the knowledge of its cause." And, since it has already been established that the mind knows some things, or possesses adequate ideas, Spinoza can conclude that "*the human Mind has an adequate knowledge of God's eternal and infinite essence*" (P37).[37]

The key to this conclusion, which is highly paradoxical from the standpoint of both traditional theology and common sense, is Spinoza's conception of God. Insofar as God is identified with the universal and necessary order of nature, it is obvious that the adequate idea of anything must "involve" (in the sense of presuppose) a knowledge of God. Why, then, do most people fail to realize this, believing instead that God is unknowable? Spinoza's answer is that it is largely because they do not correctly apply names to things (P47S). Specifically, they erroneously apply the name "God" to that anthropomorphic being who is really the product of their own imagination. Such a being is certainly not knowable, but neither is such a being really God. The important thing is always to be sure that one has a proper understanding of the meaning of one's terms, and in the present instance this can be accomplished by attending carefully to the argument of the first part of the *Ethics*.

III The Will

In the last two propositions and concluding scholium of this part of the *Ethics*, Spinoza turns from the intellect to the will. This short, but important, section both completes the analysis of the human mind and provides a bridge between the metaphysical and epistemological doctrines of the earlier parts of the work and the psychological and ethical concerns of its later portions. In addition, it contains a concise critique of Descartes's famous account of the will and of its role in the explanation of error in the Fourth Meditation. We here find applied to the human mind many of the same conclusions that have already been established with regard to the divine mind. Just as we have previously seen that God does not act from freedom of the will, that his actions are coextensive with his power, and that his intellect is identical with his will, so we now come to see that precisely the same things can be affirmed about the human mind.

Although freedom is one of the most fundamental values of Spinoza's philosophy, he had no use for the traditional conception of a free will. Thus, he declares categorically that "*in the Mind there is no absolute, or free, will, but the Mind is determined to will this or that by a cause which is also determined by another, and this again by another, and so to infinity*" (P48). The demonstration makes it clear that this follows from the very status of the human mind as a finite mode. As such, each of its particular volitions must be determined by a particular cause. Given the cause, the effect—in this case the volition—necessarily follows. A human being, in other words, may be said to choose or will something, but this choice must itself have a cause that determines it, and, therefore, it is not free. But, if this is so, then not only can we not talk about "freedom of the will" in the traditional sense, but we can no longer attach any meaning to the notion of the will as a faculty of volition that exercises choice and that "might have chosen otherwise."

Moreover, as Spinoza adds in the scholium, precisely the same line of reasoning suffices to demonstrate that there is no "absolute faculty" of understanding, desiring, loving, or anything else. In each instance we have merely particular acts of understanding, desiring, loving, and so on. There is no mysterious faculty that performs these activities and exists apart from them. Simply put, human beings, like God, are what they do; their power is coextensive with their activity. Thus, there is no room in the Spinozistic universe for any unexercised power, any potentiality. Human beings believe in such things, of course, and this is one of the basic factors underlying the prevalent belief in a free will. But here, as elsewhere, human beings are the victims of their imagination. On the basis of their experience of particular volitions, they come to form an abstract idea of a volition in general and then proceed to reify this abstraction, thereby giving birth to the fiction of a distinct faculty.

Having established that there is no faculty of will above and beyond particular volitions, Spinoza moves on to the question of whether one can even talk about particular acts of volition. As one might expect, Spinoza's answer is an unequivocal no. "*In the Mind*," he writes, "*there is no volition, or affirmation and negation, except that which the idea involves insofar as it is an idea*" (P49). The equation in this proposition of volition with affirmation and negation is a clear indication that Spinoza's specific target is Descartes. In the Fourth Meditation, Descartes distinguishes between the intellect and the will and locates the source of the possibility of error in the will's infinite capacity to affirm or deny what the intellect conceives. The basic thesis behind this division of labor is that the intellect conceives or forms the idea of something and the will decides whether or not what the intellect has conceived is to be believed. Error arises, on this view, when the will does not limit belief to what the intellect clearly and distinctly conceives.

In the demonstration of proposition 49 Spinoza mounts a two-step argument against this doctrine and, more generally, against any attempt to distinguish between acts of assent or belief and acts of understanding. Each of these steps is based on his previously discussed conception of an idea. The first is to point out that any affirmation or belief presupposes an idea of what is affirmed or believed. To cite Spinoza's own example: the mind cannot affirm that the three angles of a triangle are equal to two right angles without already having the idea of a triangle. This follows from the conception of ideas as the fundamental modifications of thought, and it is a premise that Descartes would likewise accept. The second, and crucial, step is to claim that an idea, by its very nature, already involves an affirmation. Spinoza attempts to illustrate this by appealing once again to the idea of a triangle. The point is that we do not first entertain this idea and examine it, and then, by a distinct act of volition, affirm or decide to believe that the sum of its three angles is equal to two right angles. On the contrary, this affirmation is part of the content of the idea of a triangle; so, in conceiving of a triangle, one is already affirming this and denying its contradictory. Moreover, Spinoza continues, since this example of a "volition" has been selected at random, what has been said of it can be said of any volition—namely, "that it is nothing apart from the idea."[38] Finally, since a volition is nothing apart from an idea, and, since, as we have also seen, the will is nothing apart from its volitions and the understanding nothing apart from its ideas, it follows that in human beings, as in God, "the will and the intellect are one and the same" (P49C).

Although he proceeds to discuss a number of possible objections to this view, which are shown to rest mainly on a failure to distinguish between ideas and images on the one hand and abstractions (faculties) and realities (particular ideas) on the other, and even adds a catalogue of the advantages of his doctrine vis-à-vis morality, this really completes Spinoza's analysis of the human mind. The implications of this analysis are quite revolutionary. The human mind is removed from its special place, which served only to make its activities incomprehensible, and is fully integrated into nature. As the idea of the human body, it is not a separate substance, nor does it possess distinct and mysterious powers above and beyond its activities. Nevertheless, this does not render it totally powerless. The true power of the mind consists in its ability to understand, and this is coextensive with its possession of adequate ideas. Spinoza has shown not only that the human mind possesses such power and how that is so, but also that this is nothing more than its own, limited portion of the infinite power of nature. This account is obscure at many points, especially in regard to details, and Spinoza himself, as we have seen, does not pretend to have provided an exhaustive treatment of the topic. He does claim, however, that this account is complete and clear enough for his purpose, which, as he tells us at the very end of the section, is to "have set out doctrines from which we can infer many excellent things, which are highly useful and necessary to know" (P49S). It is to these things that we now turn.

CHAPTER 5

Bondage, Virtue, and Freedom

The last three parts of the *Ethics* form a unity, and together they contain what, broadly speaking, can be characterized as Spinoza's moral philosophy. This comprises an analysis of the human emotions and how human beings are subject to them (part 3); an account of the nature of human virtue, or *ethics* in the narrow sense of the term, which includes both the presentation of rational rules for living and an analysis of the "good life" (part 4); and a theory of human blessedness, which provides a philosophical alternative to the traditional religious doctrine of salvation (part 5). These are the main consequences that Spinoza derives from the argument of the first two parts, and they form the subject matter of the present chapter.

I The Human Emotions

Despite its agreement on many points of detail with previous treatments of the subject, most notably that of Descartes, Spinoza's analysis of the human emotions is one of the more interesting and original aspects of his philosophy. This originality consists largely in the thoroughgoing naturalism of his approach. We have already seen Spinoza's naturalism at work in connection with both his analysis of the cognitive capacity of the mind and his mechanistic account of imagination and association. He treats the human emotions in precisely the same way—that is, as natural phenomena. As he says in the famous declaration in the preface to part 3 of the *Ethics*, "*I shall treat the nature and powers of the Affects, and the power of the Mind over*

124

them, by the same Method by which, in the preceding parts, I treated
God and the Mind, and I shall consider human actions and appetites
just as if it were a Question of lines, planes, and bodies."

Since he assumes that mental and physical phenomena are subject
to the same set of universal laws and are to be understood in terms of
the same model of scientific explanation, Spinoza anticipated the
method and world view of modern rational science to a much greater
degree than Descartes.[1] Thus, he states in the same preface that "*the*
way of understanding the nature of anything, of whatever kind,
must . . . be the same, viz. through the universal laws and rules of
nature." Nevertheless, here as elsewhere, Spinoza was not guided
solely, or even primarily, by theoretical considerations. His intent is
rather to give an account of the emotions that will enable us to
understand how it is possible to avoid falling victim to them, and
thereby achieve the degree of freedom of which we, as finite modes,
are capable. But before he can provide the remedy, Spinoza must first
diagnose the disease, which means that he must provide an account of
the basic mechanisms of the human emotions. Since this brings him
into direct conflict with Descartes, it will prove helpful to preface our
analysis of the opening propositions of this part of the *Ethics* with a
brief consideration of Descartes's doctrine as it is developed in *The*
Passions of the Soul.

Descartes begins his account by distinguishing between actions and
passions. Following the traditional view, which goes back to Aristotle,
he argues that these are not two distinct things, but merely two names
for the same thing. Which name is used depends on the point of view
from which they are being considered. The same occurrence can be
viewed as an action in relation to the agent (cause) and a passion in
relation to the patient (effect). Now the body acts directly and immediately on the soul in Descartes's view; hence, what in the body is an
action is in the soul a passion. From this it follows that in order to
determine the passions of the soul, it is first necessary to distinguish
the soul's functions from those of the body.

These functions are determined by means of the general Cartesian
method of appealing to clear and distinct ideas. Whatever we experi-

ence as being in us but can also conceive as existing in wholly inanimate bodies is attributed to the body alone; whereas whatever we cannot possibly conceive of as pertaining to the body of corporeal nature is attributed to the soul. On the basis of this principle, all physiological functions are attributed to the body, which Descartes regards as a machine, and the only function granted to the soul is thought. Thoughts, however, are of two sorts, termed "actions" and "passions." The former includes all our volitions, or desires, which experience teaches us proceed directly from the soul and depend on it alone. The latter encompass "all those kinds of perceptions or forms of knowledge which are found in us, because it is often not our soul which makes them what they are, and because it always receives them from the things which are represented by them."[2]

The passions, or perceptions, are themselves divided into two classes. The first consists of those which have the soul itself as a cause and includes the perceptions of our desires and imaginings and of other thoughts that depend on them—in short, the mind's awareness of its inner states. The second class consists of those passions which have the body as their cause. These, in turn, are divided into three subgroups: those which relate to external objects—for example, sense perceptions; those which relate to our own bodies and their parts—for example, the sensations of hunger, thirst, pleasure, and pain; and those which are referred to the soul itself—for example, feelings of joy and sadness, love and anger, or, in other words, emotions. These are the "passions of the soul" of which Descartes endeavors to give an account.[3]

This account is developed in terms of the interaction between the soul and the body. As noted earlier, Descartes held that this interaction, or mutual influence, occurs through the action of the pineal gland. By means of the "animal spirits," small particles of matter that it both sends through the nerves to the other parts of the body and receives back again, this gland functions as a kind of messenger service between the mind and the body. When the body is affected by external stimuli, it sends its messages through the "animal spirits" to this gland. These spirits are then relayed to the mind and produce perceptions in it. By reversing the process and sending messages through the gland to the rest of the body, the mind is able to influence the body. This is the basis of the Cartesian account of voluntary action, which enables Descartes, on the one hand, to provide a physiological analysis of how the various passions are produced in the mind as a result of changes in the body and, on the other hand, to show "that there is no soul so feeble that it cannot, if well directed, acquire an absolute power over its passions."[4]

This latter claim, which he shared with the Stoics, is the fundamental tenet of Descartes's moral philosophy. He attempts to justify it on the rather questionable grounds that the connection between our thoughts and the motions of the "animal spirits" is a consequence of custom, not nature. Thus, although a given emotion—for example, fear—is generally produced in the mind as a result of particular messages sent by the body to the pineal gland, the mind has the power to break this customary connection and to establish in its place a connection between these emotions and different ideas. For example, the physiological condition that normally gives rise to fear could, by proper training, be connected with the idea of courage. Ultimately, there is nothing to prevent the mind from attaining absolute control over its passions.

Spinoza attacks this view head-on in the preface, definitions, and initial propositions of part 3 of the *Ethics*. The first step in this attack is a redefinition of the notions of action and passion. Whereas for Descartes they refer to two ways of looking at a single occurrence, for Spinoza they characterize two distinct states of affairs. We act, he states, "when something happens, in us or outside us, of which we are the adequate cause. . . . On the other hand . . . we are acted on when something happens in us, or something follows from our own nature of which we are only a partial cause" (D2).

As the juxtaposition of adequate and partial causes clearly suggests, this doctrine is based on the distinction between adequate and inadequate ideas. An adequate cause, we are told, is one "whose effect can be clearly and distinctly perceived through it," whereas an inadequate, or partial, cause is one "through which, by itself, its effect cannot be understood" (D1). This distinction leads, in turn, to a definition of the emotions, or affects (*affectiones*). As used by Spinoza, this term has reference to *both* the mind and the body.[5] In regard to the latter, it refers to the "affections of the Body by which the Body's power of acting is increased or diminished, aided or restrained." In regard to the former, it refers to "the ideas of these affections" (D3). Emotions in the mental sense, which are largely what will concern us here, are ideas in the mind corresponding to events in the body, in which the power of that body is affected either positively or negatively. As he adds by way of explanation, if we can be the adequate cause of any of these affections (of either the mind or the body), the affect is an action; otherwise it is a passion. At the very beginning of his account, Spinoza introduces the notion of an active emotion. As we shall see, this notion will prove central to his entire ethical theory.

The immediate problem, however, is to explain how the mind can be an adequate cause of something, and hence active. Given his analysis of mind and the repudiation of the freedom of the will that this analysis entails, it is not surprising to find Spinoza affirming that "*our Mind does certain things [acts] and undergoes other things, viz. insofar as it has adequate ideas, it necessarily does certain things, and insofar as it has inadequate ideas, it necessarily undergoes other things*" (P1). When the mind conceives something adequately, it possesses its ideas completely and independently of any external causes. This, as we have seen, is the reason why Spinoza holds that when the mind has adequate ideas, it is determined from within and follows its own laws (the laws of logic, rather than the associations of things dictated by the common order of nature). From this it can be inferred that to the extent to which the mind possesses adequate ideas, it is the adequate cause of its states (emotions) and does not merely reflect external events passively. Contrary to Descartes's assumption, however, this activity of the mind does not entail any power to determine the body directly; nor does passivity entail any power of the body to determine the mind. Both are precluded by the doctrine of attributes, from which we can conclude that "*the Body cannot determine the Mind to thinking, and the Mind cannot determine the Body to motion, to rest or to anything else (if there is anything else)"* (P2).

As Spinoza goes on to note in the long, important scholium to this proposition, the problem with Descartes and with all who believe that the mind can influence the body through some mysterious act of will is simply that they have not adequately understood the nature of the body. "No one," he writes, "has yet determined what the Body can do, i.e., experience has not taught anyone what the Body can do from the laws of nature alone, insofar as nature is only considered to be corporeal." In view of Descartes's efforts to provide a purely mechanistic physiology and his consequent conception of the body as a machine, one might question whether Spinoza is here referring to him. Nevertheless, this is precisely the case. What Spinoza seems to have specifically in mind is Descartes's claim that we can determine the functions of the mind or soul by attributing to it everything that we cannot clearly and distinctly conceive as pertaining to the body—that is, everything that we cannot explain in mechanistic terms. From Spinoza's standpoint, this whole approach is far too facile, since it neglects a great truth that has already been established—namely, "that infinitely many things follow from nature, under whatever attribute it may be considered" (P2S).

But what about our ordinary experience? Does this not provide ample evidence of the mind's ability to exercise control over the body? Again Spinoza's answer is an emphatic no. "Experience," he points out sarcastically, "teaches all too plainly that men have nothing less in their power than their tongue, and can do nothing less than moderate their appetites." Moreover, people tend to believe they are free only with regard to the moderate appetites and desires that they are able to control, not with regard to their stronger desires and more violent appetites, which often prove irresistible. Yet this distinction is illusory, and it stems from an ignorance of true causes. The truth of the matter, according to Spinoza, is that there is no such thing as a volition or mental decision distinct from a bodily appetite, through which an individual either resists or yields to that appetite. On the contrary, he asserts that "all these things, indeed, show clearly that both the decision of the Mind and the appetite and the determination of the Body by nature exist together—or rather are one and the same thing, which we call a decision when it is considered under, and explained through, the attribute of Thought, and which we call a determination when it is considered under the attribute of Extension and deduced from the laws of motion and rest" (P2S).

This is the counterpart of Spinoza's conception of volition as assent to the content of an idea. Just as there is no volition extrinsic to an idea, so there is none extrinsic to a desire. As a finite modification of thought, any desire is determined by a cause and, specifically, by an idea. The decision of the mind to engage in or forego any course of action is, therefore, not a mysterious act of will, but simply another name for a specific desire. As such, it is as determined as the bodily appetite that it reflects in the attribute of thought.

The problem of understanding human action has thus been radically shifted from the form that it assumed in Descartes. The question is no longer whether or how consciousness can effect changes in the bodily mechanism, for even the possibility has been ruled out on metaphysical grounds (the doctrine of attributes). Instead, the central issue is whether the mind can ever be the sufficient, or adequate, cause of its desires. Moreover, once the question is posed in this manner, it admits of an affirmative answer. This occurs whenever these desires follow from, or are caused by, adequate ideas. We can express the same point in non-Spinozistic terms by saying that the mind acts, as opposed to being merely the passive victim of circumstances, whenever its desires, and hence its decisions, are grounded in rational considerations—for example, when it desires a particular food because of the knowledge (adequate idea) that it is nutritious. In Spinoza's own terms, "the actions of the Mind arise from adequate ideas alone; the passions depend on inadequate ideas alone" (P3).

We can now see that in the first three propositions of this section and the last two of the preceding section, Spinoza has developed what amounts to the outlines of a psychology in which human thought and activity are explicable without reference to the notion of a will. It should also be obvious, however, that, for such a radical program to succeed, Spinoza must introduce an alternative principle that can adequately account for the dynamics of human behavior. This principle is provided by the conception of *conatus*. The conatus of a thing is simply its effort to persist in its own being. This effort pertains to the nature of every finite mode, and in a human being, who is conscious of such an effort, it becomes the desire for self-preservation. Spinoza thus comes down on the side of Hobbes and many others who view the desire for self-preservation as the basic motivating force in human behavior. In characteristic fashion, however, Spinoza does not affirm this on the basis of an empirical knowledge of human nature, but rather deduces it from the very status of human beings as finite modes. This allows him to affirm not merely that this desire, as a matter of fact, is basic to human beings, but that it constitutes their very essence.

Spinoza argues for the fundamental tenet of his anthropology in an indirect and typically cryptic manner. The first point to be established is that "*no thing can be destroyed except through an external cause*" (P4). Although this seems counterintuitive, since it appears to rule out the possibility of suicide, Spinoza claims that it is self-evident. In support of its alleged self-evidence, he remarks only that the definition of any thing affirms or posits, rather than denies, that thing's essence. Consequently, insofar as we consider only the thing itself (its definition), thereby ignoring external causes, it is impossible to find anything that could destroy it.

By appealing to the definition of a thing, Spinoza appears to be making a claim about what is contained in a thing's concept or idea. So construed, the point is simply that nothing that is incompatible with the possibility of a thing can be included in its concept or definition—for example, no property incompatible with its geometrical nature can be included in the definition of a circle. The problem with this, however, is that it seems to invite the objection that Spinoza is conflating things with their concepts or definitions. Certainly, it does not seem to follow from the fact that something is not contained in the definition of a thing that it cannot pertain to the thing itself (particularly if one regards the thing as persisting through time and undergoing changes of state).[6]

This objection requires a two-part response. First, it must be emphasized that Spinoza is here referring to real definitions, which express adequate ideas, and which therefore characterize the true nature of the thing defined. Second, the claim does not refer to things in an unqualified way, but rather to things considered as they are in themselves—that is, as they are apart from their relations to other things in the order of nature. Consequently, Spinoza's full claim is that things *so considered* cannot have any properties that are not contained in the adequate ideas of them, or their real definitions.

By itself, the first point obviously does not solve the problem, because the objection can easily be restated with reference to the real definition. To continue with the same example, there is more to an actual circle than is contained in the real definition of a circle—for example, it has a radius of a certain, determinate length. Moreover, at first glance at least, the second point appears to make things even worse. Recall that for Spinoza a finite mode is not supposed to be an independent, self-subsistent thing. On the contrary, it is a part of a whole; and its particular state at any given moment—indeed, its continued duration—is a function of its relation to this whole—that is, to the external forces acting on it. Thus, to consider a thing apart from its relation to these forces would seem to require an act of abstraction that, in a certain sense, "falsifies" the situation, thereby yielding an inadequate idea.

This last point takes us to the nerve of the argument. In reality, such a claim is no more a falsification than is the principle of inertia, which states how a body would behave if, *per impossibile*, it were not acted on by other bodies. Like the latter principle, of which it is a metaphysical counterpart, Spinoza's principle is an idealization. It concerns the nature of a finite mode considered as a pure possibility, in abstraction from its relations to other such modes which determine its actual existence and duration in the order of nature. To consider a thing in this way is to consider it with respect to its intrinsic nature. Moreover, it is just this intrinsic nature, not the thing itself, that Spinoza identifies with the thing's essence, and that he claims is expressed in its real definition.

The basic point can also be expressed by noting that, although he does not use the terminology, Spinoza operates with what amounts to his own version of the traditional distinction between essential and accidental or, better, intrinsic and extrinsic, properties. The former are those properties which constitute the essential nature of a thing—that is, the nature of a thing considered as it is in itself; whereas the latter are those which pertain to it only by virtue of its relations to other things in the order of nature. Duration, for Spinoza, is a prime example of a property of the latter type. Given Spinoza's necessitarianism, both types of property are necessary; but, as we have already seen, they are necessary for different reasons: the former because their negation would contradict the concept of the thing to which they belong, the latter because their negation would contradict the necessary order of nature considered as a whole.

Finally, it is its inherent nature, or essence, not the actually existing thing, that is supposed to exclude all contrary properties. If the inherent nature of a thing is constituted by a certain proportion of motion and rest, for example, then its definition, which expresses this nature, necessarily excludes everything that is incompatible with the maintenance of this proportion—that is, everything that is incompatible with the "formula" that defines the thing.[7] Correlatively, anything that is in this sense incompatible with the thing—that is, that would tend to destroy it—must be conceived as extrinsic to it, as not part of its intrinsic nature. Spinoza makes this latter point explicit when he states: *"Things are of a contrary nature, i.e., cannot be in the same subject, insofar as one can destroy the other"* (P5).

The conatus doctrine itself emerges from the reformulation of these principles in positive terms. Central to this reformulation is the conception of things as acting.[8] Since things act, and since (by the preceding propositions) they cannot act in ways that are contrary to their nature—that is, which tend to their self-destruction—Spinoza concludes that *"each thing, as far as it can by its own power, strives to persevere in its being"* (P6). This argument has been criticized from a number of different perspectives; but the simplest way of characterizing the problem is that it seems to involve an illicit slide from the claim that things (by their very nature or definition) are necessarily opposed to whatever can destroy them to the claim that things necessarily act in self-maintaining ways. Spinoza, so it would seem, is entitled only to the former.[9]

Against this it can be retorted, first, that insofar as a thing acts, this opposition to whatever tends to destroy it is expressed as an actual resistance; and second, that for a thing to act in such a way as to resist whatever tends to destroy it is to act in a self-maintaining way. Combining this with the definition of essence as "that which, being given, the thing is also necessarily posited and which, being taken away, the thing is necessarily also taken away" (IID2), Spinoza can claim that "*the striving (conatus) by which each thing strives to persevere in its being is nothing but the actual essence of the thing*" (P7). Finally, precisely because it constitutes the essence of the thing, this striving, or endeavor, does not last for a determinate time but continues for as long as the thing endures (P8).

It still remains to apply this principle to the human mind. Such a mind, we have learned, is composed of both adequate (clear and distinct) and inadequate (confused) ideas. Since the mind's conatus constitutes its very essence, it must be reflected in all its ideas; and since the human mind is self-conscious (contains an "idea of the idea"), it must be aware of this endeavor. Thus Spinoza affirms: "*Both insofar as the Mind has clear and distinct ideas, and insofar as it has confused ideas, it strives, for an indefinite duration, to persevere in its being and it is conscious of this striving it has*" (P9). This is of great importance, for it establishes the universality of the conatus principle for the explanation of human behavior. All such behavior, whether it be an "act of the mind"—that is, a rational decision based on adequate ideas of the end to be achieved and the means to be employed—or a passive response to external stimuli based on blind impulse and imagination (merely inadequate ideas) is an expression of the effort of the individual in question to persevere in its own being.

From this we can readily see the absolute impossibility for Spinoza of what other philosophers have described as "disinterested" action. One can no more help striving to preserve one's being than a stone can help falling when it is dropped. It is simply one's nature, and nothing can violate the laws of its own being. Viewed from a psychological standpoint, this endeavor can be called "will" (*Voluntas*); thus one can, in a manner of speaking, say that human beings "will" to preserve their being. But there is nothing undetermined or free about this will. As before, this "act of will" is nothing more than the mental decision accompanying the bodily appetite. The notion of appetite (*Appetitus*), therefore, is basic in the characterization of an individual's conatus. This refers to the endeavor for self-preservation viewed in relation to both the mind and the body. Construing it in this broad sense, Spinoza claims that appetite is "nothing but the very essence of man, from whose nature there necessarily follow those things that promote his preservation. And so man is determined to do those things" (P95). Appetite in this sense can also be called desire (*Cupiditas*). The only difference is that desire implies consciousness; hence desire itself is defined as *"appetite together with the consciousness of the appetite."* Finally, given this virtual identification of desire and appetite, Spinoza can state at the end of his whole account of the emotions that "desire is man's very essence, insofar as it is conceived to be determined, from any given affection of it, to do something."[10]

At first glance this conception of conatus as the endeavor on the part of a thing to preserve its being may seem to conflict with the frequent description of it as the thing's effort to *increase* its power, or force, for existence. Moreover, this latter conception was already implicit in the "official" definition of the emotions, in which, as we have seen, Spinoza referred specifically to the increase or diminution in the organism's active power, or power of acting (*agendia potentia*). This power is the force through which the body maintains its existence (its particular proportion of motion and rest) throughout its interaction with other bodies in its environment. Spinoza also equates this force with a thing's "perfection." With regard to living organisms, however, with which we are at present concerned, it can be more easily understood as the organism's level of vitality. This force, or vitality, can be viewed as the very principle of organic unity. When it sinks below a certain level, the organism is overcome by its environment, and its particular proportion of motion and rest is destroyed; it is then said to die.[11] The endeavor of an organism to preserve its existence is thus identical with its effort to increase its perfection, power of acting, force for existence, or level of vitality. The only difference is that the initial formula refers to the organism in isolation, whereas the latter, which is much more relevant to the emotional life of a human being, considers it as involved in a constant struggle for existence with other beings in its environment.[12] From this point of view, anything that lessens an organism's power lessens its ability to preserve its being, and anything that increases its power enhances that ability.[13]

Spinoza's basic concern, however, is with the emotions, and especially the passions, insofar as they are ideas in the mind which correspond to changes in the level of vitality of the body. Essential to this analysis is the conception of the mind as the idea of the body. From this we can now see that the mind's fundamental endeavor, or basic desire, must be to affirm the existence of the body. Just as the body, in its endeavor to persist in its being, tends to reject any change or affect contrary to its nature, so the mind tends to reject the *idea* of anything contrary to the existence or well-being of the body (P10). The mind, in other words, cannot spontaneously entertain the thought of anything that would be destructive to the body and, consequently, to itself. Spinoza thus rules out in advance, as a psychological impossibility, anything like a Freudian death wish. Furthermore, since the power of thought in the mind is a function of its ability to affirm the existence of the body, it also follows that the idea of anything which either helps or hinders the body's capacity to act has a like effect on the mind (P11), and that the mind endeavors as far as possible to imagine things that are beneficial to the body (P12).

These general principles, or universal laws, of the mind's conatus provide the basis for the explication of the primary emotions: pleasure, pain, and desire. All are closely associated with the transition from one state of perfection, or level of vitality, to another. Pleasure, or joy (*Laetitia*), is "*that passion by which the Mind passes to a greater perfection*," and pain, or sorrow (*Tristitia*), is "*that passion by which the Mind passes to a lesser perfection*" (P11S).[14] Pleasure and pain thus reflect changes brought about in the organism through its interaction with the environment; and, as Spinoza notes in his subsequent analysis, the source of pleasure or pain lies in the transition itself, not in the state at which one arrives.[15]

The status of desire as a distinct primary emotion is complicated by the ambiguity of Spinoza's account. On the one hand, the official definition of desire as "*appetite together with the consciousness of the appetite*" suggests that it is equivalent to a thing's conatus. As such, it is certainly fundamental to the emotive life; nevertheless, it is not so much a distinct emotion as the basis of all the emotions, including pleasure and pain. On the other hand, Spinoza recognizes specific desires directed toward whatever the mind regards as beneficial to the body and to itself—that is, toward whatever it sees as a source of pleasure or as a means of avoiding pain. In fact, Spinoza insists that there are as many kinds of desire as there are kinds of pleasure and pain, and that there are as many kinds of these as there are objects by which the body is affected (P56). So construed, a desire is a distinct emotion; but, given its dependence on pleasure and pain, it seems not to be primary. Even granting this ambiguity, however, it still seems possible to make a case for the claim that desire in the second sense is a primary, as well as a distinct, emotion.[16] The point here is that, although a particular desire depends on what the mind deems pleasurable or at least a means of avoiding pain, the desire itself is not a pleasure or a pain. We cannot, therefore, account for the emotive life of a human being simply in terms of pleasure and pain; it is also necessary to include desire, which functions as the basic motivating force in human behavior.

The claim that pleasure, pain, and desire are distinct, primary emotions implies that all other emotions, the so-called "derivative emotions," can be explained in terms of them. The actual systematic working-out of this thesis with regard to a whole catalogue of emotions, taken mostly from Descartes, occupies the great bulk of this part of the *Ethics*. Although we cannot take time here to follow the details of this analysis and to see how it applies to very many specific emotions, we can at least delineate the basic principles underlying the discussion. A crucial point to keep in mind is that pleasure, pain, and desire, as just described, relate directly to present objects, which cause the affections in the body to which the respective emotions in the mind correspond. The derivative emotions all turn out to be species or combinations of pleasure, pain, and desire, which are directed in various ways either to objects that do not at present exist and affect the body or to objects that are not themselves directly the cause of its affections.[17]

This can be illustrated with regard to the two most basic derivative emotions, love and hate. We have already seen that the mind attempts, as far as it is able, to conceive of things that increase or aid the power of activity of the body. From this and his analysis of imagination and memory, Spinoza is able to infer that "*when the Mind imagines those things that diminish or restrain the Body's power of acting, it strives, as far as it can, to recollect things that exclude their existence*" (P13). The very idea of an object can thus itself be a source of pleasure or pain, even if the object is not actually present. This principle provides the basis for Spinoza's analysis of love and hate. The former, he argues, "*is nothing but pleasure with the accompanying idea of an external cause*, and the latter *is* nothing but *pain with the accompanying idea of an external cause.*" Moreover, like any other species of pleasure and pain, these passions are inseparable from the effort to possess and keep present the object of love and to remove and destroy the object of hatred (P13S).

As a result, Spinoza can hold that the human mind is capable of feeling love or hatred toward any number of things, and much the same can be said in regard to two other key derivative emotions, hope and fear. The former is defined as "*an inconstant pleasure which has arisen from the image of a future or past thing whose outcome we doubt,*" and the latter as "*an inconstant pain, which has also arisen from the image of a doubtful thing*" (P18S2). These emotions, like everything else in nature, do not arise capriciously, but in accordance with universal and necessary laws. In the context of his analysis, Spinoza presents two such laws, both of which are based on the previous analysis of the imagination. The first has been called the "law of the association of emotions."[18] According to this law, an object that has never been itself a cause of pleasure, pain, or desire may become such by being associated with one that has. This association can be based on similarity, contrast, or contiguity. For instance, the mind necessarily tends to love objects resembling those that it already loves, hate those that contrast sharply with them, and love and hate in turn those things which it commonly finds together with the objects that it loves and hates. The second basic law can be called the "law of the imitation of the emotions."[19] This law explains how an object that is neither an essential nor an accidental (through association) cause of pleasure, pain, or desire may become such if it happens to cause them in other human beings whose emotions we naturally tend to imitate. Here Spinoza deals for the first time with the social nature of human beings and explains emotions such as sympathy, pity, and joy in the well-being of others.

But these laws deal with the mind only insofar as it is passive—that is, only insofar as it is the inadequate, or partial, cause of its affections. To the extent that it is passive, it is subject primarily to external causes, as a result of which "we are driven about in many ways . . . and . . . like waves on the sea, driven by contrary winds, we toss about, not knowing our outcome and fate" (P59S). Nevertheless, although Spinoza repudiates the Cartesian conception of the power of the mind in terms of a free will, he no more believes that the above account tells the whole story of the emotive life of the mind than that the analysis of sense perception and imagination tells the whole story of the mind's cognitive life.

Accordingly, at the end of his long analysis of the passive emotions, or passions, Spinoza briefly introduces and describes the active emotions: "*Apart from Pleasure and Desire that are passions,*" he notes, "*there are other affects of Pleasure and Desire that are related to us insofar as we act*" (P48). These affects are grounded in the mind's adequate ideas. When the mind conceives anything adequately, it is necessarily also aware of itself. It is thus aware of its power or activity, and this gives rise to an active emotion of pleasure. This emotion is basically what other philosophers have described as "intellectual pleasure," although Spinoza is careful to point out that the source of the pleasure is the mind's sense of its own activity, not the nature of the object. Similarly, desire as an active emotion is simply rational desire, or the endeavor to preserve one's being insofar as that endeavor is guided by adequate ideas (scientific knowledge). However, there is no active analogy to pain, the third primary emotion. This emotion reflects a diminution in the mind's power or activity, which, as we have seen, can never be the result of the mind's activity, or adequate ideas, but merely of its being determined by external forces and its possession of inadequate understanding (P49).

This account closes with the suggestion that all a person's actions stemming from active emotions can be ascribed to "*strength of character (fortitudo)*." This, in turn, is divided into "*courage (animositas)*"[20] and "*nobility (generositas)*." Courage is defined as "the Desire by which each one strives, solely from the dictates of reason, to preserve his being." As we shall soon see, courage construed in this broad sense is equivalent to virtue as a whole, although it is here referred solely to actions concerned with the good of the agent. As such, it is contrasted with nobility, which is defined as "the Desire by which each one strives, solely from the dictates of the reason, to aid other men and join them to him in friendship" (P59S). This governs our actions when we are concerned with the well-being of others and provides the basis of the social virtues. Within the confines of part 3 of the *Ethics*, however, Spinoza does little more than describe and affirm the possibility of these active emotions through which the mind can escape being a slave to its passions. The actual demonstration of this claim and the development of its implications for the understanding of the moral life are the aims of part 4 of the *Ethics*, which deals with the nature of virtue.

II Human Virtue

The full and revolutionary implications of Spinoza's naturalistic-rationalistic program emerge with his analysis of virtue. Traditionally, most moral philosophers, as well as the proverbial man in the street, have viewed "moral perfection" and "goodness" as absolute values that one ought to and can realize. Within the Judeo-Christian tradition, this view has often been linked with the conception of a human being as created with a free will by a personal deity who requires obedience to a set of commandments that define the morally good. The eternal destiny of the individual is then linked to the fulfillment of these commandments (the "Divine Law"). For the past three hundred years, this religious ethic has competed with a secular, "humanistic" ethic, in which the theological trimmings have been removed but the belief that human beings have free wills and are obligated to perform certain duties quite independently of their interests and desires, remains. The conscientious performance of these duties is called "virtue" and is deemed worthy of praise, whereas the failure to perform them is considered morally blameworthy.

It should be clear from our previous consideration of his philosophy that Spinoza had little sympathy for this moral outlook in either its religious or secular form. For him, the entire outlook, as well as the conception of human nature that it entails, is a product of the imagination, rather than of reason. As such, it is based on inadequate ideas—specifically, on a failure to recognize that human beings, as finite modes, are parts of nature, and that their particular desires and values, as well as their actions, are necessary consequences of the endeavor to preserve their being. Spinoza succinctly expresses this view at the conclusion of his account of the conatus doctrine in part 3: "From all this, then, it is clear that we neither strive for, nor will, neither want, nor desire anything because we judge it to be good; on the contrary, we judge something to be good because we strive for it, will it, want it, desire it" (IIIP9S).

Spinoza develops his critique of traditional morality further in the preface to part 4. After providing a nonevaluative definition of *perfection* in terms of the completed, or finished,[21] and noting that, so construed, it applies only to artifacts, he attempts to explain how the notion and its opposite came to acquire an evaluative sense and to be applied to natural things (including human beings). This is traced to mankind's tendency, under the domination of the imagination, to form universal ideas (which are, of course, highly confused) and to regard them as norms, or models (*exemplaria*) in terms of which things and their actions are to be judged. Given such models, perfection and imperfection are now understood evaluatively in terms of conformity or lack thereof to the model—for example, the "perfect" human being is the one who realizes or comes closest to realizing the "ideal" of what it is to be a human being. The specifically moral notions of *good* and *evil* are likewise defined in terms of these models. Not surprisingly, Spinoza connects the development of this way of thinking with the belief in final causes. The basic idea here seems to be that belief in a norm or model reflects belief in a purpose for which a thing has been created. For Spinoza, however, these "purposes," together with the associated models, are really nothing more than projections of human desires. He thus concludes that perfection and imperfection, good and evil, are not intrinsic properties of things, but merely "modes of thinking"—fictions that we attribute to things insofar as we consider them in light of our desire-based model.

No sooner does Spinoza complete this critique of traditional morality, however, than he appears to take much of it back by admitting the necesssity both of appealing to a model of human nature and of defining *good* and *evil, perfect* and *imperfect* in light of it. As he puts it:

> But though this is so, still we must retain these words. For because we desire to form an idea of man, as a model of human nature which we may look to, it will be useful to us to retain these same words with the meaning I have indicated. In what follows, therefore, I shall understand by good what we know certainly is a means by which we may approach nearer and nearer to the model of human nature that we set before ourselves. By evil, what we certainly know prevents us from becoming like that model. Next, we shall say that men are more perfect or imperfect, insofar as they approach more or less near to this model.

Although this sudden reversal is perplexing and raises a number of questions regarding Spinoza's intentions, the most reasonable reading is that he is suggesting that the problem with traditional morality is not that it appeals to a model of human nature, but that it appeals to a bad model, one based on inadequate ideas. Presumably Spinoza's alternative model will be based on an adequate idea of human nature—that is, one which recognizes that human beings are finite modes and that all their activities are therefore necessary consequences of that striving for self-preservation which constitutes the essence of each finite thing.[22] Presumably, this new model will also provide the basis for a "new morality," one that is based on reason rather than imagination and that is in accord with true human needs.[23]

This attitude is reflected in the definitions offered at the beginning of part 4. Referring back to the passage from the preface cited above, Spinoza informs the reader that "by good I shall understand what we certainly know to be useful to us" (D1), and "by evil . . . what we certainly know prevents us from being masters of some good" (D2). By defining *good* and *evil* in terms of self-interest, Spinoza makes explicit the egoistic basis of all evaluation, which is obfuscated by traditional morality. A third key moral concept, virtue, undergoes a similar transformation. In sharp contrast with traditional morality, which tends to equate virtue with altruistic, disinterested behavior, Spinoza states that "by virtue and power I understand the same thing" (D8). The equation of virtue with power reflects the original meaning of the Latin term *virtus*, according to which, virtue is nothing more than the ability to act according to one's nature, to be self-determined, to be oneself the source (adequate cause) of one's states. In less metaphysical terms, this means that, for Spinoza, the virtuous person is one who has power over his emotions and is not merely a slave to his passions. Moreover, since virtuous behavior so construed involves, by definition, an increase in one's capacity to act, Spinoza can claim that virtue is inherently and necessarily pleasurable. This, in turn, enables him later to identify virtue with happiness, and to affirm, in opposition to a good deal of religious morality, that virtue is its own reward.

The essential feature of Spinoza's theory of virtue, however, is its connection with knowledge. This connection is based on the analysis of what it is to be an adequate cause. As we have seen already, one can be an adequate cause, and hence act in the full sense of the term, only insofar as one has adequate ideas. The logic of Spinoza's position thus leads directly to the identification of virtue with knowledge. Only if one lives "under the guidance of reason," to use Spinoza's frequent expression, can one control one's appetites, realize one's true being, and achieve human perfection. The real power in human existence is thus the power of reason, not of will. Reason, to be sure, can never, for Spinoza, replace desire as the motivating force in human behavior. We are essentially desire, and hence we cannot cease desiring. We can, however, through the possession of adequate ideas—that is, through the exercise of reason—come to understand our desires and their causes, discern what is truly useful for our self-preservation, and live accordingly. We can, in short, desire rationally. The possession of adequate ideas is therefore at one and the same time both the ultimate goal of all human endeavor, in the sense of being that state in which we most fully realize our essence, or nature, and the only means through which we can arrive at this goal.

Nevertheless, Spinoza was under no illusions regarding the extent of this power. Human perfection is relative only, and its achievement is a rare and difficult feat. Accordingly, the first eighteen propositions of part 4, which is significantly entitled "On Human Bondage, or the Powers of the Affects," deal in a thoroughly realistic fashion with the power of reason in its conflict with the emotions. The entire discussion is prefaced by an axiom that sets the tone for what follows: "There is no singular thing in nature than which there is not another more powerful and stronger. Whatever one is given, there is another more powerful by which the first can be destroyed" (A1).

Since a human being is just such an individual thing in nature and therefore cannot be conceived without other things, such a being is always to some extent passive (P2). Furthermore, it follows from this and the above axiom that "*the force by which a man perseveres in existing is limited, and infinitely surpassed by the power of external causes*" (P3). Consequently, human beings cannot be the adequate cause of all their modifications—that is, they cannot cease being a part of nature (P4). From this, Spinoza infers that "man is necessarily always subject to his passions, that he follows and obeys the common order of Nature, and accommodates himself to it as much as the nature of things requires" (P4C). Given this, it becomes rather difficult to see just what room there is in the Spinozistic universe for the exercise of the power of reason. This difficulty is compounded by the claim at the very beginning of the analysis that *"nothing positive which a false idea has is removed by the presence of the true insofar as it is true"* (P1).

This suggests that truth qua truth is not a weapon against false or inadequate ideas; from this it would seem to follow that truth cannot serve as a weapon against the passions. Spinoza bases his main proof of this proposition on his analysis of falsity as privation. It follows from this analysis that if the assumed positive quality of a false idea were to be removed by what is true, it would be removed by itself; and this, Spinoza contends, is obviously absurd. Realizing perhaps that this argument is not likely to prove convincing, Spinoza suggests in a scholium that his point can be grasped more clearly in terms of his account of the relation between reason and imagination. Returning to the example of the perception of the sun, he reminds us that possession of the adequate—that is, scientific—idea of the sun does not remove, but merely enables us to understand, the imaginative idea that we have of it as a disk in the sky about two hundred feet above us. Generalizing from this example, Spinoza concludes: "So imaginations do not disappear through the presence of the true insofar as it is true, but because there occur others, stronger than them, which exclude the present existence of the things we imagine" (P15).

The difficulty increases when we realize that this conclusion holds for emotions as well as imaginative ideas. As an idea through which the mind affirms of the body either a greater or a lesser force of existence than before, an emotion can arise in the mind only when the body is affected in such a way that its force is increased or diminished. In non-Spinozistic terms, every emotion is correlated with a physiological change in the organism's level of vitality. But such a change can occur only when the body is affected by an external force. Moreover, once the change has occurred, this new state tends to preserve itself (according to the principle of conatus or inertia) until the body is affected in a contrary manner by another external force. For example, a state of pleasure will tend to persist until it is replaced by another affect through a subsequent physiological change. But, since it is the corresponding modification in the attribute of thought, precisely the same can be said of the emotion. Accordingly, Spinoza can assert that "*an affect cannot be restrained or taken away except by an affect opposite to, and stronger than, the affect to be restrained*" (P7).

Combining these two propositions, Spinoza concludes that "*no affect can be restrained by the true knowledge of good and evil insofar as it is true, but only insofar as it is considered as an affect*" (P14). This proposition both expresses the essence of the problem regarding the power of reason and suggests the means for its solution. Clearly, the key point is the distinction between the "true knowledge of good and evil insofar as it is true"—that is, considered with respect to its propositional content—and the same item of knowledge considered as an emotion, or affect. The latter way of considering an item of knowledge or, better, a true idea, is possible because "*the knowledge of good and evil is nothing but an affect of Pleasure or Pain insofar as we are conscious of it*" (P8).

The proof of this crucial proposition turns on the conception of an idea of an idea. First, Spinoza reminds us that we call a thing good or evil insofar as it is either an aid or a hindrance to the preservation of our being. Since the emotions of pleasure and pain are the signs through which we recognize this, it follows that by the "knowledge of good and evil" is meant nothing more than the mind's awareness of these ideas (pleasure and pain). Consequently, this knowledge is an idea of an idea. As such, Spinoza argues, it is not actually distinct from the original idea (the emotion) but is merely the same idea *qua* consciously apprehended. From this, Spinoza concludes that such knowledge possesses the entire emotive force of the pleasure or pain that it apprehends. Finally, it is this force, pertaining to the knowledge of good and evil, that provides the basis for understanding the power of reason.

But reason remains at best a fragile power, and Spinoza proceeds to underscore this in a brief analysis of the power of the emotions. We see first that the relative strength of an emotion is a function of the modality and temporal location of its object. For example, an emotion toward an object viewed as present and necessary is stronger, other things being equal, than one toward an object viewed as future and possible, or contingent (P9–P13). These general principles are then applied to "desire which arises from a true knowledge of good and evil"—that is, rational desire. This application shows that in general such desire can be checked by many other desires by which we are often assailed (P15). More specifically, it shows that rational desire for a future object can be overcome more easily than a similar desire for a present object (P16), that such desire directed toward a contingent object is weaker still (P17), and that, other things being equal, a desire arising from pleasure is stronger than one arising from pain (P18). By means of this analysis, based on this theory of the emotions, Spinoza attempts to explain in his own terms, without recourse to either the philosophical conception of will or the religious conception of a sinful nature, a fundamental and lamentable fact of moral experience: the great difference, which we all recognize, between knowing what is good, right, or useful and doing it.

After demonstrating that reason has some, albeit very limited, power to control the emotions and explaining why it so frequently fails to do so, Spinoza is prepared to show "what reason prescribes to us, which affects agree with the rules of human reason, and which, on the other hand, are contrary to these rules" (P18S). In so doing, he provides a general account of the nature of human virtue and of the proper goal of the life of reason, together with an analysis of some specific virtues, both real and purported. These are the topics of the remainder of part 4, which contains Spinoza's "moral philosophy" in the narrow, more usual sense of the term.

The account, of course, is based on the previously articulated conception of human nature. Hence it begins with the assertion that *"from the laws of his own nature, everyone necessarily wants, or is repelled by, what he judges to be good or evil"* (P19). This claim is hardly surprising, given the conatus doctrine and what we have already learned about the knowledge of good and evil. Now, since virtue has been equated with power, and more specifically with the power to act according to the laws of one's own nature, it follows that the more one is able to seek and obtain what is useful to oneself—that is, to preserve one's being—the more virtue one possesses. Correlatively, the more one neglects one's own true interests, the more one is subject to external forces rather than to the laws of one's own nature (P20). As Spinoza notes in a scholium to this proposition, this entails that no one, unless overwhelmed by external and contrary causes, neglects to endeavor to preserve his or her own being.[24] Moreover, Spinoza continues, since no one can desire to act and live well without also desiring to act and live, no desire can be more basic than the desire to live or actually to exist (P21). Similarly, no virtue can be more basic than that manifest in the endeavor to preserve oneself (P22); nor, finally, can there be any higher goal for the sake of which we strive to preserve our being (P25).

Although the account given above may suggest the contrary, Spinoza is actually quite far from either equating virtue with survival or identifying the good with what is in one's self-interest narrowly conceived. First, a person who, through fortuitous circumstances and without really knowing what he is doing, manages to "muddle through" or "luck out," would hardly be regarded as virtuous by Spinoza. What is important to him is that the result follow from the individual's own activity. The person must be the adequate cause, which means that his behavior must be grounded in adequate ideas (P23). A person whose behavior is so grounded can be said to be acting under the guidance of reason, from which it follows that "*acting absolutely from virtue is nothing else in us but acting, living, and preserving our beings (these three signify the same thing) by the guidance of reason, from the foundation of seeking one's own advantage*" (P24). Second, what turns out to be truly advantageous is not mere life or the maximization of sensuous pleasure, but understanding. Consequently, the chief endeavor of those who live "under the guidance of reason" is to increase their understanding; hence things are deemed useful only insofar as they contribute to the attainment of that end (P26).

Given Spinoza's emphasis on the primacy of self-preservation, this identification of the true good with understanding is indeed paradoxical. In fact, it seems to contradict the claim that there is nothing for the sake of which we strive to preserve our being. Even more paradoxically, Spinoza attempts to establish this claim on the basis of the very principle of self-preservation with which it seems to conflict. According to this principle, Spinoza argues, the mind, like everything else, endeavors to persist in its being and engage in those activities which follow from the laws of its own nature. This principle holds whether a person lives under the guidance of reason or in bondage to the passions. But the essential activity of reason is clear and distinct conception or understanding. Consequently, the fundamental endeavor of the mind under the guidance of reason will be to understand, and hence it will necessarily regard as useful only those things which are conducive to its understanding. Moreover, since the highest object of knowledge is God, the very source of intelligibility, Spinoza can conclude that *"knowledge of God is the Mind's greatest good; its greatest virtue is to know God"* (P28).

This uncompromising intellectualism implies that ordinary moral virtues such as benevolence have no absolute worth, that they are valuable only to the extent to which they contribute to the power of the mind. Spinoza does not deny this implication, but he contends that these virtues do in fact contribute significantly to this power. "To man," he writes, "there is nothing more useful than man" (P18S). Among other things, this means that each of us needs the help of others if we are to realize our full intellectual potential. Moreover, since we cannot "go it alone," we must be prepared to cooperate with others and to be concerned with their well-being. Spinoza's moral theory is thus transformed from an intellectualistic egoism into a philosophy that emphasizes the social nature of man and that argues, on the basis of the principle of self-preservation, for the necessity of a genuine concern for the well-being of others.

As usual, Spinoza makes things difficult for his readers by casting his argument in a metaphysical form, deducing people's need for one another from general principles concerning the relations between all finite modes. The starting point of his analysis is the principle that no individual whose nature is completely different from our own can either help or hinder us in any way (P29). This follows from the even more general principle that things which have nothing in common cannot enter in causal relation. Since this means that they cannot affect one another at all, it is obvious that they cannot affect one another either advantageously or adversely. On the other hand, things which do have something in common with us can either help or hinder us— that is, they can either augment or check our power of activity. Something is harmful to the extent that its nature disagrees with, or is contrary to, our own (P30). Presumably, this applies to things whose efforts to preserve their own being conflict with our efforts to preserve our own being. On the biological level, one here thinks of things such as poisonous foods or predatory animals. If, howeveer, a thing is in harmony with our nature, which presumably means that its effort to preserve its own being is at least compatible with our effort to preserve our own, then, according to Spinoza, it is always useful to us (P31). On the biological level, one might here think of things such as nutritious foods and useful animals.

The next step is to apply these general principles to human social relationships. Here Spinoza's main concern is to demonstrate that, insofar as people live in harmony with reason, they live in harmony with one another, and consequently, are mutually useful to each other. But first he argues that, insofar as people are governed by their passions, they necessarily differ from, and are not in harmony with, one another. This is because they are then determined by external things, and their passions differ according to the nature of the determining objects. As a result they are at least potentially in conflict (P32–P34).

An obvious objection to this doctrine is that two or more people can love and desire the same object, thus having something in common, while at the same time being in conflict precisely because of this shared emotion. Spinoza attempts to counter this by contending that, although both may love or desire the same object, they really do not share the same emotion. One person has the idea of the loved object as present or in his possession; the other, the idea of the same object as absent. Hence, one will feel pleasure; the other, pain; and this difference is the basis of their conflict (P34S).

On the face of it, this argument is not particularly convincing. Among its many problems, it simply ignores the situation in which neither of the two (or more) jealous lovers is able to possess the desired object.[25] Nevertheless, this is incidental to Spinoza's main concern, which is to argue that things are quite different insofar as people live under the guidance of reason. In such circumstances, he argues, people will always agree in nature, because their behavior will be governed by the common laws of human nature alone, not those of external objects. Consequently, they will never be in conflict with one another (P35). Moreover, since what reason tells us is good necessarily is so, it also follows that "insofar as men live according to the guidance of reason, they must do only those things that are good for human nature and hence, for each man" (P35D).

The operative assumption in all this is that, in spite of individual differences, we share a common human nature as rational beings. Largely on the basis of this assumption, together with the identification of the good for human beings with understanding, Spinoza proceeds to claim that "*the greatest good of those who seek virtue is common to all, and can be enjoyed by all equally*" (P36). Given Spinoza's equation of the pursuit of virtue with the pursuit of one's true self-interest, his view has obvious affinities with the famous "Invisible Hand" doctrine of Adam Smith, offered a century later in defense of a capitalistic, free-enterprise system. According to Smith, the reasoned pursuit by every individual of his own economic self-interest (profit) in a competitive free market leads inevitably, by means of the Invisible Hand, to the common good. Unlike the capitalistic conception advocated by Smith, however, the Spinozistic conception of society is decidedly noncompetitive, even anticompetitive.[26] Spinoza's point is that, although everyone pursues their own self-interest, insofar as they live under the guidance of reason, people do not come into conflict with one another, because the good for which they strive—understanding—is, unlike wealth, attainable by all. In other words, knowledge is not a depletable resource, and the quest for it is not a zero-sum game. Indeed, one person's acquisition of knowledge actually enhances the capacity of others to attain it. Consequently, there can be no jealousy, envy, or competition among genuine seekers after truth; quite the contrary, "*the good which everyone who seeks virtue wants for himself, he also desires for other men; and this Desire is greater as his knowledge of God is greater*" (P37).

Spinoza offers two arguments in defense of the latter thesis, the one strictly utilitarian, the other psychological and based on his theory of the emotions. The utilitarian argument, which is implied rather than stated, holds that whoever lives under the guidance of reason, and thus pursues understanding as the highest good, necessarily desires that others do likewise, and basically for two reasons: first, so that similarly motivated individuals will not molest them out of envy, jealousy, or fear (the emotions with which philosophers have traditionally been greeted); and second, so that like-minded individuals may be of assistance in one's own pursuit of wisdom.

The psychological argument, which is based on the analysis of love offered in part 3, seems rather like an appeal to what is now called "positive reinforcement." That analysis purported to show that a good which one loves or desires for oneself will be loved more constantly and with greater strength if it is believed that others love it also. Applying this to the case of knowledge, it follows that the pursuit of knowledge by others serves to increase the zeal with which we pursue it ourselves.

By this line of reasoning, Spinoza moves from the rather unpromising premises of psychological egoism and intellectualism—that is, the identification of virtue with knowledge—to a conclusion regarding the social nature of human beings. So far, however, the scope of the argument is limited to those fortunate few who live under the guidance of reason. Moreover, Spinoza is well aware of this limitation, and he stops to remind us that "it rarely happens that men live according to the guidance of reason. Instead their lives are so constituted that they are usually envious and burdensome to one another" (P35C2S). Nevertheless, Spinoza goes on to state, albeit without supporting argument, that we cannot live solitary lives, and that a human being is

correctly defined as a "social animal." Spinoza expresses his belief in
the interdependence of the members of the human community in a
passage of uncharacteristic emotion:

> So let the Satirists laugh as much as they like at human affairs, let the
> Theologians curse them, let Melancholics praise as much as they can a
> life that is uncultivated and wild, let them disdain men and admire the
> lower animals. Men still find from experience that by helping one
> another they can provide themselves much more easily with the things
> they require, and that only by joining forces can they avoid the dangers
> that threaten on all sides—not to mention that it is much preferable and
> more worthy of our knowledge to consider the deeds of men, rather
> than those of the lower animals. But I shall treat this topic more fully
> elsewhere. [P35C2S]

These claims regarding the life of reason and our essentially social
nature form the basis of Spinoza's account of the specific virtues. Once
again, the account consists in an application of previously established
general principles. The virtues are here identified with certain emotions or states of mind (affects as expressed in the attribute of thought),
and their value is held to be a function of their capacity to enhance an
individual's conatus. As one would expect, the key role is given to two
of the primary emotions, pleasure and pain. Since pleasure is an
emotion that reflects, in the attribute of thought, an increase in the
body's power of activity, whereas pain reflects precisely the opposite
condition, it follows that the former is always good and the latter
always bad (P41). This positive attitude toward pleasure gives a
hedonistic, or at least anti-ascetic, tone to much of Spinoza's moral
philosophy, which is not always easily reconcilable with its dominant
intellectualistic thrust. Rejecting the Calvinistic austerity of many of
his countrymen, he remarks that "nothing forbids our pleasure except
a savage and sad superstition."[27] Pleasure, after all, reflects perfection, and thus, "to use things . . . and take pleasure in them as far as
possible . . . this is the part of the wise man" (P45C2S). Nevertheless,
it is crucial to distinguish between genuine pleasure, which reflects the
well-being of the organism as a whole, and mere titillation (*Titillatio*),
or localized pleasure. Although it can be good, the latter, for obvious

reasons, can also be harmful. Similarly, its opposite, grief or sorrow (*Dolor*), although bad in itself, can be beneficial if it serves to restrict titillation, thereby preventing it from becoming excessive and hindering one's ability to function.

We can see from this that the emotions can be divided into three classes. There are some that are intrinsically good and can never become excessive, some that are intrinsically bad, and finally, a large group that are good in moderation, but bad if experienced excessively. Among the emotions that are always good, Spinoza includes not only pleasure per se, which we have already discussed, but also cheerfulness, which is the opposite of melancholy (P42), and self-esteem insofar as it is grounded in reason. Spinoza's account of the latter is most interesting and reveals clearly the anti-Christian orientation of his moral philosophy. Pride, or self-esteem without any rational basis, is harmful, of course, and is to avoided at all costs. But, insofar as self-approval arises from an adequate idea of one's power, it is "*really the highest thing we can hope for*" since it is simply the conscious awareness of one's virtue (P52).

In the category of intrinsically bad emotions, Spinoza gives first place to pain and its frequent concomitant, hate. Closely associated with these and rejected in similarly unqualified terms are emotions such as envy, derision, contempt, anger, and revenge. These are all bad because they are inimical to the power of the organism and result in actions that alienate human beings from one another. More interesting is the fact that Spinoza here locates many of the traditional religious virtues—hope, fear, humility, repentance, and pity. All these emotions reflect ignorance and a lack of power in the self. None can be regarded as really good, therefore, and none has any place in the life of reason. Nevertheless, in a concession to human frailty, Spinoza does note significantly that "because men rarely live from the dictate of reason, these two affects, Humility and Repentance, and in addition, Hope and Fear, bring more advantage than disadvantage. So since men must sin, they ought rather to sin in that direction. If weak-minded men were all equally proud, ashamed of nothing, and afraid of nothing, how could they be united or restrained by any bonds?" (P54S).

Paramount among the emotions that can be either good or bad, depending on whether or not they are experienced in moderation, are titillation, desire, and love. The difficulty with the last two of these lies in their connection with titillation, which has already been discussed. Love or desire, if directed toward an object that stimulates or gratifies a part of the organism or one of its appetites at the expense of the well-being of the whole, can become excessive and hence harmful. This includes pathological states such as avarice, ambition, gluttony, and above all, lust. Contrary to his generally anti-ascetic attitude, Spinoza tended to view sexual desire as an unmitigated evil—indeed, as a form of madness (P54S).

Not surprisingly, Spinoza also insists that none of the emotions that have been accorded a provisional value for those who do not live under the guidance of reason—for example, hope, fear, shame, compassion, humility, and repentance—would have any use, "if men could easily be led to live according to the dictate of reason alone" (P58S). This follows from the connection between acting rationally and "acting" in the full sense of the term. Moreover, although a passion may more or less accidentally—Spinoza's term is "blindly"—aid in the preservation of our being, it is always possible for the same goal to be reached more efficiently by reason without the aid of the passions (P59).

In developing this account of the superiority of reason, which amounts to a philosophical defense of the "power of positive thinking," Spinoza insists that a rational desire cannot be excessive (P61). The crucial premise here, which is based on the previous account of desire, is that desire constitutes our very essence insofar as we act. Consequently, if it were excessive, this would mean that human nature had somehow exceeded itself, which is absurd (P61). Equally important is the ability of reason to view things from the standpoint of eternity and so to ignore temporal considerations. The point here is that, ideally at least, a thoroughly rational person would be totally free of any conflict between immediate and long-range goals. Such a person would therefore never succumb to the usual inclination to the present good but would invariably choose the greater good, whether this was to be found in the immediate or the distant future (P62). Moreover, unlike one who is motivated by fear, the person moved by rational desire seeks the good directly, and shuns evil indirectly and only insofar as it is perceived to stand in the way of the realization of some good (P63). Indeed, since by evil is meant the knowledge of pain, and since pain is always a passive state based on inadequate ideas, if the human mind possessed only adequate ideas, it would form no conception of evil at all (P64S). Given our status as finite modes, the latter is impossible. Spinoza insists, nevertheless, that insofar as we are guided by reason, we will invariably pursue the greater good and avoid the lesser evil (P65).

The last seven propositions of part 4 form a distinct unit and constitute what has been called the "apotheosis of the free man," who is the Spinozistic counterpart of the Stoic sage or the holy man of traditional religions.[28] Central to these propositions is the identification of life under the guidance of reason with freedom. Spinoza assumes, rather than argues for, this identification, but it is an obvious consequence of the preceding analysis. As we have already seen, Spinoza defines freedom as self-determination, rather than lack of determination. Only God is absolutely free, because only God is completely self-determined (acts from the necessity of his nature); nevertheless, finite modes are also free to the extent that their behavior follows solely from the laws of their own nature. In Spinozistic terms, one is "free" to the extent to which one is the "adequate cause" of one's state. But to be such a cause is also to "act" in the full sense of the word, so to be free and to act are likewise equivalent. We have further seen that the mind acts or is an adequate cause only insofar as it has adequate ideas. Since to live under the guidance of reason is, by definition, to be governed by adequate ideas, it follows that we are free or act just to the extent to which we live in this manner.

This conception of freedom provides the basis for Spinoza's account of the character and manner of living of the "free man." We learn first that "*a free man thinks of nothing less than of death, and his wisdom is a meditation on life, not on death*" (P67). Although this famous proposition, like many of the claims made regarding life under the guidance of reason, might seem to conflict with the primacy of the desire for self-preservation, it is really a consequence of the previously established principles that one who lives in this manner will seek the good directly and will not be governed by fear. Spinoza next tells us that "*if men were born free, they would form no concept of good and evil as long as they remained free*" (P68). This likewise follows from previously established principles; and its clear implication is that the Spinozistic free person is "beyond good and evil," at least the good and evil of traditional morality. Spinoza then asserts that "*the virtue of a free man is seen to be as great in avoiding dangers as in overcoming them*" (P69). This reflects the Aristotelian conception of courage as the mean between the extremes of excessive fear and excessive boldness. Since the same strength of mind is required to counter each of these extremes, Spinoza can claim that the virtue, or power, of the free person is manifested as fully in avoiding dangers in the first place as in facing up to them. The upshot of this, then, is the not very surprising conclusion that the free person will not be foolhardy or reckless.

The last four of these propositions deal with the free person in relation to others. The first point to be made is that, while living among the ignorant, as indeed he must, the free person will endeavor as far as possible to avoid receiving favors from them (P70). This is necessary in order to preserve one's independence. Yet Spinoza realizes that there are distinct limits to the feasibility of such a procedure. "For though men be ignorant," he notes, "they are still men who in situations of need can bring human aid" (P70S). Since even the freest among us may very well need such aid, the free person will take pains not to antagonize others. Moreover, if and when aid is given, the free person will be grateful. Thus, gratitude, or thankfulness, is included among the characteristics of a free person. Spinoza insists, however, that genuine gratitude is an emotion that only free persons can have for each other (because only they can be genuinely useful), and therefore that it differs markedly from the fickle gratitude of those who are ruled by their passions (P71).

Up to this point Spinoza's account of the life of the free person has been fairly predictable and not of great philosophical interest. The same cannot be said, however, of the next proposition and the scholium attached to it. The proposition itself, which states that "*a free man always acts honestly, not deceptively*" (P72), is not particularly surprising. But in the scholium Spinoza insists that this principle holds without exception and, therefore, even in situations in which deception is necessary to save one's life. Thus, the philosopher who begins his account of the moral life by maintaining that self-preservation is the one foundation of virtue ends up asserting that the truly virtuous person (the free man) would give up his life rather than practice deception. Moreover, Spinoza's argument for this extremely paradoxical thesis is quite problematic, even granting the principles that what one desires under the guidance of reason is not merely to live but to live actively—that is, to exercise one's rational capacity—and that the society of others is necessary in order to do this.

Spinoza begins the argument for the proposition by noting, quite consistently with his principles, that the claim that a free person could act deceptively entails that it is both in accordance with reason and virtuous to act in such a manner, This, in turn, entails that it would be advantageous—that is, virtuous or reasonable—for people "to agree only in words, and be contrary to one another in fact." But, Spinoza contends, the latter is absurd. Spinoza's point here seems to be that deceptive behavior is contrary to reason because it tends to produce social conflict, rather than harmony. Consequently, the free person, who knows what is "truly advantageous," could not engage in it. In the scholium he goes on to insist that the same principle applies when such behavior is deemed necessary to preserve oneself from the present danger of death. As he puts it, "If reason should recommend that, it would recommend it to all men. And so reason would recommend, without qualification, that men make agreements, join forces and have common rights only by deception—i.e., that really they have no common rights. This is absurd" (P72S).

The obvious problem with the argument is that it ignores the special circumstances introduced by the assumption that deceptive behavior is necessary for the preservation of life.[29] Thus, it takes the assumption that deceptive behavior is reasonable in the limiting situation in which it is necessary to preserve one's life to be equivalent to the assumption that it is reasonable under all circumstances. Even assuming that, in general, deceit is not a rational policy for self-preservation because it tends to generate conflict rather than harmony, it does not follow that it is not rational in a situation in which only such can preserve one's life. After all, a society in which people would act deceptively only in the direst emergencies would not seem to be one in which there is more conflict than harmony and in which there are no common rights. Consequently, there is no good Spinozistic reason for the free person not to be prudent in such circumstances.

Somewhat more in accord with the principles of Spinoza's philosophy is the final proposition of part 4, which states that "*a man who is guided by reason is more free in a state, where he lives according to a common decision, than in solitude, where he obeys only himself*" (P73). Spinoza here expresses his basic conviction that the truly free person is not the hermit but the citizen. We shall consider the line of argument underlying this conviction in chapter 6, in connection with an analysis of his political philosophy.

III Human Blessedness

The difference between the life of a slave and that of a free person has been described in vivid terms. The latter is guided by reason, whereas the former is driven by his appetites, which are themselves determined by inadequate, imaginative ideas of external objects. In common with many moralists, Spinoza thus maintains that the virtuous, good, happy, or free life (these terms being used more or less interchangeably) is the life of reason. In opposition to most traditional moralists, however, Spinoza also claims that the possibility of reason governing the passions is not to be explained in terms of some mysterious power of the will (in the manner of Descartes). We have learned instead that only a stronger and contrary emotion can destroy or control a given emotion, and hence, that the possibility of reason controlling the passions depends on reason itself, or adequate ideas, possessing an emotive force.

We still have not learned, however, either the specific means for the

attainment of victory over the passions or the nature of the human
condition in which the victory is attained. These are the subject matter
of the last part of the *Ethics*, which falls into two distinct portions. The
first twenty propositions present some quite specific guidelines, practical precepts, or (to use Spinoza's term) "remedies" by means of
which the intellect can maximize its control over the passions. The last
twenty-two propositions deal mainly with the nature of blessedness
(the state of victory). They contain Spinoza's discussion of the sense in
which a part of the human mind can be said to be eternal and his
account of the "intellectual love of God" (*amor intellectualis Dei*) in
which this blessedness consists. A central theme running through both
parts is the superior efficacy of the third kind of knowledge.

Spinoza begins by laying down the basic principle in terms of which
the entire discussion is to proceed: "*In just the same way as thoughts
and ideas of things are ordered and connected in the Mind, so the
affections or the body, or images of things are ordered and connected
in the body*" (P1). This follows immediately from the identity of the
order and connection of ideas with the order and connection of things.
It has been aptly called the "metaphysics of the remedy," because it
allows Spinoza to claim that the mind can have control over the
modifications of the body, even though they do not interact.[30] As the
proposition makes clear, the modifications or affections in question
are the images of the external things that affect the body and determine
its appetites. According to the above principle, it follows that insofar
as the ideas in the mind are ordered in the manner of the "order of the
intellect," the images and appetites, which are their physical correlates, will be similarly ordered.

The practical problem is how to produce the desired condition, and
its resolution actually requires nothing more than explicitly focusing
on a number of points that have already been established. In his
general approach Spinoza follows Descartes in affirming that the key
lies in the mind's ability to break established patterns of association
and replace them with new ones. Unlike Descartes, however, he views
these associations as holding between ideas, and not between ideas
and corporeal states—for example, Descartes's "animal spirits." His

analysis of the remedies for excessive love or hate is a case in point. These emotions, it will be recalled, were defined respectively as pleasure and pain accompanied by the idea of an external cause. The imagined external cause of one's pleasure or pain is the object of the emotion, and the way to overcome the emotion is to sever it from *this* idea of the external cause (P2). This can be accomplished by uniting it to the thought of another cause. For example, hate toward a particular individual who has done one some harm can be overcome, or at least be diminished, by thinking of the harmful action as only a contributing factor in one's pain and as itself conditioned by a prior cause, and this, in turn, by a prior cause, and so on. In short, rather than focusing one's attention entirely on the unique object of hatred, one comes to see it as merely a link in a causal chain. Since doing this is equivalent to forming a clear and distinct idea of the emotion, Spinoza claims that "*an affect which is a passion ceases to be a passion as soon as we form a clear and distinct idea of it*" (P3).

Furthermore, since "*there is no affection of the Body of which we cannot form a clear and distinct concept*" (P4)—that is, none which we cannot understand in terms of general laws, or "common notions"—and since an emotion is an idea of an affection, or modification, of the body, it follows that there is no emotion of which we cannot form a clear and distinct idea (P4C). This, of course, means that our emotions are capable of being understood scientifically; and this possibility provides a basis for Spinoza's recommendation that we endeavor to cultivate a detached, objective attitude toward our own emotional life. Although he naturally recognizes that there are limits to our ability to do this, he also insists that, to the extent to which we can attain such an attitude, we can gain control not only of our loves and hates, but also of our desires and appetites.

This ability is allegedly enhanced by certain features of our emotional makeup which give some advantage to the rationally grounded—that is, active—emotions in their struggle with the passions. First of all, we note that, all else being equal, our strongest emotions are toward things which we regard as free (P5). For example, we love or hate an individual with greater intensity if we believe that the person is solely responsible for our condition and acted out of free choice. Conversely, the knowledge of the necessity of a state of affairs, which is chiefly what we derive from a "clear and distinct conception," inevitably serves to weaken the force of an emotion. Our tendency to respond passionately to things is based largely on a sense that they might have been otherwise. We feel saddened by the loss of a good that we believe we might have possessed, but this feeling is mitigated, if not completely overcome, by the recognition that the loss was inevitable. Furthermore, since rationally grounded emotions are, by their very nature, directed toward the common properties of things, it follows that if we take their duration into consideration, these emotions will be stronger than passions directed toward an absent object (P7). The object of the former kind of emotion (nature and its universal laws) is always present, and the emotion can remain constant. Thus, while obviously less intense at a given moment than the hope, fear, disappointment, or regret generated by the thought of an absent object, these emotions prevail over passions in the long run. In other words, the greater endurance of a rationally grounded emotion more than compensates for its lack of intensity.

Finally, while it is obviously true that *"the more an affect arises from a number of causes concurring together, the greater it is"* (P8), such an emotion turns out to be less harmful than an equally powerful emotion that arises from fewer causes or a single cause (P9). Once again Spinoza seems primarily to have sexual love in mind. His point is that emotions of this nature lead to an obsessive concern with a few objects or one particular object, thereby hindering the mind from engaging in its characteristic activity, thought. Fortunately, however, an emotion fostered by a large number of different causes is stronger, and since this is precisely the kind of emotion associated with the scientific attitude (which is concerned with that which is common to all things), the healthy emotion has the power to overcome obsessive concern with particular objects. On this basis, Spinoza concludes confidently that *"so long as we are not torn by affects contrary to our nature, we have the power of ordering and connecting the affections of the Body according to the order of the intellect"* (P10).

The problem, of course, is that we cannot always be in that idyllic condition of detached observation. Since we are part of nature, we cannot completely avoid being assailed by dangerous emotions. Nevertheless, Spinoza maintains that it is possible to minimize the danger if, while in a detached state, we prepare for the inevitable assault by forming and committing to memory a set of rules or principles for correct living, which we can then apply as rules of thumb when the occasion demands it (P10S). This is Spinoza's therapeutic alternative to the training of the will advocated by the Stoics and Descartes. Its goal is to condition the imagination (not the will) to respond in appropriate ways.

These rules turn out to be mainly conventional bits of popular wisdom, although Spinoza does give them his own characteristic twist. For example, we have already learned that hatred should be overcome by love, and in order that "we may always have this rule of reason ready when it is needed," Spinoza suggests that we reflect often on human wrongs and how they may best be prevented by nobility. By so doing, we shall come to associate the idea of wrongness with that of love or nobility, so that, when a wrong is done to us, we shall tend to respond with the proper emotions. Similarly, if we constantly reflect on the necessity of things, we shall be better able to control the anger or hate in our reactions to personal injury; and if we reflect on courage as a means of overcoming fear, we shall be better prepared to meet the ordinary dangers of life. Most important, we must condition ourselves so that we are always moved to action by an emotion of pleasure. This is the ultimate expression of the power of positive thinking. Spinoza's point is that the proper way to free ourselves from an obsessive attachment, be it to a sexual partner, wealth, power, or whatever, is _not_ to harp constantly on the harmful features of the object. The negative approach succeeds only in breeding an attitude of envy or resentment, and, as Spinoza acutely notes, all the faults that we have convinced ourselves are to be found in the lover who has jilted us miraculously disappear as soon as we find ourselves back in his or her good favor. Hence, the only way to overcome, as opposed to repress temporarily, these emotions is to think positively about things, to concentrate on people's virtues rather than their faults.

The ultimate positive thought, and, therefore, the ultimate remedy against the passions, is the love of God. Through this love, and this love alone, the mind is able to assume control of its emotional life. The special power of this emotion is based on its connection with the third kind of knowledge (intuitive knowledge) and on the fact that it can be suggested by, and conjoined with, all our physical states. Basic to the latter point is Spinoza's contention that the more things a given emotion can be associated with, the more frequently it can be evoked, and the more constantly it can occupy the mind (P11–P13). Since there is no modification of the body or physical state of which the mind cannot form some clear and distinct idea, and since to conceive something clearly and distinctly is to conceive it in relation to God, it follows that the mind is able to refer all its bodily modifications to the idea of God (P14S). This idea can therefore be associated with all these modifications.

The real key to the argument is the contention that this third kind of knowledge is more potent than the second kind (P36S). Although Spinoza does not explain himself any further, one can assume that its greater power over the passions is a function of its greater explanatory power. First, by comprehending the essences of individual things, including the inquiring self, it goes beyond the abstract generalities of the second kind of knowledge and shows how general principles relate concretely to particular instances. Second, by comprehending these things in relation to God, it grasps them in terms of the very source of their intelligibility. Consequently, it is the highest conceivable level of understanding; and, as such, it must also be both the expression of the highest and most perfect activity of the mind and the source of the greatest intellectual satisfaction. Moreover, since this satisfaction is accompanied by the idea of God as its cause, Spinoza can call it the "love of God" and claim that "*he who understands himself and his affects clearly and distinctly loves God, and he does so more, the more he understands himself and his affects*" (P15). Finally, since this love is fostered by and associated with all states of the body, Spinoza can conclude that it must necessarily hold the chief place in the mind (P16).

So construed, the love of God is also "the highest good which we can want from the dictate of reason" (P20D). In order to understand this fully, we must consider this love in a little more detail and distinguish it from the kind of love usually associated with the religious tradition. Such consideration shows that the decisive characteristic of the Spinozistic conception of the love of God is its unrequited character. Since God is without emotions, he cannot feel pleasure or pain. Consequently, he can neither love nor hate (P17). Thus, one who loves God in the manner recommended by Spinoza, unlike the religious person, does not expect to be loved in return (P19). Moreover, this love can neither be turned into hate (P18) nor tainted by envy or jealousy (P20).

Against this, it might very well be objected that, as the cause of all things, God is also the cause of pain. Consequently, given Spinoza's definition of hate as pain accompanied by the idea of an external cause, God could very well become an object of hate. To this, Spinoza responds on the basis of his theory of the emotions that, to the extent to which we understand the cause of pain, it ceases to be a passion and therefore ceases to be pain. Moreover, insofar as we understand God to be the cause of pain, we feel satisfaction. Spinoza is not here making the absurd claim that one can get rid of pain simply by acquiring a knowledge of its cause. Nor is he merely claiming with the Stoics that the knowledge of the necessity or unavoidability of pain makes us better able to endure it. Although the latter is certainly part of what Spinoza has in mind, it is not all of it. He is also arguing that the adequate knowledge of a pain is not itself a pain; rather, like any adequate idea, it is an expression of the mind's activity and, as such, a genuine source of satisfaction.[31] This is particularly true, of course, insofar as it involves the more potent third kind of knowledge.

At this point we encounter one of those sharp and sudden shifts in the argument that are so typical of the *Ethics*. After summarizing the argument of the first twenty propositions and explicitly linking the love of God with the third kind of knowledge, Spinoza proclaims,

"With this I have completed everything which concerns this present life . . . so it is now time to pass to those things which pertain to the Mind's duration without relation to the body" (P20S). Presumably, this sets the agenda for the final twenty-two propositions of the *Ethics*, and the major item on this agenda is to show that "*the human Mind cannot be absolutely destroyed with the Body, but something of it remains (remanet) which is eternal*" (P23).

Even though, apart from one passage in which they are equated, Spinoza consistently uses the term *eternal* rather than the more usual religious expression *immortal*,[32] this claim seems to stand in glaring contradiction to the central tenets of the *Ethics*. First, the characterization of the human mind as the "idea of the body," together with the identification of the order and connection of ideas with the order and connection of things, certainly appears to imply that the human mind cannot exist apart from the body. Second, Spinoza's insistence that only God and those modes which either follow directly from God or follow from a mode that does (the immediate and mediate eternal and infinite modes) are eternal seems to conflict with the attribution of eternity to a finite mode such as the human mind. Third, the apparent connection of the mind's alleged eternity with duration apart from the existence of the body seems to contradict the sharp distinction between eternity and duration drawn at the very beginning of the *Ethics* (ID8).[33]

In order to deal with these apparent inconsistencies and thus to make progress in interpreting the highly obscure last portion of the *Ethics*, it is crucial to realize that Spinoza has not yet accomplished all that he needs to accomplish. He has provided some remedies against the passions, all of which involve knowledge of the second and third kinds. Accordingly, knowledge, including the intuitive knowledge of God, has so far been considered as a force for combating the passions. Essential to Spinoza's philosophy, however, is the doctrine that knowledge is not merely a means for escaping bondage, but that human freedom or perfection itself consists in intellectual activity. In other words, Spinoza must move from a consideration of reason (construed in a broad sense to include both the second and third kinds of knowledge) as a force for controlling the passions—that is, reason as a means—to a consideration of the life of reason as an end in itself. Moreover, considered in the latter manner, the life of reason can be identified with human blessedness.

Given what remains to be done, it is hardly surprising to find Spinoza using traditional religious language to indicate his shift in concern. By the "present life" in this context, we need understand nothing more than the life of conflict with the passions.[34] Since this conflict is between the adequate ideas in the mind and the inadequate ideas corresponding to the bodily appetites, it can certainly be said to concern the mind as it is "in relation to the body." Thus, in moving from a consideration of the use of reason as a weapon in the struggle to a consideration of rational activity as constitutive of intrinsic and ultimate satisfaction (blessedness), Spinoza is, indeed, in a certain sense, both turning from all that "concerns the present life" and considering the mind as it is "without relation to the body." Finally, since the Latin term *remanet* ("remains") can be taken as equivalent to "remainder" in arithmetic or "residue" in chemistry,[35] the claim (P23) that something of the mind "remains which is eternal" can be taken to mean simply that there is some "eternal" aspect of the mind that has not yet been considered.

In addition to the need to specify the sense in which an aspect of the mind is eternal, the main problem in all this is obviously the reference to the *duration* of the mind in connection with its alleged eternity. Now, within the Western philosophical tradition there are two competing conceptions of eternity: an essentially Platonic conception, which construes eternity as timeless, necessary existence, and an essentially Aristotelian conception, which construes it as existence at all times, or "omnitemporality."[36] While Spinoza has traditionally been regarded as a strong advocate of the Platonic conception and therefore committed to a sharp distinction between eternity and duration (even endless duration), it has been argued recently that he really adheres to the Aristotelian conception.[37] This would support a fairly literal reading of the text, according to which the claim that something of the mind is eternal means simply that it endures throughout all times (both before and after the existence of the body).

Unfortunately, this is another of those issues that are too complex to be dealt with adequately here; however, it does seem to me that the Platonic conception is more in accord with the texts.[38] Moreover, there are two passages in the last propositions of the *Ethics* in which Spinoza explicitly denies that his conception of the mind's eternity implies its endless duration. Thus, immediately after claiming that we "feel our mind, insofar as it involves the essence of the body under a species of eternity, is eternal," he adds by way of explication that "this existence it has cannot be defined by time or explained through duration." And, as if this were not explicit enough, he goes on to state that "our mind, therefore, can be said to endure . . . only insofar as it involves the actual existence of the body" (P23S). The second passage occurs within the context of the account of the intellectual love of God, where Spinoza remarks that, "if we attend to the common opinion of men, we shall see that they are indeed conscious of the eternity of their Mind, but that they confuse it with duration, and attribute it to the imagination, *or* memory, which they believe remains after death" (P34CS).

These passages make it quite clear that, in spite of the impression created by the passage from the scholium to proposition 20, Spinoza does not in fact attribute any duration to the mind apart from its relation to the body. Thus it seems reasonable to take the reference to the mind's "duration" in that passage ironically (the point of the irony being simply that the result of considering the mind "without relation to the body" is the realization that, so considered, the mind cannot be said to have any duration). Alternatively, one could perhaps take the whole expression "the Mind's duration without relation to the body" to be Spinoza's oblique way of making the point that, since we are concerned with the *duration* of the mind, we are still concerned with its activity in "this life," albeit in a way that cannot be explicated completely in terms of its relation to its body.[39]

Of perhaps greater significance, however, for the interpretation of the Spinozistic conception of the eternity of the mind is the claim that "*the mind can neither imagine anything, nor recollect past things, except while the body endures*" (P21). This follows from Spinoza's account of the relation between memory and imagination on the one hand and the affections of the body on the other. Apart from the correlation between ideas in the mind and these affections, there can be neither memory nor imagination. But without memory, there can be no notion of personal identity. If not actually constitutive of personal identity, memory is certainly an important component thereof.[40] What sense would it make to say that one is identical with a person who existed previously (perhaps in a previous incarnation) if there were no possibility of recalling that person's experiences? Thus, if the "duration" of the mind apart from the body is without any memory, then it can hardly be viewed as the continued duration of the same person.[41] Once again, then, it would seem that by explicitly excluding memory, Spinoza is providing the reader with a clear signal that he is not advocating anything like the traditional notion of personal immortality.[42]

Armed with these exegetical preliminaries, we are now in a position to consider Spinoza's official argument for the eternity of the mind. Its first step is to claim that, in spite of the lack of memory and imagination, *"nevertheless, in God there is necessarily an idea that expresses the essence of this or that human Body, under a species of eternity"* (P22). The proposition turns on the distinction between essence and existence and on the conception of God as the cause of both. Since the essence of a thing (here the human body) is "in God"—that is, it follows from, or is conceived through, an attribute of God (extension)—Spinoza contends, on the basis of his parallelism doctrine, that there must be an idea in the attribute of thought corresponding to the essence, and that this idea expresses an eternal truth.

Underlying this argument is the same conception of individual essence that we encountered in connection with Spinoza's theory of conatus. This essence is the intrinsic nature, or structure, of a thing (its "formula") considered as a pure possibility apart from its concrete realization in the order of nature. So considered, the essence of even a finite thing is eternal, in that it involves no relation to duration. The latter pertains only to its actual existence, which is determined by extrinsic factors—namely, the series of finite modes that together constitute the order of nature. Correlatively, the idea of an essence in the attribute of thought is likewise eternal in the sense that it consists of a timelessly true proposition (or set of propositions) regarding this essence. The same could be said, of course, about all finite modes expressed in all the attributes and about their corresponding ideas.

The next, decisive step is the attempt to connect the idea in God with the human mind. Thus, the key to, and the most problematic aspect of, Spinoza's argument is not the claim that there is an idea in God that expresses an eternal truth about the essence of the human body; it is rather that this idea is "necessarily something that pertains to the essence of the human mind" (P23D). It is this premise, supposedly based on the conception of the mind as the idea of the body, that enables Spinoza to conclude that "something of it [the human mind] remains which is eternal." So construed, however, the argument appears hopeless; for it seems to turn on an obvious and gross conflation of an eternal truth *about* a mind (the idea in God) with an idea *in* the mind or, perhaps even worse, with a mind itself (or a part thereof).[43] Clearly, if any sense is to be made of Spinoza's argument for the eternity of the human mind, some resolution of this problem must be found.

One approach is to insist that there is no illicit conflation here, because by the "human mind," or "idea of the body," Spinoza just means the complete set of true propositions about the body.[44] On this interpretation, presumably, the "essence" of the mind would consist in the subset of propositions that refer to the intrinsic nature of the body—that is, the body considered in abstraction from its place in the order of nature. Since this intrinsic nature is unchangeable, the subset of propositions describing it will be eternally—that is, timelessly—true; and since the essence of the human mind is identical with this subset, it too will be eternal.

This, of course, is the same interpretive move that has already been considered in connection with Spinoza's claims that "the order and connection of ideas is the same as the order and connection of things," and that all things are "animated." Not surprisingly, then, it involves precisely the same difficulty: namely, that logicizing the attribute of thought, that is, reducing the "mind" to a set of true propositions about its object, the body, effectively eliminates the mental from the Spinozistic universe. As we have seen already, it is difficult to reconcile such an interpretation with much of what Spinoza has to say about the mind in the *Ethics*. In addition, this interpretation trivializes Spinoza's claim about the mind's eternity. Since, according to Spinoza, there must be in God a set of timelessly true propositions about the essence of everything in nature, it would seem to follow that human beings (we can no longer speak of human "minds" on this interpretation) have no greater share of eternity than any other finite modes.

Fortunately, the problem posed by Spinoza's apparent identification of the human mind with an idea in God can be dealt with in another way, one that does not involve either of these implications. On the alternative reading, which can be called the "epistemological interpretation" of Spinoza's conception of the eternity of the mind, Spinoza is not literally identifying the human mind (or its essence) with the idea in God of the essence of the body. He is saying rather that this idea "pertains to the essence of the mind," in the sense that the mind (by virtue of its intrinsic nature) has the capacity to comprehend it— that is, the human mind has the capacity to form adequate ideas of the essence of its body and itself.

Now, as we have already seen and as Spinoza will emphasize further, to have an adequate idea of something is to conceive it under a species of eternity, and this is equivalent to participating in the infinite intellect of God. This, however, is a matter of epistemological accomplishment, not of ontological identification. In other words, on the epistemological interpretation, the identification of the idea in the human mind with the idea in God concerns only the content, or "objective reality," of the idea, not its actual or "formal reality" as a mental occurrence. Moreover, if this is how the identity is understood, then the eternity of the human mind turns out to be equivalent to the mind's capacity to conceive itself and the essence of its body as eternally necessitated—that is, to understand itself by the third kind of knowledge.[45] So construed, *eternity* refers to an actual capacity of the human mind, not simply a feature of certain propositions about its object. Nevertheless, the mind retains this capacity only as long as it endures, which is, of course, no longer than the duration of the body of which it is an idea.

The epistemological interpretation strongly suggests that the next item on the agenda should be to make explicit the connection between the mind's eternity and the third kind of knowledge; and this is precisely what Spinoza proceeds to do (P24–P31). His account culminates in the claim that *"the third kind of knowledge depends on the Mind, as on a formal cause, insofar as the Mind itself is eternal"* (P31). Indeed, in a scholium to this proposition, Spinoza suggests not merely that the mind's ability to know things by the third kind of knowledge depends on part of it being eternal, but also that "the Mind is eternal insofar as it conceives things under a species of eternity." If it does not actually require it, this remark certainly supports the epistemological interpretation of the mind's eternity.

We should further expect that Spinoza would not only equate the mind's capacity to conceive things, including itself and the essence of the body, by means of the third kind of knowledge with its eternity, but also with its blessedness, or perfection. Once again, this is precisely what Spinoza attempts to do. This equation, which constitutes the culmination of his philosophy, is reached by showing how the third kind of knowledge gives rise to the intellectual love of God. Since Spinoza has already emphasized the importance of the love of God as the supreme remedy against the passions, it might appear strange to find him reintroducing it in the present context. This can be understood, however, in terms of the twofold function of part 5. The love of God in the previous account was certainly "intellectual," even though Spinoza does not characterize it as such (recall that he connects it with the third kind of knowledge). But, as a force against the passions, as a weapon in the moral struggle, such love is "this-worldly" in the religious sense. In this respect at least, it is analogous to the Christian conception of divine grace as an aid in the struggle with sin. But now, having completed his analysis of that struggle and, with it, "everything which concerns the present life," it is perfectly appropriate for Spinoza to return to the topic of the love of God, this time with the intention of showing that it constitutes human blessedness. Viewed from this perspective, it provides the Spinozistic alternative to the beatific vision.

The connection between the third kind of knowledge, the intellectual love of God, and human blessedness is quite direct. Once again, the main point is that the understanding of anything in this matter is intrinsically satisfying, and since this understanding involves comprehending the thing in question in relation to God, this satisfaction is accompanied by the idea of God as its cause (P32). The equation of the satisfaction connected with such a cognitive state with the love of God depends, of course, on Spinoza's rather peculiar conception of love as pleasure accompanied by the idea of an external cause. Given this conception, anything that can serve as a cause of pleasure can be an object of love. The pleasure—or, better, mental satisfaction—associated with the third kind of knowledge is the pure joy of understanding. God is the cause of this joy in the sense that he is both the ultimate object of knowledge and the source of the very intelligibility of things. In the last analysis, then, the intellectual love of God turns out to be equivalent to the delight in the intelligibility of things that accompanies the mind's satisfaction with its own cognitive powers.[46] This same satisfaction also constitutes human blessedness.

Given this conception of intellectual love, we can also understand Spinoza's mystical-sounding and paradoxical claims that "*God loves himself with an infinite intellectual love*" (P35), and that "*The Mind's intellectual Love of God is the very Love of God by which God loves himself, not insofar as he is infinite, but insofar as he can be explained by the human Mind's essence, considered under a species of eternity*; *i.e., the Mind's intellectual Love of God is part of the infinite Love by which God loves himself*" (P36). Having been told previously that, "strictly speaking, God loves no one" (P17C), one is taken aback by these propositions. In reality, however, there is no contradiction or change of doctrine, but merely another example of Spinoza's tendency to express his rationalistic thought in traditional religious terms. Since the human mind has been shown to be a finite modification expressed in the attribute of thought and, with regard to its adequate ideas, part of the infinite intellect of God, the mind's love of God is equivalent to God's love of himself so modified. Spinoza's claim, in other words, reduces to an elaborately expressed tautology; and there is no reason to believe that he intended it to be construed otherwise.[47] By expressing himself in this convoluted and paradoxical manner, Spinoza is, in effect, saying to theologians that this is the only way one can understand their central contention that God loves mankind.

Finally, since the mind both acts and is eternal precisely to the degree to which it possesses adequate ideas, and since minds obviously differ on this score, they also differ in the degree to which they are eternal. In fact, since the capacity of the mind has been shown to be functionally (but not causally) related to the capacity of the body, Spinoza can even claim that "*he who has a Body capable of a great many things has a Mind whose greatest part is eternal*" (P39). And presumably, although Spinoza is hardly clear on this point, since every human mind has an adequate idea of God (IIP47) and therefore some degree of insight into the rational order of things, every human mind must have some vestige of the satisfaction or blessedness (intellectual love) which necessarily accompanies that insight. Unfortunately, for most of us, this is far outweighed by our imaginatively based ideas and their concomitant passions—hope, fear, and so on. For the fortunate few who are capable of attaining the third kind of knowledge, however, this satisfaction is far greater. Thus, with respect to such minds, Spinoza remarks that the part which perishes with the body "is of no moment in relation to what remains" (P38S). What perishes, of course, is the imagination and its associated passions; whereas what remains—that is, what constitutes the actuality of such minds—is rational thought.

Spinoza's whole philosophy is epitomized in the final proposition: "*Blessedness is not the reward of virtue, but virtue itself; nor do we enjoy it because we restrain our lusts; on the contrary, because we enjoy it, we are able to restrain them*" (P41). In order to understand this proposition, we need only keep in mind the connection between blessedness and knowledge on the one hand and knowledge and power on the other. Spinoza's point is simply that we do not acquire this knowledge by first controlling our lusts or passions, but that we have the power to control them only to the extent to which we already possess adequate knowledge. Thus, whereas the ignorant are perpetually tormented by their passions and seldom attain peace of mind, "the wise man, insofar as he is considered as such, is hardly troubled in spirit, but being, by a certain eternal necessity, conscious of himself, and of God, and of things, he never ceases to be, but always possesses true peace of mind." Such, then, is the good, the particular form of human existence to which the *Ethics* attempts to point the way. It is certainly hard to achieve, but as Spinoza remarks in his famous closing words: "What is found so rarely must be hard. For if salvation were at hand, and could be found without great effort, how could nearly everyone neglect it? But all things excellent are as difficult as they are rare" (P42S).

CHAPTER 6

The Individual and the State

We have learned from the *Ethics* that, despite their conatus, or fundamental drive for self-preservation, human beings are essentially social animals. From this we have been led to see that human beings can achieve freedom, or blessedness, only in association with others. The difficulty, however, is that human beings are at best imperfectly rational, and the great majority of them are hardly rational at all. They are therefore guided by what their imaginations tell them is good, rather than by what actually is so. Accordingly, they cannot live in society with one another unless they are subjected to a common set of laws and a sovereign power to enforce these laws. Human society, in other words, is possible only in a state. But this seems to preclude the possibility of achieving the very freedom that requires socialization in the first place. The problem of freedom is thus central to Spinoza's political thought, just as it was to his metaphysical and moral theory. Whereas the task of the *Ethics* (at least one of its most important tasks) was to investigate the nature and limits of human freedom and to show how it was possible in the face of the thoroughgoing determinism of nature, the major concern of Spinoza's political philosophy is to explain how freedom can be realized in a state, which, by its very nature, demands absolute obedience to law.[1]

Spinoza's basic conviction is that such freedom is both possible and desirable; indeed, that "the purpose of the state is really freedom."[2] But he also believes that liberty (freedom in the political context) can be achieved only if each individual surrenders all his power to the state. Again, the parallel to the metaphysical doctrine of the *Ethics* is striking. There, the great lesson was that one can only achieve genuine freedom (autonomy, or self-governance) by realizing that one is a completely determined part of nature, that one has no free will, and that all one's actions follow universal and necessary laws. Here, freedom is achieved only through complete subjection to the laws of the state. In both cases, freedom and subjection to law are intrinsically connected, rather than opposed. As a consequence, Spinoza was led to affirm that the most absolute state, meaning the state with the most power over its citizens, is the best state, and, paradoxically enough, that this condition is realized in a democracy.

These thoughts are developed in the *Theological-Political Treatise* and the *Political Treatise*, which, although differing greatly in style and tone, contain, with one significant exception, much the same doctrine. The former, which we have already discussed in connection with Spinoza's life, is a polemical piece, addressed to the events of the time. In the context of a devastating attack on the authority of the Bible, and hence on the authority of the clergy, he provides a classical defense of the principles of freedom of thought and speech. The latter work, which Spinoza never finished, is basically a textbook of political science. Adopting the dispassionate, analytic method of the *Ethics*, in which human behavior is considered as subject to a set of universal and necessary laws, the *Political Treatise* attempts to deduce from these basic laws of human nature the true causes and functions of the state. On the basis of these considerations, it then proceeds to show how any regime must be organized—whether it be a monarchy, an aristocracy, or a democracy—if it is to endure and preserve the peace and freedom of its citizens.

As a political thinker, Spinoza was influenced by many factors, not the least of which were his study of Machiavelli and his personal observation of the political events of his time in the Netherlands. The chief influence, however, was undoubtedly Hobbes. Spinoza's political philosophy can be profitably seen as an ongoing dialogue with Hobbes. We shall therefore begin our consideration of Spinoza's political thought with an analysis of the assumptions that he shared with Hobbes concerning the nature, legitimacy, and origin of political power. This will enable us to see precisely where the two diverge, and thus to understand better Spinoza's unique contribution to the history of political philosophy, as well as some of the limitations of his theory. Finally, we shall consider Spinoza's own application of his principles in his discussion of the best constitution for each type of government, which occupies the bulk of the *Political Treatise*.

I The State of Nature and Civil Society: Hobbes and Spinoza

As thoroughly modern men imbued with a scientific outlook, Hobbes and Spinoza both thought that political philosophy should be based on an accurate assessment of human nature. Both, therefore, condemned much of traditional political philosophy for erecting utopias that men are unfit to inhabit. Nevertheless, in so doing, both made extensive use of many of the basic conceptions of the very line of traditional political thought that they criticized. These include the notions of natural right, natural law, the state of nature, and the social contract. In order to understand their political thought, it is therefore necessary to consider these traditional conceptions, at least briefly.

All these conceptions have their roots in Greek thought, and all have been used at various times in history to support a wide variety of political theories. In modern times, however, their main function has been to support political liberalism. By liberalism is here meant the view that advocates two closely related doctrines: first, that the *sole* end of the state is to enhance the lives of its individual citizens; and second, that all government is by consent of the governed. From these principles it is generally inferred that any governmental power that is not used to benefit the citizenry, or that is not established by consent, either explicit or tacit, is illegitimate and can be justifiably resisted.

The doctrine of natural rights is one of the chief pillars of this line of thought. Its basic thrust is that all human beings are born with certain rights which the state neither confers nor can legitimately deny. The Declaration of Independence captures this thought by describing such rights as "inalienable," and it cites "life, liberty, and the pursuit of happiness" as examples thereof. Since everyone possesses such rights—that is, since "all men are created equal"—and since any violation of these rights by a governmental power is in principle illegitimate, it can be said to justify civil disobedience or even revolution.

The notion of natural law has its roots in Stoic philosophy and Roman law, and during the Middle Ages it was invoked in support of feudalism. Yet it has also played a central role in classical liberal thought, in which it is closely associated with the theory of natural rights. In this context, natural law is generally construed as a set of universally valid moral rules grounded either in reason or in the will of God, depending on whether the theory in question is secular or religious. These rules function as criteria, or norms, for judging the morality of the actions both of individuals and of states. This doctrine holds that the "positive—that is, actual—laws of every state *ought* to conform to these rules, and that the sovereign, who is often thought to be "above the law" in the sense of the civil, or positive, laws, is nonetheless obliged to follow these rules, which constitute a "higher law." Together with the theory of natural rights, this doctrine obviously provides a powerful tool for judging the legitimacy of political institutions and the exercise of sovereign power.

Much the same can be said of the theory of a social contract, whose roots reach back to the Sophists of ancient Greece. The Sophists appealed to an original contract as a means of justifying their conviction that all laws, and even society itself, are the products of human convention and have no divine authority, or sanction. Later, however, the notion of the social contract came to include two distinct doctrines, which, although closely connected, are not always held together. The first, which is called the "social contract proper," or "pact of association,"[3] asserts that the state originated when a group of individuals living in a "state of nature" agreed to join together and collectively submit to a sovereign power. It is thus a theory of the origin of the state and is grounded in an individualistic, asocial conception of human nature. Society, or political organization, in this view, is not "natural" but is the result of an express decision by human beings to leave their original asocial condition, which is termed the "state of nature."

The second doctrine affirms the need for a contract of government, or "contract of submission,"[4] by which the people reach agreement with the sovereign regarding the conditions of rule. In this situation the people pledge their obedience to the sovereign in return for the promise of protection and good government. If the sovereign fails to keep his part of the bargain, his claim to allegiance no longer exists, and the people are no longer bound to obey. The contract is thus not an agreement among the people themselves, but one between the people, who are already organized into a society, and the sovereign. As such, it serves to define the conditions of sovereignty and obedience, thereby providing a basis for theories of limited sovereignty, as well as liberal principles in general.

By ingeniously reinterpreting each of these conceptions, Hobbes used them in support of a theory of absolute sovereignty, the most efficient form of which was held to be monarchy. Far from serving to justify the rights of the individual over and against the state, as in liberal thought, they became, in Hobbes, the very means for denying that the individual has any such rights. Central to his analysis was the notion of the social contract, and, like other contract theorists, Hobbes began his argument with a consideration of the state of nature. Unlike some theorists, however, he did not regard the state of nature as an actual historical situation before the advent of civil society. Rather, he used it to refer to the condition of humanity as it is everywhere and at all times apart from the restraints and protection provided by a state.

Hobbes's description of humanity in a state of nature, which is really an analysis of human nature, is reminiscent of much that we have already seen in Spinoza. The Hobbesian person is both thoroughly determined and thoroughly egotistical. The fundamental drive is for self-preservation, although Hobbes also grants a basic role to vanity in the motivation of human behavior.[5] In this state, Hobbes argues, an individual has a "natural right" to do whatever seems necessary for self-preservation. But since everyone else possesses such a right, which is limited only by one's power, and since everyone else is motivated by the desire to appropriate everything necessary to preserve his or her being and impress others, it follows that this state is one of perpetual conflict, in which no one really possesses any rights in the sense of guaranteed protection.[6] Hobbes expressed this thought by characterizing the state of nature as a state of war of "every man, against every man," and he describes life in such a state as "solitary, poore, nasty, brutish, and short."[7]

The whole point, of course, is that such a state of affairs is intolerable and is to be avoided at all costs. Moreover, Hobbes believed that reason provides us with certain rules which, if followed, will enable us to avoid it. With typical audacity, he equated these rules for survival with natural law, or the "laws of nature," and even with "divine law." There are some fifteen such rules, but here we need only consider the first two, which form the basis of his theory of the social contract and consequently of his doctrines of sovereignty and political obligation. The first and most fundamental of these laws of nature is the maxim that "peace is to be sought after, where it may be found; and where not, there to provide ourselves for helps of war."[8] The basic question, then, is how peace is to be achieved, which is equivalent to asking how human beings are to escape from the state of nature. The answer is provided by the social contract. The necessity for such a contract emerges when one realizes that the basic source of conflict in the state of nature is the unlimited right therein of all people to all things that they deem necessary for their self-preservation. Reason dictates that peace can thus be achieved only if everyone voluntarily relinquishes or transfers their rights. Such a mutual transference of rights is a contract, and when it includes a promise of future performance, it is called a covenant.[9] The formation of such contracts, or covenants, thus seems to provide the path by means of which human beings can escape from the state of nature.

Hobbes thought that covenants create obligations where none existed before, but he also realized that in a state of nature one has no assurance that others will respect the agreement. Consequently, in order for covenants to be valid, it is first necessary to have a sovereign power capable of enforcing them. But this can be achieved only if the multitude covenant among themselves to surrender all their rights to such a sovereign power. By this act, which is what Hobbes means by a social contract, the multitude of wills becomes one will, and the multitude itself a commonwealth. This contract, therefore, is not between people and a sovereign (the pact of subjection of traditional liberal theory) but among people themselves. Moreover, it leads not to a limited, but to an absolute sovereign, whose very will is law. The absolute nature of sovereign power follows from the absolute nature of the people's surrender of their rights. In contracting among themselves, the people voluntarily give all their own rights or power to the sovereign, thereby creating for themselves an obligation of total obedience. Behind this severe theory, which seems to justify the most unyielding despotism, lies the conviction that sovereignty must be either absolute or nonexistent, and that if nonexistent, chaos and civil war will necessarily prevail. Having experienced civil war in England, Hobbes evidently felt that it is the greatest conceivable social evil, and hence that any form of government, no matter how oppressive, is preferable to it.

At first glance, Spinoza's political philosophy seems to be an only slightly modified version of Hobbes's. As in the *Ethics*, human beings are viewed as parts of nature, completely subject to its laws; and, like everything else in nature, their basic endeavor is to preserve their own being. Moreover, since they do this according to the laws of their nature, not out of free will, and since the laws of their nature are, as the *Ethics* has shown, the laws of God, they do this by "sovereign natural right." Thus Spinoza, like Hobbes, reinterprets the notion of natural right and broadens it to encompass whatever an individual does in accordance with the laws of human nature.[10] But since everything that an individual does is a necessary consequence of the laws of human nature, it follows that whatever a person does is right! Whether the individual in question acts according to the dictates of reason or is driven by passions, whether he or she is motivated by sympathy for other people or by sheer malice, are all beside the point. Either way that person is acting according to the laws of nature and has no power to do otherwise. Moreover, given this deterministic, amoral starting point, Spinoza does not hesitate to conclude "that the right and laws of nature, under which all men are born and for the most part live, forbids nothing but what nobody desires and nobody can do: it forbids neither strife, nor hatred, nor anger, nor deceit; in short, it is opposed to nothing that appetite can suggest."[11]

This interpretation of "natural right" is even more radical than that of Hobbes, who limited the right of an individual to whatever is deemed necessary for self-preservation. This would seem to rule out at least some kinds of actions, such as those grounded in mere vanity that the individual knows will not enhance self-preservation. One might therefore contend that, despite his naturalism, there remains a trace of the old, moral meaning of natural right in Hobbes.[12] Spinoza is thus the more consistent naturalist, and this will prove to be crucial for his whole critique of Hobbes and for the development of his positive alternative to the Hobbesian Leviathan state. For him, an individual's natural right is limited only by the power that he or she possesses and, indeed, is identical with this power. It is thus Spinoza, not Hobbes, who affirms unequivocally that "might makes right."

Spinoza's conception of the state of nature follows logically from this basic premise concerning natural right. Human beings in this condition strive, as they do everywhere, to preserve their own being. Here, however, there is no authority except that which is grounded in fear, and no basis for mutual trust. Human beings are thus naturally enemies, and in such a situation literally "anything goes." Spinoza expresses this latter point by contending, against Hobbes, that people have a natural right to break promises. Since there is no external authority to enforce obedience, it is both natural and rational for an individual to honor an agreement only insofar as it is profitable to do so. But since the individual is the only judge of this, Spinoza reasons: "So if he judges that his pledge is causing him more loss than gain—and it makes no difference whether he judges truly or falsely, for to err is human—then, since it is the verdict of his own judgment that he should break it, he will break it by the right of nature."[13]

Spinoza does not go quite as far as Hobbes and equate the state of nature with a state of war, but he does affirm that in this situation human beings are always subject to the threat of war and thus have no security. Ultimately, this is due to the fact, already noted by Hobbes, that isolated individuals are really powerless, and that they are unable to preserve their being, either in the sense of fully protecting themselves from attack by others or adequately fulfilling their needs. Moreover, since right is equivalent to power, Spinoza can also say with Hobbes that, despite their unlimited natural rights, individuals in this situation really have no rights at all. The hopelessness of this situation renders necessary the transition to civil society, which is regarded by both Hobbes and Spinoza as the only condition in which human beings can effectively exercise their rights or power. However, in his analysis of the benefits to be derived from membership in civil society, Spinoza goes considerably beyond Hobbes. He does so by supplementing the latter's emphasis on security and escape from a state of war with a consideration of the advantages of such membership. These range all the way from an increase in material comfort, gained through the division of labor, to the possibility of philosophy itself; and all this reflects the rather un-Hobbesian notion that nothing is more useful to human beings than other human beings. The actual mechanism of the transition from a state of nature to civil society is somewhat uncertain, however, since Spinoza offers divergent accounts in the *Theological-Political Treatise* and the *Political Treatise*.

In the former, Spinoza sides with Hobbes in appealing to the social contract as the means whereby human beings move from a state of nature to civil society. Unlike Hobbes, however, he seems to regard this as an actual historical occurrence. For example, in repudiating the notion that, despite the lack of civil law, human beings in a state of nature still stood under an obligation to God—that is, to natural law— Spinoza asserts that the state of nature is prior both in time and in nature to religion.[14] Moreover, after reflecting on the misery inherent in this condition in which everyone must constantly be on guard against everyone else, Spinoza suggests that "each must have firmly resolved and contracted to direct everything by the dictate of reason alone (which no one dares to oppose openly lest he appear to lack understanding), to bridle his appetite when it suggested anything harmful to another, to do to nobody what he would not wish done to himself, and, finally, to defend his neighbour's right as if it were his own."[15]

Above and beyond this, however, these same individuals seem to have already realized what we have just learned, namely, that human beings can be expected to honor a contract only as long as they deem it advantageous to do so, and therefore that a lasting union of human beings cannot be built on a foundation as fragile as good faith. Consequently, they must have further agreed that everyone should transfer all their rights to society as a whole. Since society as a whole, rather than any individual or group therein, as in Hobbes, is given power by this pact of submission, the resulting state is called a democracy. Nevertheless, society thus empowered will possess the natural right or sovereign power to work its will on its individual members, "and everyone will be bound to obey it either in freedom of spirit or from fear of the supreme penalty."[16]

In the *Political Treatise*, on the other hand, not only is all reference to such a pact of submission dropped, but it is affirmed that "since all men, savage and civilized alike, everywhere enter into social relations and form some sort of civil order, the causes and natural foundations of the state are not to be sought in the precepts of reason, but must be deduced from the common nature or constitution of men."[17] It is thus not reason, but some common passion such as hope or fear, that leads men to join together.[18] Consequently, the origin of society must be seen as the inevitable outcome of human passions, not as the product of deliberate design by rational men. Within this changed perspective, the requirement of complete submission and obedience to sovereign power is maintained, but it is now viewed as a necessary condition for the existence of an enduring state, not as a historical event through which a state is created.

This change can be seen as either the result of a genuine development in Spinoza's thought[19] or, as is more likely, a reflection of the exoteric polemical character of the *Theological-Political Treatise*.[20] Since this work is to a large extent historical, and since in its political portions it focuses on the Hebrew commonwealth, or theocracy, which was, after all, alleged to have originated at a particular moment in time with an explicit covenant, it would be natural for Spinoza to treat the origin of the state *as if* it were a historical event. The important point, however, is that the thesis that the state began with an explicit covenant between rational individuals is not only not required by, but is actually incompatible with, the basic outlines of Spinoza's philosophy. We have already seen that it is a cardinal tenet of the *Ethics* that the life of reason is possible only in a society. One could therefore hardly expect Spinoza to assume that the existence of rational, autonomous, "free" individuals was a precondition of society itself. Moreover, as Spinoza makes quite explicit, if human beings were in fact led by the dictates of reason, the sanctions imposed by a state would be unnecessary, and a society of rational human beings would never submit to them. Finally, as we have seen, Spinoza explicitly rejects any notion of an obligation independent of utility, such as seems to be required by the historical, or factual, form of the contract theory.[21]

Nevertheless, apart from all questions about a historical contract, it remains the central teaching of Spinoza's political philosophy, a teaching common to both political treatises, that the very possibility of a civil society requires the total surrender by all individuals of their right—that is, power—to society as a whole. In the state that results, as in the state of nature, individuals are still governed by hope and fear and by the desire to preserve their being; but in the civil state "all fear the same things, and all have one and the same source of security, one and the same mode of life."[22] For this to be possible, it is absolutely crucial that the surrender include the right to decide what is just or unjust. If the multitude is to be guided "as if by one mind, and, in consequence, the will of the commonwealth be taken for the will of all, what the commonwealth decides to be just and good must be regarded as having been so decided by every citizen."[23] Only by such means can anarchy be avoided. For if individuals retain the right of private judgment, there is no common standard of justice to which one can appeal, and therefore no unifying social bond. "Thus," Spinoza concludes, "no matter how unfair a subject considers the decrees of the commonwealth to be, he is bound to carry them out."[24]

A more uncompromising argument for absolutism can hardly be imagined. Individuals seem to have no rights except those granted them by the state. Those who attempt to reserve additional rights for themselves or who challenge the authority of the state are to be regarded as enemies of the state and treated as such. Yet, we are struck by the paradox that the same philosopher who argues in this manner also claims that the goal of the state is liberty, champions the freedom of thought and speech, and holds, at least in one of his works, that democracy is the best form of government. The reconciliation of these claims is the basic task of any interpretation of Spinoza's political philosophy, and it is to this task that we now turn.

II The Limits and Uses of Political Power

We have already suggested that Spinoza arrived at these results through adoption of a more consistently naturalistic, "amoral" position than Hobbes himself. The best place to begin is thus with a consideration of Spinoza's own account of the relationship between his thought and that of Hobbes. Fortunately, such an account is available; for, in a letter to his friend Jarig Jelles, who evidently requested information on just this point, Spinoza writes: "With regard to Politics, the difference between Hobbes and me, about which you enquire, consists in this, that I ever preserve the natural right intact so that the Supreme Power in a State has no more right over a subject than is proportionate to the power by which it is superior to the subject. This is what always takes place in the State of Nature."[25]

By the claim that, unlike Hobbes, he preserves natural right intact, Spinoza apparently means that he consistently equates right with power, which Hobbes does not. This point is well taken, at least as a criticism of Hobbes, and it underscores a basic inconsistency in the argument through which Hobbes establishes his absolutist conclusions. This inconsistency concerns the weight given to contracts, which, in turn, reflects an inconsistency in Hobbes's conception of natural law. As we have seen already, Hobbes equates natural law with a set of precepts or practical maxims which rational beings ought to follow if they desire to escape from a state of nature. They are, therefore, essentially rules for self-preservation, maxims of prudence. This is quite different from the traditional conception of such laws as a body of "higher laws," or moral principles, above and beyond the civil laws of any state, to which both the citizens and the sovereign are morally obligated. With his conception of the state of nature and his correlative notion of sovereign power as the source of all law and justice, Hobbes, like Spinoza, repudiates *this* doctrine of natural law. Nevertheless, when discussing the social contract, Hobbes contends that it creates an unconditional obligation to obey, and he justifies this in terms of the "law of nature" that covenants ought to be kept.[26] Such an obligation, it turns out, is independent not only of the wisdom and justice of the sovereign's commands, but also of his power. Thus, the very same law of nature that teaches us what to do for our self-preservation, places us under an absolute obligation to obey the sovereign power, even when doing so is obviously not in our best interests.

This partial moralization of natural law was no doubt motivated by Hobbes's deep conviction that civil war is an unmitigated evil, to be avoided at all costs. But given his conception of human beings as driven by a desire for self-preservation, he obviously cannot maintain this obligation to obey the sovereign in an unqualified form. Since, in his view, individuals enter into the social contract only in order to preserve their being, these individuals cannot be expected to abide by it when to do so threatens their very lives. Hobbes is therefore forced to admit that individuals have a "right" to resist the sovereign power when their lives are in immediate danger.[27] Furthermore, he cannot stop with this single exception, but must acknowledge many other "rights" which individuals reserve for themselves and which the sovereign power cannot justifiably threaten. Thus we are told that the subject reserves the right to resist for "bodily protection, free enjoyment of air, water and all necessaries for life";[28] that a subject cannot be commanded to kill a parent; and that "there are many other cases in which obedience may be refused."[29] These and other passages that add further qualifications reflect the tension between the naturalistic and the "moral" elements in Hobbes's theory of natural right and provide vivid illustrations of the contradictions that emerge when he attempts to unite both elements in support of his theory of absolute sovereignty.[30]

Spinoza avoids these pitfalls by the simple expedient of eliminating all reference to a moral element that creates an obligation above and beyond the actual arrangement of power. The key to his position lies in the recognition that the right of the sovereign, like that of everything else in nature, is coextensive with his power, and that since this power is not infinite, neither is his right. The sovereign, in other words, does not have the right to do what he does not have the power to do. Now, sovereign power is largely exercised in the promulgation of laws and regulations, and Spinoza's point is that there are some laws which a sovereign literally does not have the power to enforce. This conclusion is derived from the realization that everyone is motivated by the desire for self-preservation and, consequently, will always choose that course of action which is believed to be most advantageous. People who live according to the dictates of reason will recognize the desirability of obeying the law, but since such individuals are few and far between, the force of the law rests largely on its sanctions—that is, on fear of punishment or hope of reward. By properly applying these sanctions, a sovereign can, of course, gain considerable control over a populace. There are, however, at least according to Spinoza, certain acts that run so counter to human nature that no threat or promise of reward can lead an individual to perform them. As examples, Spinoza cites forcing people to testify against themselves, torture themselves, kill their parents, or make no attempt to avoid death.[31] Laws or commands requiring these or similar deeds are therefore ineffective, and thus, "keeping natural right intact," one can claim that the sovereign has no "right" to promulgate them.

Spinoza, however, does not stop with such extreme cases, which by themselves do not go very far toward mitigating the evils of tyranny. He also shows a keen awareness of the inherent limitations of legislative power with regard to beliefs and private morality. Such things should not, because they cannot, be legislated. As he notes in the *Theological-Political Treatise*: "He who seeks to determine everything by law will aggravate vices rather than correct them. We must necessarily permit what we cannot prevent, even though it often leads to great harm."[32] But if this holds true for obvious evils, such as extravagance, envy, greed, and drunkenness, which a government might legitimately wish to eliminate, "much more then must we allow independence of judgment; for it is certainly a virtue, and it cannot be suppressed."[33] Spinoza thus argues for freedom of thought, not only on the basis of its benefit for society, a view that we shall consider shortly, but also because a government is powerless to prevent it. This belief may seem somewhat naive in light of our current knowledge of thought control and "brainwashing," but Spinoza himself was not totally unaware of the ability of a government to influence public opinion. He nevertheless felt that there were distinct limits to this power, and that in the last analysis one cannot be forced to believe other than one believes or to judge other than one's reason dictates.[34] Laws governing opinion are ineffectual and therefore violate natural right.

Above and beyond this, Spinoza also recognized that there are some things which a government can accomplish by brute force, but that in doing them, it inevitably undermines its own authority. Since a government cannot do these things with impunity, Spinoza argues that it does not, strictly speaking, have the power or right to do them at all.[35] Behind this claim is the contention that for a law to be effective—that is, to command obedience—it must not do too much violence to the public's sense of what is to its own advantage. Although a government can for a time, by the use of force and propaganda, institute policies which run completely counter to prevailing public opinion, the attempt to do so will succeed only in arousing widespread opposition, which will lead in the end to the government's downfall. Public opinion, or what the majority regards as in its own best interests, thus functions as a real check on governmental power. To function effectively, and even to stay in power, a government must consider the will of the people.

Spinoza's political philosophy is not primarily devoted to telling us what a government cannot do at all or what it cannot do with impunity, however, but to determining what it *ought* to do if it is to realize the end for which it was established. In basic agreement with Hobbes, Spinoza defines this end as peace and security; he also acknowledges that this cannot be achieved without a force strong enough to guarantee compliance with the law. Unlike Hobbes, however, he contends that the state ought to be construed not merely as a device for preventing people from killing one another, but also as a positive instrument, one that has an essential role to play in the creation of the conditions necessary for a meaningful human existence. "A commonwealth," he writes, "whose subjects are restrained from revolting by fear must be said to be free from war rather than to enjoy peace." And again, "A commonwealth whose peace depends on the apathy of its subjects, who are led like sheep so that they learn nothing but servility, may more properly be called a desert than a commonwealth."[36] The point of all this is that peace is not to be construed with Hobbes as the mere absence of war, for the sake of which almost any degree of tyranny and oppression would be tolerable, but rather as a positive condition in which people can exercise their virtue. The goal of the state is thus to create this condition, a goal that Spinoza clearly affirms in his conclusion to the discussion: "Thus when I say that the best state is one in which men live in harmony, I am speaking of a truly human existence, which is characterized, not by the mere circulation of blood and other vital processes common to all animals, but primarily by reason, the true virtue and life of the mind.[37]

By identifying "truly human existence" with the life of reason, Spinoza is underlining the basic practical conclusion of the *Ethics*. But if human beings are to exercise their reason properly and thus achieve the freedom described in the *Ethics*, it is obviously necessary for them to develop independent judgment. A regime that proscribes opinions is therefore not one in which people can readily realize their true nature and live fully human lives. This is the point of the claim in the *Theological-Political Treatise* already cited that "the purpose of the state is really freedom." Here, freedom must be understood primarily as freedom of thought and speech, and it is argued that while governmental power can and ought to be used to limit the actions of subjects, it should not be used to limit their thoughts (which is impossible) or their freedom to express these thoughts. Moreover, not only is suppression of these basic freedoms harmful to the individual who is attempting to live according to the dictates of reason, it is also harmful to the state itself. In recognition of the history of both the Dutch republic and the Marranos in Spain and Portugal, Spinoza contends that attempts to suppress these freedoms succeed only in producing hypocrites and martyrs. The great lesson of Spinozistic political science is thus: "If honesty, then, is to be valued above servility, and sovereigns are to retain full control, without being forced to yield to agitators, it is necessary to allow freedom of judgment, and so to govern men that they can express different and conflicting opinions without ceasing to live in harmony."[38]

Finally, the emphasis on freedom of thought and expression leads Spinoza in the *Theological-Political Treatise* to his conception of democracy as "the most natural form of state," meaning the form that comes "nearer to preserving the freedom which nature allows the individual."[39] The point here is that although a democracy, like any other form of government, requires that all individuals transfer their natural right to the sovereign and agree to obey the laws, it at the same time gives them a say in determining the laws that they are obliged to obey. Thus, every citizen has, at least in theory, an equal voice in the affairs of the state, and "in this way," Spinoza claims, "all remain equal as they were before in the condition of nature."[40] Moreover, in no other form of government are the benefits of freedom more apparent. Since every citizen has a stake in the decision-making process, and since the will of the majority becomes law, a democracy does not merely tolerate, but actually requires freedom of thought and expression. A democracy, in other words, more than any other form of government has a vested interest in the rationality of its subjects; for that reason it would seem to be the form of government under which one could most readily lead the kind of life described in the *Ethics*.

Here, then, is the liberal element in Spinoza's political thought, the element by virtue of which he both differs most profoundly from Hobbes and stands firmly in the tradition of Locke and Rousseau as one of the founders of modern liberal democratic thought. Yet, in coming to grips with Spinoza's political philosophy, one must constantly keep in mind that this liberal element is found in an uneasy juxtaposition with another strand that is much more akin to Hobbes. This other, less than liberal, strand is reflected in the demand for total obedience and in the adoption of the Hobbesian doctrine that the state, as the source of civil law, can in the strict sense do no wrong. Spinoza, to be sure, attempts to avoid some of the more unpleasant consequences of this view with his analysis of the limits of governmental power. As we saw in our discussion of that analysis, for a law to be effective, it must not clash too violently with the majority's sense of its own best interests. A law requiring universal suicide would be universally disobeyed, and any government that tried to enforce such a law would be "rightly" overthrown. The problem with this is that the multitude seldom, if ever, operates under the guidance of reason. What the majority at any time regards as advantageous is not necessarily so, from which it follows that there can be valid laws, approved at least tacitly by the majority, which are nevertheless grossly unjust and yet demand obedience.[41]

Spinoza himself was very much aware of this problem, and his attempts to deal with it reveal the deepest motivations of his thought, as well as its basic conflicts. Typical is the following passage from the *Theological-Political Treatise*, in which an effort is made to reconcile the right of free speech with the demand for total obedience to the law:

> For example, suppose a man shows that some law is contrary to sound reason, and thus maintains that it should be repealed; if he at the same time submits his opinion to the judgment of the sovereign (which alone is competent to pass and repeal laws), and meanwhile does nothing contrary to what that law demands, then, of course, he ranks with all good citizens as a benefactor of the state. But if he breaks the law in order to accuse the magistrate of injustice and to stir up mob hatred against him, or makes a seditious attempt to repeal the law against the magistrate's will, he is simply an agitator and a rebel.[42]

This passage expresses in graphic form the limits of Spinoza's political philosophy, limits that seem to follow from his rigid separation of thought and action. In particular, it makes clear that despite his great advance over Hobbes in finding room for the rights of the individual in an authoritarian state, he was not able to show how these rights could be fully reconciled with political power and the demand for total obedience to the law. When confronted by an unreasonable or "unjust" law, an individual has the "right" to reason with the authorities and try to convince them of their folly. If he fails, however, he must remain silent and obey. Moreover, the rational person will do so voluntarily, and the state has the right to treat as an enemy and execute for the crime of treason anyone who does not.

But why should Spinoza, who assigned to the state the function of providing the social conditions necessary for the realization of human freedom and rationality, so narrowly limit the rights of the individual against the state? Otherwise expressed, why, according to Spinoza, should rational subjects obey laws that they know to be counter to their true self-interest? The answer lies in Spinoza's profound and unshakable sense of the irrationality of the multitude, a sense that is constantly in conflict with his liberal political tendencies. We have already seen, from our discussion of the *Ethics*, that the life of reason is not attainable by the masses, and that human freedom is a fragile thing, difficult to attain and easily destroyed by external forces. This belief was certainly confirmed for Spinoza by the fate of the De Witts. It was not generated by that event, however, for we find it clearly expressed in the *Theological-Political Treatise*, where Spinoza writes, very much in the spirit of Hobbes: "There is no doubt that devotion to country is the highest form of piety a man can show; for once the state is destroyed nothing good can survive, but everything is put to hazard; anger and wickedness rule unchallenged and terror fills every heart."[43] Nevertheless, as one might expect, the sharpest expression of this point of view is to be found in the *Political Treatise*. Here, after reflecting on the fact that human beings are liable to passions, Spinoza concludes:

> And so the more a man is guided by reason, the more free he is, the more steadfastly will he observe the laws of the state and carry out his sovereign's commands. Finally, the political order is naturally established to remove general fear and to dispel general suffering, and thus its chief aim is one which every rational man would try to promote in the state of nature; though his efforts in that state would be useless. Hence

> if the rational man has sometimes, by order of the commonwealth, to
> do what he knows to be opposed to reason, this inconvenience is far
> outweighed by the advantage which he derives from the actual exist-
> ence of the political order: reason, we must remember, also bids us
> choose the lesser evil.[44]

This whole line of thought is epitomized by Spinoza's extremely
negative views on revolution. As a political scientist, he points out that
revolutions tend to occur whenever a tyrannical government foolishly
seeks to extend its authority beyond its actual power. He denies that
they are ever effective, however, in the sense of leading to a genuine
amelioration of the human condition. All that ever happens is the
replacement of one form of tyranny by another that is usually even
more severe. In the *Theological-Political Treatise* Spinoza explicitly
draws this moral from his analysis of the history of the Hebrew nation
and presents it as a warning to his contemporaries. While the people
held power, he notes, there was only one civil war, and even this was
not bitterly contested, which made possible a peaceful settlement.
"But after the people, though quite unused to kings, changed the state
into a monarchy, there was almost no end to civil wars, and the battles
they fought were of a fierceness unparalleled in history."[45] Moreover,
lest one erroneously believe that the problem lay with the monarchy,
rather than with the change in form of government, he goes on to
emphasize that it is equally dangerous to remove a monarch, even if he
is universally regarded as a tyrant. This is because, having become
accustomed to royal power, the multitude will refuse to acknowledge
any lesser authority. The removal of one tyrant thus leads inevitably to
the installation of another, and Spinoza reflects: "This is why peoples,
though often able to change their tyrants, have never been able to abolish
them and replace monarchy by a different form of constitution."[46]

III Forms of Government

Although Spinoza's view of human nature seems to have precluded the
possibility of a beneficial change in the form of government of any
given state, he believed that each form of government could be

constituted so as to ensure both the security of the state and the liberty of its subjects. The analysis and demonstration of the appropriate principles of organization (the constitutions) for each form of government is the main task of the *Political Treatise*. The account is based on the classical division of governments into monarchies, aristocracies, and democracies, a division that Spinoza took to be exhaustive. The analyses of monarchy and aristocracy are complete, but unfortunately, the treatment of democracy remains a mere fragment. The entire discussion is based on the principle that, for each form of government, "it is necessary to organize the state so that all its members, rulers as well as ruled, do what the common welfare requires whether they wish to or not, that is to say, are compelled to live according to the precept of reason, if not by inclination, then by force or necessity—as happens when the administration is arranged so that nothing which concerns the common welfare is wholly entrusted to the good faith of any man."[47]

A. Monarchy. The successful functioning of a monarchy depends on its limited constitutional nature. Against Hobbes and as a warning to the Orangists in his own country, Spinoza challenged the myth of the security and stability of an absolute monarchy. The inherent weakness of this form of government lies in the fact that "the power of one man is far too small to bear so great a burden."[48] The absolute monarch necessarily depends on others, "so that the state which is believed to be a pure monarchy is really an aristocracy in practice, but a concealed and not an open one, and therefore of the very worst type."[49] Moreover, not only is such a monarch often ruled by his advisers, who are in turn ruled by their desire to please him, but in his efforts to preserve his power, he will come to fear and oppress his own subjects. Oppression is counterproductive, however, and eventually leads to the monarch's demise.

The main goal of Spinoza's analysis is to describe those institutions that will effectively limit the monarch, so that he will be able both to preserve his power and to serve the best interest of the people. The most important of these institutions is a large council, with members drawn from all clans and classes of the realm. Each member of this council must be over fifty years of age and should serve a limited term. The body should be so constituted that it reflects all shades of public opinion and so that the private affairs and interests of its members depend on the preservation of peace. Here again Spinoza makes no optimistic assumptions about human nature. All his recommendations are designed to ensure that the members of the council serve the common good and are neither motivated by the desire for perpetual power nor corrupted by bribes. The primary function of the council is to defend the fundamental laws of the realm and to give advice about the administration of the state to the king, so that he may know what the common good requires. The king, for his part, "is not allowed to make a decision about any matter without hearing the opinion of this council."[50] Since the makeup of the council ensures that its majority opinion reflects the views of the majority of the populace, the king is always obliged to confirm that opinion or, in the case of a badly split council, to attempt to reconcile their differences.[51] The institution of the council thus limits the power of the king in such a way that there is at least a reasonable guarantee that he will act in the public interest.

A second essential institution in a stable monarchy is state-owned land. "The fields and the whole territory—and, if possible, the houses also—should be owned by the state, i.e. by the sovereign; who should let them out at an annual rent to the citizens, i.e. to the city-dwellers and farmers. These should be subject to no other form of taxation in time of peace."[52] This radical proposal, by virtue of which Spinoza has been described as a forerunner of Henry George,[53] was formulated in the interests of peace and security. Without a landed gentry and with all subjects engaged in commerce, everyone will have a basically equal risk in war. The majority of both the council and the people will thus tend to oppose war unless absolutely necessary. As a result, such a commonwealth will not involve itself in costly and destructive wars, which are among the chief causes of the undoings of states.

Finally, in agreement with Machiavelli, Spinoza argues for a citizens' militia and underlines the extreme danger of mercenary troops in a monarchy.[54] Spinoza here shows a keen awareness of the dangers of militarism—that is, of a strong professional army that can either lead the nation into unnecessary wars or be used by the monarch as a means of oppressing the people.[55] A people's militia is therefore the best protection of their liberty. Such a militia will fight only when necessary and even then, only in defense of liberty, rather than out of desire for gain. Moreover, since no one is to be exempt from service in this militia, everyone will have not only an equal stake, but also an equal part in the preservation of the commonwealth. Given these, as well as other institutions that we have not been able to touch on, Spinoza concludes that "a people can maintain a fair amount of freedom under a king as long as it ensures that the king's power is determined by its power alone, and preserved only by its support."[56]

B. *Aristocracy.* Whereas Spinoza seems grudgingly to admit only that a properly constituted monarchy can function as a viable form of government, his attitude toward aristocracy is far more positive, and his discussion thereof ends with the claim that if any state can last forever, it will be an aristocracy.[57] In fact, his whole treatment of the subject can be seen as a defense of this form of government, together with an analysis of why it failed in the Netherlands and how such failure can be avoided in the future.[58] This analysis consists largely of an appeal to certain features of the constitution of the Venetian republic, modified to fit the situation in the Netherlands.

Aristocracy, as defined by Spinoza, is a form of government in which political power is held "not by one man, but by certain men chosen from the people, whom I shall henceforth call patricians."[59] Whereas an aristocracy differs from a monarchy in respect to the number of those who are in power, it differs from a democracy with regard to the method of selection. The key point is that in an aristocracy the patricians are expressly elected, whereas in a democracy the right to vote, and thus political power, is automatically granted to every person who meets certain stipulated conditions. These conditions could be so stringent that very few could meet them—for example, a very considerable amount of wealth—whereas in an aristocracy those elected might constitute a substantial proportion of the population. Nevertheless, the former would still be a democracy, the latter an aristocracy. Furthermore, not only is a large number of patricians a theoretical possibility, but it is a practical necessity if the aristocracy is to avoid either degenerating into a monarchy or splitting into factions.

Spinoza's task, as already noted, is to determine the best constitution for an aristocratic government; but before proceeding, he stops to catalogue the advantages that a properly constituted aristocracy has over a monarchy. There are four of these. First it has adequate numbers and hence sufficient power to govern. Unlike a king, therefore, it does not stand in need of counselors. Second, whereas kings are mortal, councils are everlasting. An aristocracy is thus not subject to periodic upheaval. Third, because of old age, sickness, minority, or other causes, a king's power is often only on sufferance, but the power of a council always remains the same. Fourth, an aristocracy does not suffer from the extreme disadvantage of having its laws based on the inevitably fluctuating will of a single person. Thus, although in a monarchy, "every law . . . is the king's declared will . . . not everything the king wills should be law"; whereas in an aristocracy, with a sufficiently numerous council, "its declared will must necessarily be law in every case."[60]

Theoretically, the power of an aristocracy is thus much greater than that of a monarchy. In practice, however, aristocracies have been limited by the fact that the multitude has often maintained a certain independence and has therefore become an object of fear. Spinoza concludes from this that the greatest need of an aristocratic regime is that the multitude be deprived of all power, that it "retains no freedom save that which must necessarily be allowed it by the constitution of the state itself, and which is therefore not so much a right of the people as a right of the whole state, enforced and preserved by the patricians as their own exclusive concern."[61] As one commentator has pointed out, this amounts to the demand for a *dictatorship of the commercial aristocracy*, and all the constitutional safeguards and conditions for stability that Spinoza includes in his discussion of aristocracy work toward this end.[62] Nevertheless, although such a government is in fact a dictatorship, Spinoza believes that it would inevitably be a benevolent one, and that the people would have nothing to fear: "For the will of so large a council must be determined by reason rather than by caprice; since evil passions draw men in different directions, and they can be guided as if by one mind only in so far as they aim at ends which are honourable, or at any rate appear to be so."[63]

Once again the problem is how such a regime can best be constituted. The analysis of monarchy provides the point of departure, and the guiding question is what changes must be made in monarchical institutions in order to establish a successful aristocracy. In dealing with this question, Spinoza shows a keen understanding of the organic connection between institutions in various types of states. What is appropriate in a monarchy is not necessarily so in an aristocracy. Moreover, as he proceeds to point out, one of the basic reasons for the demise of the Dutch republic was failure to realize this. It was mistakenly thought that all that was necessary was to get rid of the king, and there was never any thought of changing the underlying organization of the state.[64] The analysis of aristocracies, however, is complicated somewhat by the fact that there are two distinct kinds. One, like that of Venice, comprises a single city and its territories; another, like that of the United States of the Netherlands, comprises several relatively autonomous cities. Spinoza felt that the latter was superior, largely because of its greater power,[65] but he devotes much of his attention to the former. Only after completing his analysis of the single-city situation does he turn to the question of what modifications would be necessary in an aristocratic state composed of several cities.

It is absolutely essential to the success of an aristocracy of any form that the supreme council, which is composed of all the patricians, be sufficiently strong. The recommended size is 2 percent of the population. The function of this council, which must meet regularly at a fixed location, is to pass and repeal laws and to choose patrician colleagues as well as ministers of state.[66] But since stable government requires that nothing be left to chance or to the good faith and rationality of the governors, Spinoza also felt it necessary that there be a supplemental body of patricians, subordinate to the supreme council, charged with the duty of seeing to it that the constitution is preserved and order maintained in the supreme council. Such bodies are called syndics, and they are in effect the watchdogs of the council. Spinoza goes into great detail concerning the appropriate number, age, involvement, and length of service of the syndics, all for the purpose of ensuring that their self-interest will lead them to pursue the general good.[67] Moreover, precisely the same principle is operative in determining the other institutions. Chief of these are the senate and the judiciary. The senate, which is a second council subordinate to the supreme one, is assigned the task of transacting public business. The most important part of this business is the ordering of the fortifications of the cities and the conferring of military commissions. Since it is so directly involved with the military operations of the state, it is vital that it be composed of men who have more to gain from peace than war.[68] The judiciary has the job of deciding disputes between private parties. It must therefore be constituted so as to be as impartial as possible and not subject to bribes.[69]

A successful aristocracy, however, differs from a monarchy in other areas besides the organization of its governing bodies. Thus, Spinoza advocates two institutions that he had deemed inappropriate for a monarchy—namely, mercenaries and private property. Since an aristocratic government possesses absolute power, the danger, inherent in a monarchy, of hiring foreign mercenaries does not exist; and since the people have no power and are more appropriately termed "subjects" than "citizens," they can hardly be expected to serve in the army without pay.[70] A similar line of reasoning is used to justify private ownership. Since the people have no say in the government of the state, without the possession of property they would have no interest in its survival. Such property thus functions as an incentive to support the government.[71]

Most of the above-mentioned institutions are relevant to aristocracies of both types. The greatest modification required for an aristocratic republic composed of several cities must be in the supreme council. Here things must be organized so that the authority of each city in the union is strictly proportionate to its power. Each city should have its own supreme council and a good deal of autonomy. The senate and judiciary should be the main links between the cities, with the senate having charge of all intercity affairs. The state will have a supreme council, of course, but this should not have a role in the ordinary affairs of state, and it should only convene at moments of national danger, when the very union itself is threatened. Such an aristocracy is thus, like the United States of the Netherlands, far more a loose federation for common defense than a genuine nation. Its obvious weakness would seem to lie in the difficulty of joining together for concerted action and the danger of degenerating into a mere debating society. Although Spinoza was well aware of this weakness and of the charge that it was the cause of the demise of the United States of the Netherlands, he denied that this was in fact the case, arguing instead that its demise was due to "its defective condition and the fewness of its rulers."[72]

C. Democracy. As we have noted earlier, Spinoza's discussion of democracy in the *Political Treatise* is merely a fragment. Democracy is defined in a manner consistent with how it was previously contrasted with aristocracy, as a state in which the supreme council or ruling body is composed of all those who fulfill certain stipulated criteria. This is different from one in which the members of the council are elected. This suggests that democratic governments can take many forms; but Spinoza tells us that he plans to deal only with what we might call a broad-based democracy—that is, one in which all citizens who are independent and who live honestly have the right to vote in the supreme council and to hold offices of state. The qualification of independence, we are told, is intended to exclude women and servants, who are subject to their husbands and masters respectively, as well as children and wards. The text ends with a discussion of why women should be excluded from participation in a democracy. It is based largely on the claim that women are naturally inferior to men in terms of intellectual ability and physical strength, although this is combined with the reflection that men are usually attracted to women through lust and thus cannot effectively govern conjointly with them.[73]

Spinoza's attitude toward women makes an interesting contrast with that of Hobbes, who, as we have seen, is generally much less "liberal" in his views. However, the latter explicitly argues that women, in a state of nature, have equal rights with men, and that their "inequality of natural force" is not so great as to undermine their basic equality with men. In support of this contention, Hobbes points to the Amazon women, who actually waged war against men, and to the fact that "at this day in diverse places, women are invested with the principal authority."[74] Spinoza, on the other hand, seems to reflect the feminist contention that men tend to regard women merely as sex objects. Unfortunately, his comments about the intellectual inferiority of women lead one to believe that he might have thought this somewhat justified. In any event, these brief remarks, as well as the occasional references to women in the *Ethics*, make it quite clear that this is one issue on which Spinoza was not ahead of his time.

In addition to the general definition of a democracy, and the remarks concerning the exclusion of women, we do find the reflection that although an aristocracy is theoretically the best regime, as it involves the rule of the best for the benefit of all, in practice a democracy is just as good. This, we are told, is because the patricians do not in fact act for the common good, but are instead driven by their passions (a situation which, on Spinoza's own grounds, should be taken as a reflection of the inadequacy of the existing aristocratic institutions, not as a mark of the intrinsic weakness of this form of government). We are not provided, however, with any information about the specific institutions that Spinoza felt would be required for a viable democracy. This is certainly unfortunate, especially when we consider that the *Theological-Political Treatise* contended that democracy was the most natural form of government and strongly suggested that it was the best form. Such a view contrasts sharply with the analysis of aristocracy in the *Political Treatise*, an analysis that stresses the importance of depriving the people of all power and that clearly reflects Spinoza's abiding distrust of the masses. This analysis raises serious questions not only about the superiority of democracy, but also about whether a viable democratic regime is even possible. Perhaps, as one commentator has suggested, the *Political Treatise* remained unfinished not because of Spinoza's untimely death, but because he had come upon a problem that is insoluble in terms of his basic assumptions concerning human beings and the state.[75]

CHAPTER 7

Revelation, Scripture, and Religion

W e have already considered the political setting and the specific concerns underlying the composition and publication of the *Theological-Political Treatise*. Moreover, in the last chapter we discussed many of its specifically political teachings. It is no doubt true that the theological discussion and analysis of the Bible found in this work were developed largely for the sake of the political message. Spinoza's critique of revelation allows him to deny it any authority over people's minds, and this allows him both to repudiate the pretensions of the Calvinist clergy and to advance his argument for freedom of thought and speech. Nevertheless, even when abstracted from the political context, the analysis and critique of revealed religion contained in the *Theological-Political Treatise* constitute an important and highly influential element in Spinoza's philosophy, one that certainly deserves consideration in its own right. This is especially true of his critique of the Bible, by virtue of which Spinoza is generally recognized as the founder of "higher criticism"—that is, the scientific, historical approach to the Bible. This critique is developed in the context of a systematic assault on the claim of divine revelation, and it can best be understood within this broader framework. Accordingly, we shall first consider the basic outlines and motivations of Spinoza's critique of revelation and then, in light of this, discuss his general approach to the Bible. Finally, in order to complete our account of Spinoza's view of religion, we shall touch briefly on his attempt to distinguish between religion and superstition and then consider the social function that he attributes to the former.

I The Critique of Revelation

Spinoza's general attitude to the claims of revealed religion is already
clear from our consideration of the *Ethics*. Basically, belief in the
teachings of traditional religions, as generally construed, is equated
with superstition. The source of such belief is the imagination, and its
hold on the mind of the masses is explained in terms of its connection
with the passions of hope and fear. Hence, not only does Spinoza
maintain that this belief lacks any rational basis; he also holds that the
"virtues" which its proponents affirm—for example, fear of God, a
sense of guilt, repentance, humility, and so on—are largely at vari-
ance with the dictates of reason.[1] Such a critique is external, however,
and rests on philosophical assumptions that theologians deny in the
name of a superior revealed truth. In order to convince theologians—
and we should keep in mind that this was his avowed goal—Spinoza
must meet their arguments on their own grounds.[2] This means that he
must examine the central theological claim that the Scripture, whether
the Jewish or Christian version, contains the authoritative word of
God, to which reason must be subjected.

Now, according to Spinoza, there is only one way in which the
authority of Scripture can be justified, and this is by means of an
appeal to Scripture itself. Ignoring the obviously circular nature of any
such process of reasoning, he affirms as a fundamental principle of
biblical exegesis that the sense of Scripture must be taken from
Scripture itself.[3] The crucial point, which is an application to such
exegesis of the basic principle of Cartesian method, is that nothing
may be claimed to be in the text that is not clearly and distinctly
perceived to be contained in it. In light of this governing principle,
Spinoza rejects out of hand both the Calvinist doctrine "that the light
of nature has no power to interpret Scripture, but that a supernatural
faculty is required for the task,"[4] and the basic tenet of Maimonidean
rationalism that "if the literal meaning clashes with reason, though the
passage seems in itself perfectly clear, it must be interpreted in some
metaphorical sense."[5] Both these approaches are not only dangerous
politically, because they lead to the establishment of spiritual

authorities, but they are useless for determining the actual meaning of
Scripture and thus for justifying its authority.[6]

Having rejected both these approaches, Spinoza centers his attention on the evidence traditionally adduced for the divinity of Scripture.
This evidence is of two sorts. First, there is the authority of the
prophets, whom Spinoza construes broadly to encompass the apostles
and even Christ, as well as the Hebrew prophets. This enables him to
include both the New Testament and the Old Testament in his analysis.
Second, there are miracles, which allegedly serve as signs of divine
revelation. Spinoza's critique of revelation thus contains a systematic
analysis of both prophecy and miracles. With specific reference to
Judaism, however, and perhaps in defense of his own break with the
religion of his fathers, he also includes a critique of the Jewish
conception of the Law and of the claim of the Jews to be the chosen
people.

Prophecy, which is equated with revelation, is defined by Spinoza
as "sure knowledge revealed by God to man."[7] Spinoza notes in
passing that this definition could very well include ordinary knowledge, but that in general such knowledge is not attributed to prophecy.
His concern is solely with the extraordinary, superhuman knowledge
that is traditionally held to be the unique result of prophetic insight.
Following Maimonides, Spinoza agrees that prophetic insight is based
on a superior imagination, rather than a superior intellect. But
whereas Maimonides, the Aristotelian, used the superiority of imagination to justify a real superiority of insight, Spinoza, in accordance
with the basic principles of his theory of knowledge, uses it to draw
just the opposite conclusion. Once it is established that the authority of
the prophets depends merely on their superior imaginative capacity
and not on their intellect, Spinoza can conclude that their views are of
no import in theoretical matters. The overall strategy and intent of the
work prevents him from merely deducing this result from his metaphysical and epistemological principles, however, and requires
instead that he derive it from a consideration of Scripture.

The first step is obviously to demonstrate that Scripture itself
clearly teaches that prophetic power is a function of the imagination.

In line with the traditional Jewish insistence on the primacy of the Mosaic revelation, Spinoza shows, by considering a number of biblical texts, that only Moses was held to have heard a real voice or received a direct revelation from God. All the other prophets encountered God through dreams and visions—that is, through the mediation of their imagination. The one exception is Christ, who "communed with God mind to mind,"[8] and whose knowledge of God is thus attributed to his intellect rather than his imagination. On the basis of his analysis of the express teachings of Scripture, Spinoza concludes that, with the exception of Moses and Christ, it was only by virtue of their vivid imagination and upright character that the prophets were held to possess the "spirit of God," which is equivalent to being recipients of divine revelation.[9]

The next step is to show that, precisely because the prophets rely on imagination, they cannot be taken as authorities in theoretical or speculative matters. This, of course, is a logical consequence of the analysis of imagination found in the *Ethics*, but we have already seen that Spinoza's strategy does not permit him to present it in this fashion. Here, however, he also obviously cannot show that the prophets themselves teach this conception of the imagination. Instead, what he can and does do is to demonstrate that, not only the doctrines and conceptions, but even the imagery and style of the various prophets differ markedly, and that these differences can be understood in terms of their dispositions, backgrounds, and ways of life. For example, Spinoza points out that the rustic prophets such as Amos and Ezekiel tend to depict God in rustic images and in a crude style, whereas a far different kind of imagery and a much more polished style are to be found in the prophecies of the "courtly Isaiah." Spinoza further shows that this explains the specific differences between the visions of Ezekiel and those of Isaiah, and he presents these differences as graphic examples of disagreement among the prophets. In his own cryptic language, which is intended to sum up the whole issue: "Isaiah saw seraphim with six wings, Ezekiel beasts with four wings; Isaiah saw Him in the likeness of a fire; each doubtless saw God under the form in which he usually imagined Him."[10]

Such discrepancies were, of course, a great source of embarrass-
ment to traditional defenders of the faith, and one standard tactic was
to attempt to reconcile these differences by interpreting the passages in
question in some nonliteral manner. Against this, Spinoza simply
points out that by such means one could read anything into Scripture,
"for every absurd and evil invention of human perversity could thus,
without detriment to Scriptural authority, be defended and fostered."[11] Consequently, the only reasonable thing to do is to acknowledge frankly that the prophets disagree, and that their individual
insights and visions reflect merely their own opinions and backgrounds and not some mysterious "higher" truth. However, while
Spinoza uses this obvious disagreement to undermine the authority of
the prophets in speculative matters, he also points out that they all
agree in teaching the virtues of justice and charity. He thus grants their
moral teachings an authority he denies to their speculative insights.
This result, as we shall see, plays a central role in his systematic
attempt to separate theology from philosophy and genuine religion
from superstition.

The appeal to miracles and to reports thereof constitutes the second
traditional basis for establishing the divine origin and authority of
Scripture. Miracles are here construed as events that violate, or at least
transcend, the laws of nature. As such, they function as signs which
authenticate the claims of prophets (taken in the broad sense) to be
emissaries of God and bearers of divine revelations. Since the prophets supported their teachings with miracles, these teachings and the
Scripture in which they are contained are thus to be viewed as the
authoritative word of God. Such a conception obviously runs completely counter to the whole tenor of Spinoza's metaphysics, which
expressly rules out the possibility of anything contravening the universal laws of nature. Once again, however, his strategy does not allow
him simply to refute this conception by a metaphysical argument, but
requires that he also show that this conception is not in accord with, or
at least not derivable from, an unbiased reading of Scripture. Nevertheless, as he himself is forced to acknowledge, the question of
miracles is not quite the same as the question of prophecy. The nature

of prophecy, he notes, is a "purely theological question," by which is meant a question as to what Scripture actually teaches; whereas the question of miracles deals not only with this, but also with the matter of their intrinsic possibility.[12]

Some metaphysical considerations are therefore necessary in dealing with miracles, but Spinoza is careful to separate these considerations from the specifically anti-theistic tenets of the *Ethics*. Here, as elsewhere in the work, his concern is to formulate the argument in terms that theologians might accept, or at least not reject out of hand with cries of "atheism." Nevertheless, despite his conciliatory intent, Spinoza begins by describing the common attitude toward miracles in contemptuous terms. Central to this attitude is the belief that the power of God is somehow more evident and more worthy of adulation when manifested in unusual and inexplicable events than when it is found in the ordinary course of nature. This power is therefore distinguished from the power of nature, and God is viewed as a kind of royal potentate who orders things for the benefit of man. Spinoza sums up his whole attitude toward the subject by reflecting: "What pretension will not people in their folly advance! They have no single sound idea concerning either God or nature, they confound God's decrees with human decrees, they conceive nature as so limited that they believe man to be its chief part!"[13]

As this passage makes clear, one of the underlying causes of the common belief in miracles is failure to grasp the infinity of nature, to understand "that the power of nature is infinite, and that her laws are broad enough to embrace everything conceived by the Divine intellect."[14] Students of the *Ethics* will, of course, realize immediately that this failure is itself the result of an illicit separation between God and nature. In our analysis of that work we saw that the infinity of nature follows logically from the very conception of God, or nature, as the one substance which contains within itself everything that is possible. (*"Whatsoever is, is in God, and without God nothing can be, or be conceived,"* [IP15].) Since nature contains within itself everything that is possible, miracles, which by definition violate the laws of nature, are logically impossible. Moreover, this same conception of nature as an infinite and necessary system of laws is shown to be the true meaning of Maimonides' assertion that the intellect and the will of God are identical. Here Spinoza begins with the acceptable theological formula "It is the same thing to say that God wills a thing, as to say that He understands it."[15] From this he infers that the universal laws of nature reflect perfectly both the divine understanding and the divine will. Once theologians admit this, however, they must also admit that anything which contravenes the laws of nature would also contravene the will (and intellect) of God. In willing a miracle, God would be acting contrary to His own nature, which is absurd. Thus, by a process of argument based on accepted theological principles, Spinoza proceeds to reduce the doctrine of miracles to an absurdity.

Furthermore, Spinoza continues, even if one were to acknowledge the existence of miracles, this could serve only to undermine, rather than confirm, our knowledge of the existence of God. The point here is simply that an appeal to events which contravene the laws of nature casts doubt on the very principles of our reasoning and thus leads inevitably to a hopeless skepticism. If we cannot be certain of these laws, or "primary ideas" (the "common notions" of the *Ethics*), then we cannot be certain of anything, including the existence of God. However, given these laws—that is, given the uniformity of nature— the existence of God can confidently be inferred. Thus, once again Spinoza turns the argument of the theologians against them, showing that it is the lawfulness of nature, not the alleged exceptions to this lawfulness, that provides a basis for inferring the existence of God.

There is another conception of miracles, however, which is not subject to these objections. In this view, miracles are events that cannot be explained through natural causes because we or whoever witnesses them are not in possession of the requisite knowledge. They do not transcend the laws of nature, therefore, but merely our knowledge of these laws. This conception of a miracle is certainly meaningful. In fact, Spinoza claims that it is precisely the sense of miracle found in Scripture, "that what is meant in Scripture by a miracle can only be a work of nature, which surpasses, or is believed to surpass,

human comprehension."[16] The only problem with miracles understood in this way is that they cannot fulfill the function assigned to
them. How, after all, can any such event, which by definition surpasses human understanding, serve as a source of knowledge? Moreover, even assuming that some inferences could legitimately be drawn
from miracles, we could certainly not appeal to them to infer the
existence of God. God, if he is anything, is an infinite being, and
miracles are particular, finite events. But from a finite effect, we can
never infer an infinite cause.[17]

Finally, in accordance with his general strategy, Spinoza supple-
ments his philosophical critique with a further consideration of the
actual biblical teaching concerning miracles. As already noted, the
Bible views miracles merely as events that surpass human comprehension. As Spinoza points out, however, this means that what counts as a
miracle is determined by the particular level of knowledge possessed
by the narrator or witness. But since the ancient Hebrews had a very
limited amount of scientific knowledge, they naturally regarded as
miraculous many events which, from the superior standpoint of seventeenth-century science, could easily be explained. Furthermore, the
prevalence of miracles in the Bible is also explicable in terms of the
poetic manner of expression and the religious intent of the various
authors. This intent often led them to ignore secondary causes and to
refer things directly to God. As a result, many events are described in
ways that suggest miraculous intervention on the part of God, when
the authors themselves had no such thought in mind. The moral that
Spinoza draws from this is that the interpretation and evaluation of
biblical miracle stories requires, among other things, an understanding of the level of knowledge, motivation, and manner of expression of
the authors. Far from serving as a basis for claiming the authority of
Scripture, or as a ground of faith, miracles are seen as a reflection of
the limited understanding of the biblical authors.

The analysis of prophecy and miracles constitutes the essence of
Spinoza's general critique of revealed religion; but this is supplemented by a lengthy critique of Judaism, a critique that in all probability dates back to the days of his excommunication. It repudiates the

claim of the Jews to be a chosen people, elected by God for a special destiny, possessing unique virtues, and, above all, subject to a special discipline (the Torah). Spinoza prefaces his treatment of this topic with a reflection that lies at the very heart of his moral philosophy: "Every man's true happiness and blessedness consist solely in the enjoyment of what is good, not in the pride that he alone is enjoying it, to the exclusion of others."[18] The Jewish people would, after all, be none the less blessed if God conferred his favors equally on all human beings. The fact that the ancient Hebrews thought otherwise, that they prided themselves on being especially chosen, is merely a reflection of their childish understanding and rather crude moral standpoint.

Nevertheless, the Bible does speak of the election of the Jews, and once again Spinoza's overall strategy requires that he explain what legitimate sense this can have. As one might expect, this sense turns out to be consistent with the basic principles of his philosophy. First, he deals with the general question of the nature of divine aid, or grace. Since the "will of God" is perfectly manifest in (really identical with) the laws of nature, these very same laws can also be called "decrees of God." It thus turns out to be strictly equivalent to say that everything happens according to the laws of nature or the will of God. Hence, any and all human accomplishment, since it occurs in accordance with the fixed laws of nature, can, if one wishes, be seen as the result of divine aid. In other words, the notion of divine aid is allowed, but only in a form in which it is merely another name for purely natural occurrences.

On the basis of this principle, Spinoza is able to explain the peculiar achievement of the Hebrew people, by virtue of which they can be said to have been chosen by God. Denying that they possessed any superiority over other nations in either knowledge or virtue, Spinoza concludes that their "election" can refer only to their unique social organization, which enabled them to survive in a hostile environment for such a long period of time. This, however, turns out to be far from complimentary; for the attribution of this organization to divine election merely reflects the fact that it is inexplicable how such a crude and ignorant people could have arrived at it by rational planning. There is, of course, nothing really supernatural in all of this; but it is so incomprehensible, Spinoza ironically notes, that it could even be called miraculous![19]

This then is the only sense in which one can meaningfully talk about the Jews as a "chosen people." Even the gift of prophecy, which was traditionally viewed as a sure sign of Jewish uniqueness, or divine favor, is of no significance in this regard. For Scripture itself clearly teaches, explicitly in the story of Balaam and implicitly in many other places, that the ability to prophesy was commonly attributed to individuals of other nations. Spinoza can thus reaffirm his contention that the election, or superiority, of the Jews concerns only their social order—and from this can draw the inference "that the individual Jew, taken apart from his social organization and government, possessed no gift of God above other men, and that there was no difference between Jew and Gentile."[20] Finally, since this social order—that is, the Hebrew commonwealth—no longer exists, Spinoza arrives at the obvious conclusion that "at the present time, therefore, there is absoutely nothing which the Jews can arrogate to themselves beyond other people."[21]

It could be argued, however, that in doing so, Spinoza is ignoring the obvious fact that, despite all their oppression and suffering, the Jews have managed to survive as a people with a sense of identity and a common hope for the future. Just as Christian apologists often cited the incredible growth of Christianity in the oppressive atmosphere of the Roman Empire as a sign of divine favor, and hence as evidence of the truth of the Christian faith, so too, Jewish thinkers have tended to appeal to the very survival of Judaism as evidence of the divine election of the Hebrew people. Spinoza meets this issue head-on, and his treatment is a masterpiece of concise sociological analysis. Two factors are presented in explanation of Jewish survival: Gentile hatred and the sign of circumcision. Far from destroying them, the experience of hatred and oppression unified the Jews and kept them in their traditional faith. Spinoza illustrates this by noting the different fate of the Jews in Spain and in Portugal. In both countries they were compelled either to embrace Catholicism, the state religion, or go into exile. In Spain, those who converted were made full-fledged citizens, with all the rights and privileges thereof, with the predictable result "that they straightway became so intermingled with the Spaniards as to leave of themselves no relic or remembrance."[22] In Portugal, on the other hand, the Jews were forced to live apart and were considered unworthy of civic honors, and as a result they steadfastly maintained their traditional faith. Curiously enough, Spinoza seems to attach even greater importance to circumcision. With regard to this traditional Jewish rite, he reflects: "The sign of circumcision is, as I think, so important, that I could persuade myself that it alone would preserve the nation for ever. Nay, I would go so far as to believe that if the foundations of their religion have not emasculated their minds they may even, if occasion offers, so changeable are human affairs, raise up their empire afresh, and that God may a second time elect them."[23]

To complete his critique of traditional Judaism, Spinoza had to deal directly with the Mosaic law, or Torah. After all, it is largely because they are the recipients of this law, and not by virtue of any special moral or intellectual powers, that the Jews lay claim to being a chosen people with a unique historical mission. This law contains not only moral principles, but also rules for worship, social organization, and diet. Indeed, it provides precepts governing almost every phase of daily life. During the Middle Ages, Jewish thinkers such as Maimonides attempted to explain and justify some of these rules which did not seem to serve any explicitly moral purpose—for example, the dietary laws—by suggesting that they had a spiritual sense. The goal of these efforts was always to demonstrate that, apart from the laws concerning worship in the Temple, which obviously could not be observed after its destruction, all these laws were obligatory for all Jews.

The requirement to observe a large number of apparently arbitrary laws concerning such morally indifferent matters as what one may or may not eat was obviously ridiculous to a philosopher of the rigidly rationalist cast of mind of Spinoza. Nevertheless, rather than simply rejecting the entire corpus of Jewish law on the basis of an independent philosophical perspective, Spinoza attempts to analyze the actual significance of this law for the Hebrew people. Central to this analysis is the distinction between the divine and the ceremonial laws, both of which are contained in the revelation to Israel.

By "divine law" Spinoza means those moral rules, dictated by reason, that describe what is necessary for the realization of human blessedness. This law is divine, because blessedness, as we have seen from the *Ethics*, consists in the love of God, and because it follows from the idea of God that is within us. The chief precept is simply to love God as the highest good, and not out of fear or in expectation of some further reward.[24] Since this precept is universal and is, in fact, deduced from human nature, it is more properly described as an eternal truth than a command. The Israelites, however, "did not adequately conceive God's decrees as eternal truths."[25] Because of their crude, anthropomorphic conception of the Deity, they viewed the divine law as the command of a sovereign. Thus, although the prophets taught the genuine divine law (love of God), they did not present it in its proper, spiritual sense. Spinoza suggests that it was Christ, who was sent to teach not only the Jews but the whole human race, who first taught the true sense of the law. That Christ was able to do this was because he possessed adequate ideas, or, in the carefully chosen language of the *Theological-Political Treatise*, he "perceived truly what was revealed."[26] Thus, Spinoza, apostate Jew and friend of many members of the Mennonite and Collegiant communities, assigns Christ a unique place in the religious history of the human race.

The situation with regard to the ceremonial laws is somewhat different. Ceremonies are defined as morally indifferent actions, which are called good or bad only by virtue of their institution—that is, the fact that they have been commanded by God. Since ceremonies are by their very nature morally indifferent, they do not play an intrinsic or necessary role in the achievement of human blessedness. Consequently, the law commanding such practices (the ceremonial law) cannot, like the divine law, be viewed as an expression, however inadequate, of eternal truths. Nevertheless, it had significance for the Jewish state, since its precepts constituted the civil legislation of the state. Moreover, Spinoza shows in considerable detail how various aspects of this legislation—for example, the laws concerning sacrifice and economic arrangements—were important in maintaining the stability of the state. The upshot of the analysis, however, is that, since the significance of this law is limited to its function in the ancient Jewish state, and since this state no longer exists, no contemporary Jew is under any obligation to keep the law.[27]

II The Interpretation of Scripture

This thoroughgoing critique of revelation and of the special claims of Judaism rests, to a considerable extent, on an appeal to what Spinoza claims to be the express teachings of Scripture. The presentation and justification of the proper method for determining this sense is therefore an integral part of Spinoza's project, forming the subject matter of chapters 7–10 of the *Theological-Political Treatise*. Spinoza first (chapter 7) explains the basic principles of his exegetical method, then, in the succeeding chapters, applies these principles to the entire canon of the Old Testament and to some of the Epistles in the New Testament. Although we cannot go into many of the details of Spinoza's analysis, which reveals a deep knowledge of the Bible, particularly of the Old Testament, we can and must consider the main outlines of Spinoza's revolutionary approach.

Its essence is concisely expressed in the famous formula: "The method of interpreting Scripture does not widely differ from the method of interpreting nature—in fact, it is almost the same."[28] This is, indeed, a revolutionary statement in the history of biblical interpretation. The Bible, which had been viewed previously as the literal word of God and hence as equally sacred in every syllable, is now to be construed as a natural phenomenon, the product of purely human capacities and endeavors. In other words, it is to be interpreted in precisely the same manner as any other ancient text. Now, with regard to any other text, the goal would obviously be to arrive at the clear intent of the author; and any interpretation that twisted the sense of a given passage in order to make it conform to a previously accepted truth would be rejected out of hand. The Bible, according to Spinoza, is not to be viewed as an exception to this rule, regardless of the consequences for traditional theological doctrines. Just as Descartes, in his *Discourse on Method*, had argued that the proper method in the sciences must begin with clear and distinct conceptions, which serve as the foundation of all truth, so Spinoza, in what amounts to a discourse on the method for arriving at the true meaning of the Bible, points to the clear meaning of the text as the ultimate standard and source of interpretation.

The first step in the development of a science of biblical interpretation, then, is to determine the proper method for the interpretation of nature, which, as Spinoza tells us in typically oblique fashion, "consists in the examination of the history of nature, and therefrom deducing definitions of natural phenomena on certain fixed axioms."[29] By the "history of nature," Spinoza seems to mean the sequence of actual events (in the language of the *Ethics*, the series of finite modes). He therefore appears to be describing an essentially inductive procedure, in which one moves from particular events to general laws ("certain fixed axioms") and from these back to the phenomena to be explained. With regard to the Bible, the phenomena requiring explanation are the particular passages under consideration. The goal is to determine the true intentions of the authors of these passages, and these intentions are to be derived from fundamental principles. These principles, or general exegetical rules, are themselves to be based on a consideration of the history of Scripture. "By working in this manner," Spinoza reflects, "everyone will always advance without danger of error—that is, if they admit no principles for interpreting Scripture, and discussing its contents save such as they find in Scripture itself."[30]

Under the general rubric of the "history of Scripture," Spinoza had in mind three quite specific things. The first is a linguistic, or philological, analysis. Since the interpretation of any text requires an understanding of its language, it is obviously necessary to investigate "the nature and properties of the language in which the books of the Bible were written, and in which their authors were accustomed to speak."[31] A thorough knowledge of the ancient Hebrew language is thus the first prerequisite for accurate biblical exegesis, and it was no doubt with this in mind that Spinoza attempted to write a Hebrew grammar. Furthermore, Spinoza adds in a reflection that suggests considerable historical insight, this requirement holds not only for the Old Testament, but also for the New, since the latter, although written in Greek, contains Hebrew modes of thought and speech.[32]

Second, it is necessary to analyze each book and to arrange its topics under appropriate headings. This provides a general frame of reference for the interpretation of obscure passages. As an example of an obscure passage and of the proper way to handle it, Spinoza cites two statements attributed to Moses: "God is a fire," and "God is jealous." Each of these is perfectly clear in and of itself, although taken literally, both are absurd. The problem, therefore, is to determine whether they are in fact to be understood in a literal fashion. This requires a comparison of these passages with other relevant passages relating to Moses and a consideration of the ways in which these expressions were commonly used by biblical authors. The important point, which Spinoza emphasizes over against the defenders of the "reasonableness" of Scripture (the Maimonideans), is that if an alternative reading cannot be found by the above method, then the literal meaning must be accepted as the expression of the author's intent, no matter how absurd it may seem from the standpoint of a more "rational" conception of God. Applying this principle to the above statements, we find that the notion of fire is used to denote anger and jealousy in the Old Testament. We can thus easily reconcile the two statements and conclude that, in describing God as fire, Moses was merely trying to indicate, through a common metaphor, that God was jealous. With regard to jealousy itself, the situation is somewhat different. We can find no textual evidence to support the claim that Scripture denies that God has passions. Hence, despite the completely unphilosophical nature of this doctrine, we must conclude that Moses actually taught that God was jealous and not try to read some more acceptable sense into the passage by interpreting it metaphorically or allegorically.

Third, one must consider certain topics relevant to the composition of each book. More specifically, we need information about the life, times, and situation of the author, as well as some knowledge of the purpose and occasion for which the book in question was written. The crucial importance of this kind of information is obvious from the analysis of prophecy, where it was shown that the teachings of the prophets reflect their dispositions, circumstances, and backgrounds. Finally, it is also necessary to inquire into the history of each book, including how it was first received, how many different versions existed, and how it became part of the canon. In short, it is essential to have an accurate historical knowledge of both the author and the text; for it is only in light of such knowledge that the true meaning of the text can be determined and the "divinity" of Scripture established.

Unfortunately, a number of difficulties prevent the attainment of this knowledge; although Spinoza is quick to point out that they concern only the interpretation of the speculative teaching of the prophets—for example their conception of God—and not their moral teachings, which are clear even to the unlearned.[33] Among these difficulties are the very limited nature of our historical knowledge and an almost total lack of knowledge of the nuances of the ancient Hebrew language. Moreover, above and beyond the difficulties that arise from the limitations of our knowledge lies the problem that the very traditions and sources on which this knowledge is based are unsound. Spinoza is here referring to received, orthodox views concerning the authorship of the various books of the Bible, the dates of their composition, their internal agreement, and the histories of the texts. The orthodox view of these matters, in both the Jewish and the Christian traditions, was based on the assumption of the absolute infallibility of the text. Accordingly, each book in the canon is regarded as a unitary work, written in its entirety by the designated author; moreover, the text is held to have remained unaltered from the time of its composition until the present. Such views, according to Spinoza, effectively reduce the Bible to nonsense. Thus, he includes within the *Theological-Political Treatise* a detailed discussion of the authorship and history of the main books of the Old Testament and some brief considerations regarding some of the Epistles of the New Testament.

Typical of Spinoza's approach is his treatment of the Pentateuch, often referred to as the "Five Books of Moses." Following the thinly veiled suggestion of the commentator Eben Ezra and the more explicit statements of radical critics such as Isaac de la Peyrère,[34] Spinoza points out a number of obvious reasons why Moses cannot possibly have been the author of the entire Pentateuch. Furthermore, as an alternative explanation, he suggests that these books, as well as many others in the canon, were compiled from a variety of sources by Ezra, the scribe who, together with Nehemiah, is traditionally credited with the reconstruction of the Temple and the revival of the religious tradition after the exile. Spinoza believes that this explains the unity of theme and language found in the various books. But since this unity is far from complete and the various books contain a number of alternative and incompatible narratives, Spinoza also suggests that Ezra did not put the finishing touches on these narratives but merely collected them from a variety of sources "and sometimes simply set them down, leaving their examination and arrangement to posterity."[35]

The remaining books of the Old Testament, the prophetic books and the wisdom literature, are dealt with in a similar fashion, although in far less detail. Here Spinoza's general statement must suffice: "An examination of these [the prophetic books] assures me that the prophecies therein contained have been compiled from other books, and are not always set down in the exact order in which they were spoken or written by the prophets, but are only such as were collected here and there, so that they are but fragmentary."[36]

The New Testament is treated in an extremely sketchy fashion. The Gospels are completely ignored, and the main point emphasized is that the obvious disagreements between the apostles must not be resolved by any appeal to a mystical exegesis but should simply be recognized as a perfectly natural consequence of the fact that each of the apostolic authors was a teacher as well as a prophet and, as such, was concerned to communicate the Christian faith *as he understood it*. Thus, basic disagreements, such as that between James and Paul regarding the roles of faith and works in salvation, are not to be explained away, but frankly accepted as expressions of different philosophical viewpoints.

Many of the inconsistencies in the various biblical narratives to which Spinoza points were, of course, well known to the rabbinic tradition, and most of his specific interpretations and historical views have been rendered obsolete by subsequent research. This does not minimize Spinoza's achievement in the field of biblical criticism, however; for this achievement does not rest on his actual results or specific interpretations, but on the presentation of a method and a program for research through which a genuine, scientific knowledge of the Bible is alone possible.

III Faith and Superstition

Spinoza presents his elaborate critique of revelation, the Jewish claim to divine election, and the infallibility of Scripture as part of an endeavor to separate true religion from superstition and to determine the respective spheres of religion, so conceived, and philosophy. Moreover, as we have already seen, one of his reasons for publishing the *Theological-Political Treatise* was his desire to answer the charges of atheism that had been raised against him (an endeavor that if seriously intended by Spinoza, must be ranked as one of the greatest failures in the history of Western thought). Indeed, Spinoza constantly affirms within the work that his arguments relate only to superstition, that they do not undermine true religion or the public peace. Accordingly, to complete our picture of Spinoza's views on religion, the analysis of his critique must be supplemented by some consideration of what he considers to be "true religion" and the function that he attributes to it.

Actually, Spinoza's position on this point is quite simple, and, in one respect at least, is rather straightforwardly presented in the *Theological-Political Treatise*. Genuine, or true, religion, the religion taught by all the prophets and the apostles, is morality. This morality, however, is presented in a form in which the multitude can appreciate it. In effect, this means that the Bible presents moral principles by appealing to the imagination, rather than the intellect, and hence as decrees of God, rather than eternal truths. Since the multitude is led by imagination and is not really capable of reason, religion has a necessary social function. Such a view of religion was, of course, hardly original with Spinoza. It had already been formulated explicitly by the Arabian philosopher ibn-Rushd, or Averroës, in the twelfth century[37] and had found expression in many subsequent politically minded thinkers, most notably Machiavelli.[38] Nevertheless, although not original with Spinoza, it is still an integral part of his political thought, since it allows him at once to "save religion" and to guarantee the autonomy of philosophy.

As before, Spinoza's strategy requires that he show that this conception of religion and its function is derived from, rather than imposed on, Scripture. To this end he emphasizes the fact that, despite vast internal disagreement in speculative matters, the Bible in its entirety teaches the same moral doctrine. This doctrine is the demand to love God above all things and one's neighbor as oneself. But since, as it turns out, love of God is manifested only in love of neighbor, the moral teaching of the Bible really reduces to the latter demand. Other moral doctrines found in Scripture, such as those contained in the Ten Commandments, are held to be derived from this principle. This love is thus the genuine kernel of true religion that survives all historical and philosophical criticism. To the extent to which the Bible teaches this love, and to this extent alone, it can be viewed as the word of God. Moreover, since both the prophets and the apostles addressed their messages to the masses, this moral teaching is expressed in a simple form, easily comprehensible by everyone. The obvious implication of this is that one should not try to find in the Bible more than is there. It does contain a sound moral teaching, expressed in a popular form, and this enables it to inculcate piety and voluntary obedience (really two expressions for the same thing). But it does not contain any speculative truths and should not be treated as an authority on such matters.

On the basis of this conception of the Bible as a textbook of public morality, the function of which is to inspire voluntary obedience, Spinoza proceeds to develop a doctrine of religious faith and even to

delineate the basic articles of the "true Catholic faith." This faith, we
are told, "consists in a knowledge of God, without which obedience to
Him would be impossible, and which the mere fact of obedience to
Him implies."[39] The point is simply that a willingness to obey God,
or, what for Spinoza amounts to the same thing, a disposition to
practice justice and charity toward one's neighbors, seems to entail
certain beliefs. These beliefs, not taken as beliefs in themselves, but
veiwed as vehicles for fostering the appropriate disposition, are the
articles of faith. Spinoza lists seven such "dogmas" that are allegedly
contained in Scripture. They are:

> I. That God or a Supreme Being exists, sovereignly just and merciful,
> the Exemplar of the true life; that whosoever is ignorant of or dis-
> believes in His existence cannot obey Him or know Him as a Judge.
> II. That He is One. Nobody will dispute that this doctrine is absolutely
> necessary for entire devotion, admiration, and love towards God. For
> devotion, admiration, and love spring from the superiority of one over
> all else.
> III. That He is omnipresent, or that all things are open to Him, for if
> anything could be supposed to be concealed from Him, or to be
> unnoticed by Him, we might doubt or be ignorant of the equity of His
> judgment as directing all things.
> IV. That He has supreme right and dominion over all things, and that
> He does nothing under compulsion, but by His absolute fiat and grace.
> All things are bound to obey Him. He is not bound to obey any.
> V. That the worship of God consists only in justice and charity, or love
> towards one's neighbour.
> VI. That all those, and those only, who obey God by their manner of
> life are saved; the rest of mankind, who live under the sway of their
> pleasures, are lost. If we did not believe this, there would be no reason
> for obeying God rather than pleasure.
> VII. Lastly, that God forgives the sins of those who repent. No one is
> free from sin, so that without this belief all would despair of salvation,
> and there would be no reason for believing in the mercy of God. He who
> firmly believes that God, out of the mercy and grace with which He
> directs all things, forgives the sins of men, and who feels his love of
> God kindled thereby, he, I say, does really know Christ according to the
> Spirit, and Christ is in him.[40]

The articles of this brief creed are very close to the list of "fundamentals" which were taught by liberal Christians of the time, such as the Latitudinarians in England and the Collegiants and Mennonites in the Netherlands, with whom, as we have seen, Spinoza had a close association. The above-mentioned groups held these fundamentals to be the essential doctrines necessary for salvation. This approach resulted in a simplified, ethically oriented Christianity, with considerable toleration of differences of opinion with regard to the nonessential, or "indifferent," teachings of the various denominations. In reality, however, Spinoza's Averroistic conception of religion is far more radical than these liberal versions of Christianity. For, although these liberal groups desired to simplify doctrine in the interest of both a more sincere faith and a more harmonious society, they adhered in a straightforward way to this simplified faith. Spinoza, on the other hand, distinguishes sharply between the truth of these dogmas and their effectiveness in inculcating obedience. Moreover, his concern is solely with the latter. "Faith," he writes, "does not demand that dogmas should be true as that they should be pious—that is, such as will stir up the heart to obey."[41]

Nevertheless, we are far from the intellectual love of God of the *Ethics*, and it is only Spinoza's Averroism that can reconcile such a creed with the basic principles of his metaphysics. The God of religious faith, unlike the God of philosophy, is decked out in human attributes and functions as a lawgiver and judge. Moreover, the religious person views salvation as a reward for virtue, rather than virtue itself and requires a belief in the mercy and forgiveness of God, without which one would despair of this salvation. The point, however, is that such faith does not contradict, but rather operates on an entirely different level from, philosophical truth. Its articles are necessary to inculcate piety, or virtue, not in the free individual or philosopher, who lives according to the dictates of reason, but in the multitude, who can never rise above the first level of knowledge. Religion, therefore, appeals to the imagination. It presents moral rules as the commands of a personal God, reinforces these rules with signs and wonders, and connects them with the powerful passions of hope and fear, which are the chief moving forces for the great majority of human beings. In the end, true religion differs from superstition not in its truth value, but merely in its usefulness for inculcating obedience and mutual love in the multitude. Superstition, by its very nature, is divisive; it breeds intolerance and social chaos. Genuine, or ethically oriented, religion, on the other hand, is not only a desirable social force, but a necessary ingredient in any society that is not composed entirely of philosophers.

It is only in light of this conception of religion that we can understand the role that Spinoza assigns to religion in the state and the fact that he grants to the sovereign power supreme right in matters of public worship. This latter point, which seems to contradict his advocacy of freedom of thought, is a logical consequence of the social function that Spinoza attributes to religion. This function is to inspire voluntary obedience, and so it is only appropriate that religion be under the control of that power to whom obedience is due—namely, the sovereign. Moreover, far from violating liberty of thought, such secular control serves to guarantee it. As the situation in the Netherlands made perfectly clear to Spinoza, ecclesiastical control of public affairs was the great enemy of personal liberty. After all, it was the Calvinist clergy who were intolerant and demanded a share of sovereign power. Nor did Spinoza see this demand for political power as a peculiar aberration of Calvinism, but rather as a typical attitude on the part of any religious orthodoxy which holds that human beings can be saved only by adherence to its particular creed. Thus, like Hobbes, Spinoza saw in secular control over religion a check on ecclesiastical power and on the fanaticism that the exercise of such power inevitably incites in the masses. Finally, since sovereign power can control only actions and not thought, its control over religion is limited to observances, or ceremonies. But since these are really indifferent, that is, not intrinsically connected with beliefs—the sovereign's control over such matters serves only to keep the public peace and does not interfere with anyone's freedom of thought. Thus Spinoza, an apostate Jew living in a Christian country, advocates an official state religion as the best protection of the freedom of philosophy.

NOTES

1 The Life of Spinoza

1. The following biographical sketch is based on accounts of Spinoza's life in some of the standard sources. These include the contemporary account *The Life of the Late Mr. de Spinoza*, generally attributed to J. M. Lucas, translated and edited by A. Wolf as *The Oldest Biography of Spinoza*; John Colerus, *The Life of Benedict de Spinoza*, English translation (London, 1706) reprinted as an appendix to Sir Frederick Pollock, *Spinoza: His Life and Philosophy*; Pollock's own account in the above-mentioned work; J. Freudenthal, *Spinoza Leben und Lehre*, 2d ed., edited by Carl Gebhardt; A. Wolf, "The Life of Spinoza," in the introduction to his edition and translation of *Spinoza's Short Treatise*; and Lewis Samuel Feuer, *Spinoza and the Rise of Liberalism*.

2. This material is based on the account in H. Graetz, *Popular History of the Jews*, trans. A. B. Rhine, 5th ed., vol. 5, pp. 48–75, and Freudenthal, *Spinoza Leben und Lehre*, pp. 3–16.

3. For an interesting analysis of both the broad culture and the Jewish commitment of these men, see Richard H. Popkin, "The Historical Significance of Sephardic Judaism in 17th Century Amsterdam," *American Sephardi*, Journal of the Sephardic Studies Program of Yeshiva University, vol. 5, nos. 1–2 (1971): 18–27.

4. Feuer, *Spinoza and the Rise of Liberalism*, p. 5.

5. Ibid., pp. 8–9.

6. Freudenthal, *Spinoza Leben und Lehre*, pp. 32ff.

7. For a discussion of Van Den Ende and his relationship to Spinoza, see Feuer, *Spinoza and the Rise of Liberalism*, pp. 18–20.

8. Ibid., pp. 4–9, 24–37.

9. Lucas, *Oldest Biography*, p. 52.

10. Wolf, *Spinoza's Short Treatise*, pp. 149–50.

11. For a most interesting discussion of the whole debate over method at the time, see Leroy E. Loemker, *Struggle for Synthesis and the Seventeenth Century Background of Leibniz's Synthesis of Order and Freedom*, esp. chap. 7.

12. *Spinoza Opera*, ed. C. Gebhardt, vol. 2, p. 8, and *The Collected Works of Spinoza*, vol. 1, ed. and trans. E. Curley, p. 11 (hereafter cited as Gebhardt and Curley, respectively).

13. Freudenthal, *Spinoza Leben und Lehre*, pp. 112ff.

14. Letter 8, in Gebhardt, vol. 4, pp. 38–41, and *The Correspondence of Spinoza*, trans. A. Wolf, pp. 101–05 (hereafter cited as Wolf).

15. Letters 9 and 10, in Gebhardt, vol. 4, pp. 42–47, and Wolf, pp. 105–09.

16. Letter 28, in Gebhardt, vol. 4, pp. 162–63, and Wolf, p. 202. Spinoza here says that he

will send Bouwmeester the text up to the eightieth proposition of the third part. Since the
third part in the final version does not have that many propositions, it is assumed that
Spinoza originally intended the *Ethics* to be divided into three parts, and that the
proposition referred to thus falls in what eventually became the fourth part.

17. Letter 29, in Gebhardt, vol. 4, p. 165, and Wolf, p. 204.
18. Letter 30, in Gebhardt, vol. 4, p. 166, and Wolf, p. 205.
19. See Wolf, *Life of Spinoza*, pp. lxxviiff.
20. Ibid., p. lxxxii.
21. Ibid., p. lxxxvi.
22. Ibid., pp. lxxxvii–lxxxix.
23. Feuer, *Spinoza and the Rise of Liberalism*, pp. 146–47.
24. Letter 47, in Gebhardt, vol. 4, pp. 234–35, and Wolf, p. 267.

2 Spinoza's Philosophy in Its Historical Context

1. The classic study of the influences on Spinoza is Stanislaus von Dunin-Borkowski, *Der junge De Spinoza*.
2. Two important discussions of this theme are by E. A. Burtt, *The Metaphysical Foundations of Modern Science*, and Alexandre Koyré, *From the Closed World to the Infinite Universe*.
3. Trans. and cited by Burtt, *Metaphysical Foundations*, p. 75.
4. Ibid., pp. 83–90.
5. Descartes, *Principles of Philosophy*, pt. 1, principle 51, in *Philosophical Works*, vol. 1, p. 239.
6. Ibid., p. 150.
7. Letter to Princess Elizabeth, 28 June 1643, in *Descartes' Philosophical Letters*, p. 142.
8. Descartes, *The Passions of the Soul*, pt. 1, articles 34–38, in *Philosophical Works*, vol. 1, pp. 345–49.
9. *Descartes' "Principles of Philosophy,"* in Gebhardt, vol. 1, pp. 32–33, and Curley, p. 230.
10. See Martial Gueroult, *Spinoza I*, pp. 11ff.
11. For an interesting comparison of Spinoza and Freud on this point, see Stuart Hampshire, *Spinoza*, pp. 106–09.
12. Reply to the Second Set of Objections, *Philosophical Works*, vol. 2, pp. 52–59.
13. One of the best examples of this was provided by Thomas Hobbes, who exerted a tremendous influence on Spinoza, not only in the area of political philosophy, but also in epistemology and psychology. In the Dedicatory Epistle to the Earl of Devonshire attached to his *De Cive*, Hobbes advocates the application of the geometrical method to the understanding of human actions and moral problems. See Thomas Hobbes, *De Cive, or The Citizen*, trans. and ed. Sterling P. Lamprecht, pp. 3ff.
14. In favor of the intrinsic connection, we can cite as examples, without attempting to be exhaustive, J. Freudenthal, *Spinoza Leben und Lehre*, pt. 2, pp. 110–11; H. H. Joachim, *A Study of the Ethics of Spinoza*, pp. 12–13; Geuroult, *Spinoza I*, pp. 15ff. Against such a

connection, we can cite Leon Roth, *Spinoza*, pp. 37–39; Hampshire, *Spinoza*, p. 21; and especially H. A. Wolfson, *The Philosophy of Spinoza*, vol. 1, pp. 32–60.

15. Letter 9, in Gebhardt, vol. 4, p. 43, and Wolf, p. 106.

16. For an interesting defense of the opposite view, see R. J. Delahunty, *Spinoza*, pp. 91–96.

17. This interpretation is most forcefully presented by Gueroult, *Spinoza I*, pp. 21ff.

18. *Treatise on the Emendation of the Intellect*, in Gebhardt, vol. 2, p. 35, and Curley, pp. 39–40.

19. Ibid., in Gebhardt, vol. 2, p. 34, and Curley, p. 39.

20. The significance of genetic definitions for Spinoza is emphasized by Gueroult, *Spinoza I*, pp. 33ff., and by Ernst Cassirer, *Das Erkenntnisproblem in der Philosophie und Wissenschaft der neueren Zeit*, vol. 2, pp. 90ff.

21. See H. Höffding, *Spinozas Ethica: Analyse und Charakteristik*, p. 6.

22. *Treatise on the Emendation of the Intellect*, in Gebhardt, vol. 2, p. 36, and Curley, p. 41. The expression "objective essence" is used by both Descartes and Spinoza. It means the essence of a thing as grasped by thought, which is equivalent to the adequate idea of the thing. The topic will be discussed in chapter 4 in connection with Spinoza's account of ideas.

23. Ibid., in Gebhardt, vol. 2, pp. 115–16, and Curley, p. 19.

3 God

1. Aristotle, *Categories*, chap. 5, 4a.

2. Ibid., chap. 5.

3. See chap. 2, n. 5.

4. Descartes, Reply to the Second Set of Objections, *Philosophical Works*, vol. 2, p. 53.

5. Descartes, *Principles of Philosophy*, pt. 1, principle 53.

6. Ibid., principles 56, 61, 64, and 65.

7. The above analysis of the Spinozistic critique of the Cartesian conception of substance, as well as the arguments sketched in the next paragraph, are based largely on the account of Curley, *Spinoza's Metaphysics*, pp. 14–20.

8. This is connected with Descartes's strange doctrine that the will of God is the source of eternal truths. For the best recent discussions of this aspect of Descartes's thought, see Margaret Wilson, *Descartes*, esp. pp. 120–31, and 136, and Curley, "Descartes on the Creation of Eternal Truths."

9. This thesis is argued quite forcefully by Curley, *Spinoza's Metaphysics*, pp. 36ff. Another commentator who denies, albeit on somewhat different grounds, the Cartesian basis of the Spinozistic conception of substance is H. F. Hallett, *Creation, Emanation and Salvation*, esp. pp. 44–48. According to Hallett, Spinoza did not regard substance as a thing but as an "infinite potency-in-act" (p. 46).

10. John Locke, *An Essay Concerning Human Understanding*, bk. 2, chap. 22.

11. In this account of individual things, or finite modes, if not in the positive characterization of substance, I am again following Curley, *Spinoza's Metaphysics*, chap. 1. The main issue underlying the exegetical question can be traced back at least as far as the famous "refutation" of Spinoza by Pierre Bayle in his *Historical and Critical Dictionary*, pp.

288–338. Starting with the assumption that Spinoza held to an essentially Cartesian conception of substance, Bayle claimed that his monism committed him to the absurdity that only substance is real and that finite modes, including human beings, are merely its ephemeral accidents. Curley argues that the whole critique rests on an erroneous reading of Spinoza. Recently Bennett has argued to the contrary that, for Spinoza, bodies can indeed be regarded as predicates of extended substance, or, equivalently, as "adjectival on the world" (*A Study of Spinoza's Ethics*, pp. 92–106). In support of this interpretation, he develops an interesting and sophisticated "field metaphysic," which is then used to attack Curley's interpretation. One problem with the interpretation, which Bennett notes (p. 94) is that it can only be applied plausibly to extended things; another is that it does not seem to do justice to Spinoza's conception of an individual.

12. The best overall account of this controversy is by Gueroult, *Spinoza I*, pp. 428–61. For helpful and up-to-date English language discussions, see Delahunty, *Spinoza*, pp. 116–24, and Moltke S. Gram, "Spinoza, Substance, and Predication."

13. See *Short Treatise*, pt. 1, chap. 2, in Gebhardt, vol. 1, p. 25, and Curley, p. 71; letter 9, in Gebhardt, vol. 2, p. 46, and Wolf, p. 108.

14. This analogy is offered by Léon Brunschvicg, *Spinoza et ses Contemporains*, pp. 67–68; cited by Curley, *Spinoza's Metaphysics*, p. 144.

15. This is suggested by Emile Bréhier, *The History of Philosophy*, p. 168.

16. I am here ignoring the problems raised by the contrast between logical and psychological aspects of the attribute of thought. This topic will be taken up in the next chapter.

17. For an account of Leibniz's argument, see Curley, p. 410.

18. This is claimed by Curley; see preceding note.

19. The point is convincingly made by Bennett, *Spinoza's Ethics*, p. 69.

20. Bertrand Russell, *A Critical Exposition of the Philosophy of Leibniz*, p. 59.

21. Spinoza's fullest discussion of the topic is in his famous letter to Meyer entitled "On the Nature of the Infinite," letter 12, in Gebhardt, vol. 4, pp. 52–62, and Wolf, pp. 115–22. Gueroult's authoritative account of this letter (*Spinoza I*, pp. 500–28) is published in an English translation in M. Grene, ed., *Spinoza, A Collection of Critical Essays*, pp. 182–212.

22. For Descartes, however, extension is indefinite rather than infinite. This reflects his contention that the term *infinite* pertains to God alone. See *Principles of Philosophy*, pt. 1, principles 26 and 27.

23. This account of the connection between having more reality and more attributes was suggested to me by Michelle Gilmore.

24. See Alan Donagan, "Essence and the Distinction of Attributes," p. 173.

25. See George Kline, "On the Infinity of Spinoza's Attributes."

26. This is emphasized by Bennett in support of his "dualistic" reading of Spinoza, *Spinoza's Ethics*, pp. 75–79.

27. See particularly the *Short Treatise*, Appendix 2, in Gebhardt, vol. 1, p. 119, and Curley, pp. 154–55, and the correspondence with Schuller and Tschirnhaus, letters 63–66 and 70. For an interesting, albeit speculative, discussion of the "unknown attributes," see Curley, *Spinoza's Metaphysics*, pp. 144–52.

28. Nicholas Malebranche, *De la Recherche de la Verité*, bk. 3, chap. 10.

29. Descartes, *Philosophical Works*, vol. 1, p. 181.
30. For a quite different interpretation of the argument, see Willis Doney, "Spinoza's Ontological Proof."
31. The famous formula "God *or* Nature" (*Deus seu Natura*) occurs in the preface to pt. 4, in Gebhardt, vol. 2, p. 206, and Curley, p. 544.
32. The distinction between *natura naturans* and *natura naturata* also occurs in the *Short Treatise*, pt. 1, chaps. 8 and 9, in Gebhardt, vol. 1, pp. 47–48, and Curley, p. 91.
33. This discussion of the argument is suggested by Gueroult, *Spinoza I*, pp. 243–44.
34. Letter 82, in Gebhardt, vol. 4, p. 334, and Wolf, p. 364.
35. Letter 83, in Gebhardt, vol. 4, pp. 334–35, and Wolf, p. 365.
36. See Wolfson, *Philosophy of Spinoza*, vol. 1, p. 332.
37. Ibid., vol. 1, pp. 347–69. This is a controversial point, to which we shall return in chapter 5 in connection with Spinoza's argument for the eternity of the human mind.
38. See *Theological-Political Treatise*, pt. 3, in Gebhardt, vol. 3, p. 45, and Elwes, vol. 2, p. 44.
39. See Wolfson, *Philosophy of Spinoza*, vol. 1, pp. 372–76.
40. See Curley, p. 429, n. 59, for a discussion of this point.
41. *Short Treatise*, pt. 1, chap. 9, in Gebhardt, vol. 1, p. 48, and Curley, p. 911.
42. Letter 64, in Gebhardt, vol. 4, p. 278, and Wolf, p. 308.
43. See Pollock, *Spinoza*, p. 142; Höffding, *Spinozas Ethica*, p. 44; Parkinson, *Spinoza's Theory of Knowledge*, p. 79; and Bréhier, *History of Philosophy*, p. 165.
44. *Treatise on the Emendation of the Intellect*, in Gebhardt, vol. 2, p. 37, and Curley, p. 41.
45. Ibid.
46. This account is located between propositions 13 and 14 of part 2. We shall consider it in the next chapter in connection with the analyses of Spinoza's doctrine of the mind-body relationship.
47. See Joachim, *Ethics of Spinoza*, pp. 84–85, and Gueroult, *Spinoza I*, p. 324.
48. See Höffding, *Spinozas Ethica*, pp. 41ff.
49. From the scholium to lemma 7 in pt. 2; in Gebhardt, vol. 2, p. 102, and Curley, p. 462.
50. This is convincingly shown by Curley, *Spinoza's Metaphysics*, chap. 2.
51. The thunder example is borrowed from Bennett, *Spinoza's Ethics*, p. 113.
52. For discussions of this issue, see Curley, *Spinoza's Metaphysics*, chap. 3; W. Matson, "Steps Towards Spinozism"; and Bennett, *Spinoza's Ethics*, chap. 5. The argument against the claim that Spinoza is a necessitarian which I present and criticize is taken largely from these sources.
53. Spinoza gives his official definition of *contingency* in pt. 4, p. 3, where it is stated: "I call singular things contingent insofar as we find nothing, while we attend only to their essence, which necessarily posits their existence or which necessarily excludes it." Proposition 29 should not, of course, be taken as denying that things are contingent in *this* sense.
54. Much of this is suggested by Delahunty, *Spinoza*, pp. 163ff. Delahunty is one of the few recent commentators to insist that Spinoza is committed to necessitarianism, not simply to determinism
55. For a different analysis of this issue, see Bennett, *Spinoza's Ethics*, pp. 117–19.

56. See Gueroult, *Spinoza I*, pp. 355–58.

57. The idea that there might be more than one perfect world, so that God would still have a choice in the matter, is suggested by Matson, "Steps Towards Spinozism." Presumably such a possibility would be ruled out by the identity of indiscernibles.

58. This is suggested by Höffding, who argues for the importance of this proposition for Spinoza's psychology and ethical theory (*Spinoza Ethica*, p. 45). It should be noted, however, that its only subsequent appearances are in IIP13, IIIP1, IIIP3, and VP4S.

4 The Human Mind

1. Two interesting treatments of Spinoza's doctrine from the point of view of contemporary mind-body identity theory are by W. I. Matson, "Spinoza's Theory of Mind," and D. Odegard, "The Body Identical with the Human Mind: A Problem in Spinoza's Philosophy."

2. See Matson, "Spinoza's Theory of Mind," pp. 53–54.

3. The importance of Hobbes in this regard is emphasized by E. Cassirer, *Das Erkenntnisproblem*, vol. 2, pp. 99–102.

4. This fairly standard view has been challenged, however, by J. Bernadete, "Spinozistic Anomalies." In addition, it has been argued by S. Hampshire, *Freedom of Mind*, pp. 225–26, and E. Curley, "Behind the Geometrical Method," pp. 50–56, that Spinoza can be read as a materialist of a nonreductive sort. For a critique of the materialist reading of Spinoza, see R. J. Delahunty, *Spinoza*, pp. 196–97.

5. The problem concerns Spinoza's doctrine of the strict equivalence of the attributes. By acknowledging that the attribute of thought contains ideas corresponding to the modes of each of the infinite attributes, Spinoza seems to give the attribute of thought an infinitely greater population than any other attribute. In addition, he creates the problem of explaining how it is that the human mind has ideas only of modes as expressed in the attributes of extension and thought. See letter 65 of Tschirnhaus, in Gebhardt, vol. 4, p. 27, and Wolf, pp. 309–10, and Spinoza's cryptic response, letter 66, in Gebhardt, vol. 4, p. 28, and Wolf, p. 310. For a detailed discussion of the problem, see H. H. Joachim, *Spinoza's Tractatus de Intellectus Emendatione*, pp. 74ff., and for a more recent account, Richard Aquila, "The Identity of Thought and Object in Spinoza."

6. For a discussion of Spinozistic ideas as beliefs, see Bennett, *Spinoza's Ethics*, pp. 162–67.

7. Ibid., p. 129.

8. The classic formulations of this charge are those of F. Pollock, *Spinoza: His Life and Philosophy*, pp. 124ff.; H. Barker, "Notes on the Second Part of Spinoza's Ethics, II," pp. 140ff.; and A. E. Taylor, "Some Incoherences in Spinozism, II," p. 305. Some recent and sophisticated variations on this theme are offered by M. D. Wilson, "Objects, Ideas, and 'Minds': Comments on Spinoza's Theory of Mind." Among the defenders of Spinoza on this issue are H. F. Hallett, "On a Reputed Equivoque in the Philosophy of Spinoza," and Dasie Radner, "Spinoza's Theory of Ideas."

9. Spinoza's fullest account of this distinction is in the *Treatise on the Emendation of the Intellect*, in Gebhardt, vol. 2, pp. 14–15, and Curley, pp. 17–18.

10. This is not quite the same as the formulation in the *Ethics*, and there is still another formulation (presumably an earlier version) in letter 7. These discrepancies are noted and commented on by Delahunty, *Spinoza*, p. 202.

11. The problem is posed in slightly different forms by Bennett, *Spinoza's Ethics*, p. 129, and Delahunty, *Spinoza*, pp. 198–209, both of whom take an extremely critical stance toward the argument of P7. My own account, to a large extent, is an attempt to meet their objections.

12. Bennett suggests the possibility that P7 could be established on the basis of P3, but then rejects this idea on the grounds that P3 entails necessitarianism (*Spinoza's Ethics*, p. 131). Although it certainly does have this consequence, this is hardly a problem for the present interpretation.

13. See G. H. R. Parkinson, *Spinoza's Theory of Knowledge*, pp. 110–11.

14. The issue here is whether by *individual* Spinoza means the same as *thing*, or whether he reserves the former for entities with a certain level of complexity. The latter view is advocated by Gueroult, *Spinoza II*, esp. pp. 164–65. Bennett seems to give tentative approval to this (*Spinoza's Ethics*, pp. 138–39), but then goes on to criticize Gueroult's account. A quite different view is offered by A. Matheron, who argues that simple bodies are the limiting cases of individuals, so that the claim applies to all things, including simple bodies (*Individu et Communauté chez Spinoza*, p. 22). A similar view is expressed by Curley, "Behind the Geometrical Method," p. 49.

15. See Bennett, *Spinoza's Ethics*, p. 138.

16. This is argued forcefully by Bennett, ibid., pp. 53–54, 128–29.

17. The most recent advocate of this reading is Curley, "Behind the Geometrical Method," pp. 49–50. The present account is based largely on his analysis.

18. *Metaphysical Thoughts*, pt. 1, chap. 6, in Gebhardt, vol. 1, p. 260, and Curley, p. 326.

19. This is Spinoza's definition of an *individual*. It is located between axioms 2 and 3, in Gebhardt, vol. 3, p. 100, and Curley, p. 460.

20. See H. Jonas, "Spinoza and the Theory of Organism."

21. Recent challengers include Delahunty, who devotes the first three chapters of his book *Spinoza* to Spinoza's epistemology, and R. Walker, "Spinoza and the Coherence Theory of Truth."

22. For a discussion of this topic, see Willis Doney, "Spinoza on Philosophical Skepticism."

23. Letter 60, in Gebhardt, vol. 4, p. 270, and Wolf, p. 300.

24. For accounts of Spinoza as a correspondence theorist, see T. C. Mark, *Spinoza's Theory of Truth*, and Curley, *Spinoza's Metaphysics*, chap. 4.

25. See Walker, "Spinoza and the Coherence Theory of Truth," for a rigorous statement of this view.

26. *Descartes' "Principles of Philosophy*," Prolegomenon, in Gebhardt, vol. 1, pp. 146–49, and Curley, pp. 236–39. *Treatise on the Emendation of the Intellect*, in Gebhardt, vol. 2, pp. 29–30, and Curley, pp. 34–35.

27. Perhaps the best discussion of this whole issue is by Radner, "Spinoza's Theory of Ideas." Radner distinguishes between the object of an idea and that which the idea represents. Although I am in general agreement with the main thrust of her analysis, I

take issue with her regarding some of the consequences she derives from it (see n. 37 below).

28. For a detailed discussion of Spinoza's conception of the imagination, see Parkinson, *Spinoza's Theory of Knowledge*, pp. 138–62.

29. The imagination as a power is emphasized by Gueroult, *Spinoza II*, pp. 217–22.

30. This was the view advocated by Curley, *Spinoza's Metaphysics*, pp. 126–28.

31. This criticism is made by Wilson, "Objects, Ideas and 'Minds'," p. 116. In his most recent discussion of the topic, Curley seems to accept this criticism ("Behind the Geometrical Method," p. 49).

32. In this context one might try to develop a suggestion made to Wilson by Peggy Nicholson. According to Nicholson, as reported by Wilson ("Objects, Ideas and 'Minds'," p. 116), Spinoza might have intended to account for self-awareness by the following distinction: "The ideas of ideas belonging to the human mind are in God in so far as he constitutes the nature of the human mind, whereas the ideas of ideas of non-human minds are in God but not in so far as he constitutes these minds." Although Wilson acknowledges that this is a "natural move to try," she claims to be unable to find any textual warrant for it. This is certainly the case, if by such a warrant is meant an explicit reference in the text. If, however, one attributes to Spinoza something like the organic complexity doctrine sketched above, then it would be a reasonable next step to claim that the ideas of the ideas belonging to the human mind are in God *qua* constituting the nature of that mind because of the nature of the human body.

33. The most famous statement of this line of criticism is that of John Locke, *An Essay Concerning Human Understanding*, bk. 1.

34. Descartes, "Notes against a Program," in *Philosophical Works*, vol. 1, p. 442.

35. I am here following Parkinson, *Spinoza's Theory of Knowledge*, p. 165.

36. On this topic, see Gueroult, *Spinoza II*, pp. 333–39.

37. Although on the whole she is quite sympathetic to Spinoza, Radner is critical of this central claim ("Spinoza's Theory of Ideas," pp. 357–58). According to Radner, Spinoza's argument at this point turns on a misuse of the principle that what is common to everything and is equally in the part and in the whole can only be conceived adequately. That it is a misuse is because Spinoza never claims that God's essence is common to every individual. On the contrary, he maintains only that the *idea* of every individual "involves" God's essence. Moreover, it is clear from pt. 1 that the idea of each individual involves God's essence in a different way. Thus there is no genuine commonality at work. Against this, the interpretation offered here suggests that Spinoza's argument is really from the possession of adequate ideas to the adequate idea of God as their common source or logical ground. In other words, the possession of adequate ideas is a premise of the argument and appeals to a common feature of all such ideas.

38. An important analysis of this proposition and of the general issues it raises is provided by Curley, "Descartes, Spinoza and the Ethics of Belief." In his analysis of Spinoza's actual argument (pp. 168–69), he points out quite correctly that the basic problem lies in the assumptions that the example of the idea of the triangle really is random and that what holds of the essential properties of the triangle would also hold of its "accidental" properties. He goes on, however, to provide an interesting defense of Spinoza's claim, as well as a valuable account of the points at issue between Descartes and Spinoza.

5 Bondage, Virtue, and Freedom

1. See S. Hampshire, *Spinoza*, pp. 59–62.
2. Descartes, *The Passions of the Soul*, pt. 1, article 19, in *Philosophical Works*, vol. 1, p. 340.
3. Ibid., article 25, p. 343.
4. Ibid., article 50, p. 355.
5. The proper translation of *Affectus* is a controversial issue. Some translators, including Elwes, whom I followed in the first edition, render it as "emotion"; others, including Curley, translate it as "affect," simply anglicizing the Latin. Since I am here using Curley's translation, I render it as "affect" when quoting; but, I frequently use "emotion" when discussing Spinoza's doctrine, since it is more familiar to the English reader. Also, at times I use "passion" to refer to a passive emotion. For a balanced discussion of the advantages and disadvantages of each reading, see Curley, p. 625. One of the main advantages of "affect," which Curley notes, is that, unlike "emotion," it refers to states of the body as well as the mind.
6. This objection is raised by Bennett, *Spinoza's Ethics*, pp. 231–37.
7. Much of this is suggested by Matheron's analysis of Spinoza's conception of an individual essence and its relation to his conatus doctrine (*Individu et Communauté chez Spinoza*, esp. pp. 9–24).
8. Ibid., p. 11.
9. See Bennett, *Spinoza's Ethics*, pp. 244–45. Bennett's actual formulation of the criticism involves the charge that Spinoza illicitly relies on a teleological version of the self-preservation principle.
10. "Definition of the Affects," D1, in Gebhardt, vol. 2, p. 190, and Curley, p. 531.
11. Spinoza discusses this conception of death in an interesting scholium to IVP39.
12. D. Bidney contends, on the contrary, that Spinoza simply adhered to two distinct and inconsistent theories (*The Psychology and Ethics of Spinoza*, pp. 88–98).
13. Spinoza may have been influenced in this regard by Hobbes, who insisted that a person's quest for power never ceases, "because he cannot assure the power and means to live well, which he hath present, without the acquisition of more" (*Leviathan*, pt. 1, chap. 11). The point for both is that human beings (and, for Spinoza, everything in nature) must constantly endeavor to increase their power, merely to preserve their actual level of existence.
14. There is a good deal of disagreement regarding the proper translations of *Laetitia* and *Tristitia*. Curley renders them as "joy" and "sorrow" respectively. I shall follow the more common practice of translating them as "pleasure" and "pain," however.
15. "Definition of the Affects," D3, in Gebhardt, vol. 2, p. 191, and Curley, pp. 531–32.
16. See J. Martineau, *A Study of Spinoza*, p. 260.
17. See H. A. Wolfson, *The Philosophy of Spinoza*, vol. 2, p. 212.
18. Ibid., p. 213.
19. Ibid., p. 215.
20. *Animositas* is another controversial term. I am here differing from Curley, who translates it as "tenacity." Another possibility is "strength of character." For Curley's account of the issue, see *The Collected Works of Spinoza*, p. 658.

21. As Curley points out, in Latin, this definition amounts to a tautology (ibid., p. 543).
22. Bennett argues that Spinoza's appeal here to the notion of a model is merely a survival from an earlier stage and plays no role in the actual argument of part 4 (*Spinoza's Ethics*, p. 296). Although he is certainly correct in pointing out that there is no further explicit reference to a model of human nature, I believe that it is reasonable to claim that it is implicit in what follows.
23. How best to characterize the theory offered by Spinoza as an alternative to traditional morality is another controversial topic. W. K. Frankena argues that Spinoza is offering a rational guide to life, which is not a morality because it fails to recognize nonegoistic considerations as justifications for courses of action ("Spinoza's 'New Morality': Notes on Book IV"). Curley argues that Spinoza is an ethical naturalist of a peculiar sort, and that his moral theory is based on hypothetical imperatives with necessary antecedents ("Spinoza's Moral Philosophy"). P. Eisenberg offers a balanced and sensitive account of the points at issue ("Is Spinoza an Ethical Naturalist?"). A somewhat different view, with which I am in general agreement, is offered by S. Hampshire, who emphasizes that the fundamental value for Spinoza is freedom, construed as rationally grounded activity rather than goodness ("Spinoza and the Idea of Freedom"). Thus the basic contrast is "free–slave," not "good–bad."
24. In this scholium (IVP20S) Spinoza argues that all those who commit suicide are in some sense compelled to kill themselves. As examples, he cites the case of someone who stabs himself with a sword because his hand is under the control of someone else who forces him to direct the sword to his heart and the famous case of the Stoic Seneca, who was supposedly "forced" by the command of Nero to kill himself rather than to face disgrace. For a discussion of the topic and its relation to IIIP4, see Bennett, *Spinoza's Ethics*, pp. 237–40.
25. See ibid., pp. 301–02.
26. L. S. Feuer emphasizes the anticompetitive thrust of Spinoza's thought (*Spinoza and the Rise of Liberalism*, esp. pp. 40–52).
27. On Spinoza's anti-Calvinism, see ibid., pp. 200–01.
28. See Wolfson, *The Philosophy of Spinoza*, vol. 2, p. 285.
29. See Bennett, *Spinoza's Ethics*, p. 317. I disagree, however, with Bennett's suggestion that there is a close kinship between the argument of Spinoza and the Kantian appeal to universalizability. The fundamental difference is that Spinoza's argument, unlike Kant's, is supposed to rest on the identification of the good with what is in one's self-interest.
30. See Wolfson, *The Philosophy of Spinoza*, vol. 2, p. 265.
31. For a very different interpretation, see Delahunty, *Spinoza*, pp. 248–50.
32. The one place is at P41S. Spinoza does refer to the "immortality of the soul," however, in the *Short Treatise*, vol. 2, chap. 23, in Gebhardt, vol. 1, pp. 103–04, and Curley, pp. 140–41.
33. These three problems are noted by Delahunty, *Spinoza*, pp. 280–86.
34. See Joachim, *A Study of the Ethics of Spinoza*, p. 296.
35. This is noted by Delahunty, *Spinoza*, p. 293, who is here following E. E. Harris, "Spinoza's Theory of Human Immortality," p. 250, and C. L. Hardin, "Spinoza on Immortality and Time," p. 136.

36. The classic discussion of this topic is that of Wolfson, *The Philosophy of Spinoza*, vol. 1, pp. 358–59, but there is an important, more recent discussion by M. Kneale, "Eternity and Sempiternity."

37. The Aristotelian reading has been defended by Kneale, "Eternity and Sempiternity"; A. Donagan, "Spinoza's Proof of Immortality"; and Bennett, *Spinoza's Ethics*, pp. 204–07.

38. The Platonic reading has been assumed in the discussions of eternity in chapters 3 and 4. An excellent analysis of this issue is provided by Delahunty, *Spinoza*, pp. 282–300.

39. This reading was suggested by Michelle Gilmore. Both readings seem superior to that of Joachim, who suggests, somewhat incongruously, both that the expression is a "momentary slip" and that Spinoza has two different conceptions of duration: one that is sharply opposed to duration and another that makes it a "general term, of which eternal existence and temporal existence are forms" (*A Study of the Ethics of Spinoza*, pp. 294–98).

40. The precise connection between memory and personal identity is a controversial topic. Here, I am making only the minimal claim that in a situation in which the possibility of recollection of one's previous stage or activity is *in principle* denied (as it is by Spinoza), one can no longer speak meaningfully of the survival of the same person. The claim that memory is actually constitutive of personal identity was made by John Locke, *An Essay Concerning Human Understanding*, bk. 2, chap. 27.

41. For a diametrically opposed analysis of this proposition, see Donagan, "Spinoza's Proof of Immortality," pp. 256–57.

42. Spinoza himself suggests as much in his interesting discussion of death in IVP395.

43. The problem is posed in a sharp form by Bennett, *Spinoza's Ethics*, pp. 359–61.

44. This was suggested to me by Nicholas Jolley. It rests on the conception of the mind attributed to Spinoza by Curley in *Spinoza's Metaphysics*.

45. A similar interpretation is offered by E. E. Powell, *Spinoza and Religion*, pp. 268–69. Powell also points out that Spinoza had some Neo-platonic predecessors who interpreted the eternity of the mind in analogous fashion.

46. Ibid., p. 257.

47. Ibid., pp. 263–65. For a quite different account of this doctrine, see Bennett, *Spinoza's Ethics*, pp. 370–71.

6 The Individual and the State

1. The fullest account of the connection between the doctrines of the *Ethics* and Spinoza's political theory is that of A. Matheron, *Individu et Communauté chez Spinoza*.

2. *Theological-Political Treatise*, XX, in Gebhardt, vol. 3, p. 241, and *Benedict de Spinoza: The Political Works*, ed. and trans. A. G. Wernham, p. 231 (hereafter cited as Wernham).

3. J. W. Gough, *The Social Contract*, p. 2.

4. Ibid., p. 3.

5. Hobbes, *De Cive or The Citizen*, trans. S. P. Lamprecht, pt. 1, chap. 1, p. 24.

6. Ibid., p. 28.

7. Hobbes, *Leviathan*, pt. 1, chap. 13, p. 97.

8. Hobbes, *De Cive*, pt. 1, chap. 2, p. 32.

9. Ibid., pp. 35–36.

10. Matheron emphasizes the connection between Spinoza's theory of natural right and his conception of the human conatus (*Individu et Communauté chez Spinoza*, p. 270 and *passim*).

11. *Political Treatise*, II, §8, in Gebhardt, vol. 3, p. 279, and Wernham, p. 273.

12. See Wernham, pp. 14–15, and R. J. McShea, *The Political Philosophy of Spinoza*, p. 138.

13. *Political Treatise*, II, §12, in Gebhardt, vol. 3, p. 280, and Wernham, p. 275.

14. *Theological-Political Treatise*, XVI, in Gebhardt, vol. 3, p. 198, and Wernham, p. 143.

15. Ibid., in Gebhardt, vol. 3, p. 191, and Wernham, p. 129.

16. Ibid., in Gebhardt, vol. 3, p. 193, and Wernham, p. 133.

17. *Political Treatise*, I, §6, in Gebhardt, vol. 3, p. 275, and Wernham, p. 265.

18. Ibid., VI, §3, in Gebhardt, vol. 3, pp. 297–98, and Wernham, p. 315.

19. See Wernham, p. 216; Matheron, *Individu et Communauté chez Spinoza*, pp. 287ff.; and C. E. Vaughan, *Studies in the History of Political Philosophy Before and After Rousseau*, vol. 1, p. 71.

20. This is implied by McShea, *The Political Philosophy of Spinoza*, pp. 85–90, and is strongly suggested by Spinoza's own remarks in the *Political Treatise* to the effect that he is merely explicating and giving a formal proof of doctrines already expressed in the *Theological-Political Treatise* and the *Ethics* (II, §I, in Gebhardt, vol. 3, p. 276, and Wernham, p. 267).

21. See Wernham, p. 26.

22. *Political Treatise*, III, §3 in Gebhardt, vol. 3, p. 285, and Wernham, p. 287.

23. Ibid.

24. Ibid.

25. Letter 50 in Gebhardt, vol. 4, pp. 238–39, and Wolf, p. 269.

26. Hobbes, *De Cive*, pt. 1, chap. 3, pp. 43–44.

27. Ibid., pt. 1, chap. 3, pp. 39–40.

28. Ibid., pt. 1, chap. 6, p. 51.

29. Ibid., pt. 2, chap. 6, p. 79.

30. For a discussion of this topic, see McShea, *The Political Philosophy of Spinoza*, p. 142.

31. *Political Treatise*, III, §9, in Gebhardt, vol. 3, p. 282, and Wernham, p. 291.

32. *Theological-Political Treatise*, XX, in Gebhardt, vol. 3, p. 243, and Wernham, p. 235.

33. Ibid.

34. Ibid., in Gebhardt, vol. 3, p. 239, and Wernham, p. 227.

35. Ibid., in Gebhardt, vol. 3, p. 240, and Wernham, p. 229.

36. *Political Treatise*, V, §4, in Gebhardt, vol. 3, p. 290, and Wernham, p. 311.

37. Ibid., V, §5, in Gebhardt, vol. 3, p. 290, and Wernham, p. 311.

38. *Theological-Political Treatise*, XX, in Gebhardt, vol. 3, p. 245, and Wernham, p. 239.

39. Ibid., XVI, in Gebhardt, vol. 3, p. 195, and Wernham, p. 137.

40. Ibid.

41. On this issue, see G. Belaief, *Spinoza's Philosophy of Law*, esp. pp. 73ff.
42. *Theological-Political Treatise*, XX, in Gebhardt, vol. 3, p. 241, and Wernham, p. 231.
43. Ibid., XIX, in Gebhardt, vol. 3, p. 232, and Wernham, p. 211.
44. *Political Treatise*, III, §6, in Gebhardt, vol. 3, p. 286, and Wernham, p. 289.
45. *Theological-Political Treatise*, XVIII, in Gebhardt, vol. 3, p. 224, and Wernham, p. 195.
46. Ibid., in Gebhardt, vol. 3, p. 227, and Wernham, p. 201.
47. *Political Treatise*, VI, §3, in Gebhardt, vol. 3, pp. 297–98, and Wernham, p. 315.
48. Ibid., V, §5, in Gebhardt, vol. 3, p. 298, and Wernham, p. 317.
49. Ibid.
50. Ibid., V, §17, in Gebhardt, vol. 3, p. 301, and Wernham, p. 323.
51. Ibid., VII, §11, in Gebhardt, vol. 3, p. 312, and Wernham, pp. 343–45.
52. Ibid., VI, §12, in Gebhardt, vol. 3, p. 300, and Wernham, p. 321.
53. See Feuer, *Spinoza and the Rise of Liberalism*, p. 188.
54. Niccolò Machiavelli, *The Prince*, chaps. 12–13; *The Discourses*, bk. 2, chap. 20.
55. Feuer points out that the use of a professional army and the hiring of mercenaries were policies of the Orangist party (*Spinoza and the Rise of Liberalism*, p. 188).
56. *Political Treatise*, VII, §31, in Gebhardt, vol. 3, p. 323, and Wernham, p. 365.
57. Ibid., X, §9, in Gebhardt, vol. 3, p. 357, and Wernham, p. 437.
58. See Feuer, *Spinoza and the Rise of Liberalism*, pp. 182–92.
59. *Political Treatise*, VIII, §1, in Gebhardt, vol. 3, p. 323, and Wernham, p. 367.
60. Ibid., VIII, §3, in Gebhardt, vol. 3, p. 325, and Wernham, p. 371.
61. Ibid.
62. Feuer, *Spinoza and the Rise of Liberalism*, p. 165.
63. *Political Treatise*, VIII, §7, in Gebhardt, vol. 3, p. 326, and Wernham, p. 373.
64. Ibid., IX, §14, in Gebhardt, vol. 3, p. 352, and Wernham, p. 427.
65. Ibid., IX, §§14–15, in Gebhardt, vol. 3, pp. 352–53, and Wernham, pp. 425–27.
66. Ibid., VIII, §§11–19, in Gebhardt, vol. 3, pp. 328–31, and Wernham, pp. 377–83.
67. Ibid., §§20–28, in Gebhardt, vol. 3, pp. 332–35, and Wernham, pp. 403–07.
68. Ibid., §§31–34, in Gebhardt, vol. 3, pp. 336–39, and Wernham, pp. 393–401.
69. Ibid., §§37–41, in Gebhardt, vol. 3, pp. 340–43, and Wernham, pp. 403–07.
70. Ibid., §9, in Gebhardt, vol. 3, pp. 327–28, and Wernham, pp. 373–77.
71. Ibid., §10, in Gebhardt, vol. 3, p. 328, and Wernham, p. 377.
72. Ibid., IX, §14, in Gebhardt, vol. 3, pp. 351–52, and Wernham, p. 427.
73. Ibid., XI, §4, in Gebhardt, vol. 3, pp. 359–60, and Wernham, pp. 443–95.
74. Hobbes, *De Cive*, pt. 2, chap. 9, p. 106.
75. Feuer, *Spinoza and the Rise of Liberalism*, esp. pp. 196–97.

7 Revelation, Scripture, and Religion

1. This is not completely true, however, for, as noted in chapter 5, section II, Spinoza does accord a kind of provisional value to "virtues" such as repentance or humility for those

not living under the guidance of reason. Thus, they are dictated by reason for those who are not themselves capable of full rationality.

2. Many of the remarks in this chapter concerning Spinoza's strategy in the *Theological-Political Treatise* have been suggested by the analysis of Leo Strauss, *Spinoza's Critique of Religion*, esp. pp. 107–46.

3. *Theological-Political Treatise*, VII, in Gebhardt, vol. 3, pp. 111–17, and *The Chief Works of Benedict de Spinoza*, trans. R. H. M. Elwes, vol. 1, pp. 113–19 (hereafter cited as Elwes). All quotations from this work in the present chapter will be from the Elwes translation. The Wernham translation cited in the last chapter contains only the political portions of the text.

4. Ibid., in Gebhardt, vol. 3, p. 112, and Elwes, p. 114.

5. Ibid., in Gebhardt, vol. 3, p. 113, and Elwes, p. 115.

6. Ibid., in Gebhardt, vol. 3, pp. 113–16, and Elwes, pp. 115–18.

7. Ibid., I, in Gebhardt, vol. 3, p. 15, and Elwes, p. 13.

8. Ibid., in Gebhardt, vol. 3, p. 21, and Elwes, p. 19.

9. Ibid., in Gebhardt, vol. 3, p. 26, and Elwes, p. 24.

10. Ibid., II, in Gebhardt, vol. 3, p. 34, and Elwes, pp. 31–32.

11. Ibid., in Gebhardt, vol. 3, p. 37, and Elwes, p. 34.

12. Ibid., VI, in Gebhardt, vol. 3, p. 95, and Elwes, pp. 95–96.

13. Ibid., in Gebhardt, vol. 3, p. 82, and Elwes, p. 82.

14. Ibid., in Gebhardt, vol. 3, p. 83, and Elwes, p. 83.

15. Ibid.

16. Ibid., in Gebhardt, vol. 3, p. 87, and Elwes, p. 87.

17. Ibid., in Gebhardt, vol. 3, p. 86, and Elwes, p. 81.

18. Ibid., III, in Gebhardt, vol. 3, p. 44, and Elwes, p. 43.

19. Ibid., in Gebhardt, vol. 3, p. 47, and Elwes, p. 46.

20. Ibid., in Gebhardt, vol. 3, p. 50, and Elwes, p. 49.

21. Ibid., in Gebhardt, vol. 3, p. 56, and Elwes, p. 55.

22. Ibid., in Gebhardt, vol. 3, p. 56, and Elwes, p. 56.

23. Ibid., in Gebhardt, vol. 3, p. 57, and Elwes, p. 56.

24. Ibid., IV, in Gebhardt, vol. 3, pp. 60–61, and Elwes, p. 60.

25. Ibid., in Gebhardt, vol. 3, p. 64, and Elwes, p. 63.

26. Ibid., in Gebhardt, vol. 3, p. 65, and Elwes, p. 64.

27. Ibid., V, in Gebhardt, vol. 3, pp. 69–80, and Elwes, pp. 69–80.

28. Ibid., VII, in Gebhardt, vol. 3, p. 99, and Elwes, p. 99.

29. Ibid.

30. Ibid.

31. Ibid., in Gebhardt, vol. 3, pp. 99–100, and Elwes, p. 101.

32. Ibid., in Gebhardt, vol. 3, p. 100, and Elwes, p. 101.

33. Ibid., in Gebhardt, vol. 3, p. 111, and Elwes, pp. 112–13.

34. For a discussion of Isaac de la Peyrère and his relation to Spinoza, see Strauss, *Spinoza's Critique of Religion*, pp. 64–85.

35. *Theological-Political Treatise*, IX, in Gebhardt, vol. 3, p. 129, and Elwes, p. 133.

36. Ibid., X, in Gebhardt, vol. 3, p. 142, and Elwes, p. 147.
37. Averroës expressed this view most clearly in his classic work *On the Harmony of Religion and Philosophy*. For a clear statement of the Averroistic position and its influence in the West, see E. Gilson, *Reason and Revelation in the Middle Ages*, pp. 37–66.
38. For a discussion of Machiavelli's religious views in relation to those of Spinoza, see Strauss, *Spinoza's Critique of Religion*, pp. 48–49.
39. *Theological-Political Treatise*, XIV, in Gebhardt, vol. 3, p. 175, and Elwes, p. 184.
40. Ibid., in Gebhardt, vol. 3, pp. 177–78, and Elwes, pp. 186–87.
41. Ibid., in Gebhardt, vol. 3, p. 176, and Elwes, p. 185.

BIBLIOGRAPHY

I. Primary Sources
(*editions and translations of the works of Spinoza and other major philosophers cited in the text*)

Aristotle. *The Works of Aristotle Translated into English*. Edited by W. D. Ross. Vol. 1. London: Geoffrey Cumberley, 1928.

Descartes, René. *Philosophical Works of Descartes*. Translated by Elizabeth S. Haldane and G. R. T. Ross. 2 vols. New York: Dover, 1955.

Hobbes, Thomas. *De Cive or The Citizen*. Translated by Sterling P. Lamprecht. New York: Appleton-Century Crofts, 1949.

————. *Leviathan*. Oxford: Clarendon Press, 1958.

Spinoza Opera. Edited by Carl Gebhardt. 4 vols. Heidelberg: Carl Winter, 1925.

The Chief Works of Benedict de Spinoza, vol. 1. Translated by R. H. M. Elwes. New York: Dover, 1951.

The Collected Works of Spinoza, vol. 1. Edited and translated by Edwin Curley. Princeton: Princeton University Press, 1985.

The Correspondence of Spinoza. Translated by A. Wolf. London: Frank Cass, 1966.

Benedict de Spinoza: The Political Works. Edited and translated by A. G. Wernham. Oxford: Clarendon Press, 1958.

II. Secondary Sources
(*works cited in the notes, as well as a few that were cited in the first edition that have significantly influenced my views on specific aspects of Spinoza's thought*)

Aquila, Richard. "The Identity of Thought and Object in Spinoza." *Journal of the History of Philosophy* 16 (1978): 271–88.

Barker, H. "Notes on the Second Part of Spinoza's *Ethics*" (3 parts). In *Studies in Spinoza*, edited by S. P. Kashap, pp. 101–49.

Bayle, Pierre. *Historical and Critical Dictionary*. Selections, edited and translated by Richard H. Popkin and Craig Brush. Indianapolis: Bobbs-Merrill, 1965.

Belaief, Gail. *Spinoza's Philosophy of Law*. The Hague: Mouton, 1971.

Bennett, Jonathan. *A Study of Spinoza's Ethics*. Indianapolis: Hackett, 1984.

Bernadete, José. "Spinozistic Anomalies." In *The Philosophy of Baruch Spinoza*, edited by R. Kennington, pp. 53–71.

Bidney, David. *The Psychology and Ethics of Spinoza*. 2d ed. New Haven: Yale University Press, 1940 Reprint. New York: Russell and Russell, 1962.

Bréhier, Emile. *The History of Philosophy: The Seventeenth Century*. Translated by W. Baskin. Chicago: University of Chicago Press, 1966.

Brunschvicg, Léon. *Spinoza et ses Contemporains*. 3d ed. Paris: Librairie Felix Alcon, 1923.

Burtt, E. A. *The Metaphysical Foundations of Modern Science*. Rev. ed. New York: Doubleday, Anchor Books, 1954.

Caird, John. *Spinoza*. Edinburgh and London: W. Blackwood, 1888.

Cassirer, Ernst. *Das Erkenntnisproblem in der Philosophie und Wissenschaft der neueren Zeit*, vol. 2. Berlin: Bruno Cassirer, 1911.

Colerus, John. *The Life of Benedict de Spinoza*. In Pollock, *Spinoza: His Life and Philosophy*, pp. 386–418.

Curley, Edwin M. "Behind the Geometrical Method." Unpublished draft manuscript.

———. "Descartes on the Creation of Eternal Truths." *Philosophical Review* 93 (1984): 569–97.

———. "Descartes, Spinoza and the Ethics of Belief." In *Spinoza, Essays in Interpretation*, edited by E. Freeman and M. Mandelbaum, pp. 159–89.

———. *Spinoza's Metaphysics: An Essay in Interpretation*. Cambridge, Mass.: Harvard University Press, 1969.

———. "Spinoza's Moral Philosophy." In *Spinoza, A Collection of Critical Essays*, edited by M. Grene, pp. 354–76.

De Deugd, C. D. *The Significance of Spinoza's First Kind of Knowledge*. Assen: Van Gorcum, 1966.

Delahunty, R. J. *Spinoza*. The Arguments of the Philosophers. London: Routledge and Kegan Paul, 1985.

Delbos, Victor. *Le Spinozisme*. Paris: Librairie Philosophique J. Vrin, 1968.

Donagan, Alan. "Essence and the Distinction of Attributes." In *Spinoza, A Collection of Critical Essays*, edited by M. Grene, pp. 164–81.

———. "Spinoza's Dualism." In *The Philosophy of Baruch Spinoza*, edited by R. Kennington, pp. 89–102.

———. "Spinoza's Proof of Immortality." In *Spinoza, A Collection of Critical Essays*, edited by M. Grene, pp. 241–58.

Doney, Willis. "Spinoza on Philosophical Skepticism." In *Spinoza: Essays in Interpretation*, edited by E. Freeman and M. Mandelbaum, pp. 139–57.

———. "Spinoza's Ontological Proof." In *The Philosophy of Baruch Spinoza*, edited by R. Kennington, pp. 34–51.

Dunin-Borkowski, Stanislaus von. *Der junge De Spinoza*. 2d ed. Münster: Aschendorffschen Verlagsbuchhandlung, 1933.

Dunner, Joseph. *Baruch Spinoza and Western Democracy*. New York: Philosophical Library, 1955.

Eisenberg, Paul. "Is Spinoza an Ethical Naturalist?" In *Speculum Spinozanum, 1677–1977*, edited by S. Hessing, pp. 145–64.

Feuer, Lewis Samuel. *Spinoza and the Rise of Liberalism*. Boston: Beacon Press, 1958.

Frankena, William, K. "Spinoza's 'New Morality': Notes on Book IV." In *Spinoza, Essays in Interpretation*, edited by E. Freeman and M. Mandelbaum, pp. 85–100.

Freeman, Eugene, and Mandelbaum, Maurice, eds. *Spinoza, Essays in Interpretation*. La Salle, Ill.: Open Court, 1975.

Freudenthal, J. *Spinoza Leben und Lehre*. 2d ed. Edited by C. Gebhardt. *Bibliotheca Spinoza curis Societatis Spinozanae*, vol. 5. Heidelberg: Carl Winter, 1927.

Friedmann, George. *Leibniz et Spinoza*. 2d ed. Paris: Gallimard, 1962.

Gilson, Etienne. *Reason and Revelation in the Middle Ages*. New York: Scribner, 1938.

Gough, J. W. *The Social Contract*. 2d ed. Oxford: Clarendon Press, 1957.

Graetz, H. *Popular History of the Jews*. Translated by A. B. Rhine. 5th ed. Vol 5. New York: Jordan Publishing, 1935.

Gram, Moltke S. "Spinoza, Substance, and Predication." *Theoria* 3 (1968): 222–44.

Green, T. H. *Lectures on the Principles of Political Obligation*. London, 1882. Reprint. Ann Arbor: University of Michigan Press, 1967.

Grene, Marjorie, ed. *Spinoza, A Collection of Critical Essays*. Garden City, N.Y.: Doubleday, Anchor Books, 1973.

Gueroult, Martial. *Etudes sur Descartes, Spinoza, Malebranche et Leibniz*. Hildesheim: Georg Olms, 1970.

——. *Spinoza I, Dieu (Ethique, I)*. Paris: Aubier, 1968.

——. *Spinoza II, L'Ame (Ethique, II)*. Hildesheim: Georg Olms, 1974.

Hallett, H. F. *Creation, Emanation, Salvation: A Spinozistic Study*. The Hague: Nijhoff, 1962.

——. "On a Reputed Equivoque in the Philosophy of Spinoza." In *Studies in Spinoza*, edited by S. P. Kashap, pp. 168–88.

Hampshire, Stuart. *Freedom of Mind*. Oxford: Oxford University Press, 1972.

——. *Spinoza*. London: Faber, 1951.

——. "Spinoza and the Idea of Freedom." In *Studies in Spinoza*, edited by S. P. Kashap, pp. 310–31.

Hardin, C. L. "Spinoza on Immortality and Time." In *Spinoza: New Perspectives*, edited by R. S. Shahan and J. J. Biro, pp. 129–38.

Harris, Errol E. "Spinoza's Theory of Human Immortality." In *Spinoza, Essays in Interpretation*, edited by E. Freeman and M. Mandelbaum, pp. 245–62.

Hessing, S., ed. *Speculum Spinozanum, 1677–1977.* London: Routledge and Kegan Paul, 1977.

Höffding, Harald. *Spinozas Ethica: Analyse und Charakteristik.* Heidelberg: Curis Societatis Spinozanae, 1924.

Joachim, H. H. *A Study of the Ethics of Spinoza.* London, 1901. Reprint. New York: Russell and Russell, 1964.

———. *Spinoza's Tractatus de Intellectus Emandatione.* Oxford: Clarendon Press, 1940.

Joel, M. *Spinozas theologisch-politischer Traktat.* Breslau: Schletter, 1870.

Jonas, Hans. "Spinoza and the Theory of Organism." In *Spinoza, A Collection of Critical Essays*, edited by M. Grene, pp. 259–78.

Kashap, S. Paul, ed. *Studies in Spinoza: Critical and Interpretive Essays.* Berkeley: University of California Press, 1972.

Kennington, Richard, ed. *The Philosophy of Baruch Spinoza.* Studies in Philosophy and the History of Philosophy, vol. 7. Washington, D.C.: The Catholic University of America Press, 1980.

Kline, George, "On the Infinity of Spinoza's Attributes." In *Speculum Spinozanum, 1677–1977*, edited by S. Hessing, pp. 333–52.

Kneale, Martha. "Eternity and Sempiternity." In *Spinoza: A Collection of Critical Essays*, edited by M. Grene, pp. 227–40.

Koyré, Alexandre. *From the Closed World to the Infinite Universe.* New York: Harper, 1957.

Loemker, Leroy E. *Struggle for Synthesis and the Seventeenth Century Background of Leibniz's Synthesis of Order and Freedom.* Cambridge, Mass.: Harvard University Press, 1972.

Lucas, J. M. *The Life of the Late Mr. de Spinoza.* Translated and edited by A. Wolf, as *The Oldest Biography of Spinoza.* London, 1927. Reissue. Port Washington, N.Y., and London: Kennikat Press, 1979.

Mark, Thomas Carson. *Spinoza's Theory of Truth.* New York: Columbia University Press, 1972.

Martineau, James. *A Study of Spinoza.* London: Macmillan, 1882.

Matheron, Alexandre. *Individu et Communauté chez Spinoza.* Paris: Les Editions de Minuit, 1969.

Matson, Wallace I. "Spinoza's Theory of Mind." In *Spinoza, Essays in Interpretation*, edited by E. Freeman and M. Mandelbaum, pp. 49–60.

———. "Steps Towards Spinozism." *Revue internationale de philosophie* 119–20 (1977): 69–83.

Mattern, Ruth M. "An Index of References to Claims in Spinoza's *Ethics.*" *Philosophy Research Archives* 5, no. 1358 (1979).

McShea, Robert J. *The Political Philosophy of Spinoza.* New York: Columbia University Press, 1969.

Odegard, Douglas. "The Body Identical with the Human Mind: A Problem in Spinoza's Philosophy." In *Spinoza, Essays in Interpretation*, edited by E. Freeman and M. Mandelbaum, pp. 61–83.

Parkinson, G. H. R. *Spinoza's Theory of Knowledge.* Oxford: Clarendon Press, 1954.

Pollock, Sir Frederick. *Spinoza: His Life and Philosophy.* 2d ed. London, 1899. Reprint. New York: American Scholar Publications, 1966.

Popkin, Richard H. "The Historical Significance of Sephardic Judaism in 17th Century Amsterdam." *American Sephardi*, Journal of the Sephardic Studies Program of Yeshiva University, V, nos. 1–2 (1971): 18–27.

Powell, Elmer Ellsworth. *Spinoza and Religion.* Chicago: Open Court, 1906.

Radner, Dasie. "Spinoza's Theory of Ideas." *Philosophical Review* 80 (1971): 338–59.

Roth, Leon. *Spinoza.* London: Allen and Unwin, 1954.

———. *Spinoza, Descartes, Maimonides.* Oxford: Clarendon Press, 1924.

Russell, Bertrand. *A Critical Exposition of the Philosophy of Leibniz.* London: Allen and Unwin, 1900.

Shahan, R. W., and Biro, J., eds. *Spinoza: New Perspectives.* Norman, Okla.: University of Oklahoma Press, 1979.

Stein, Ludwig. *Leibniz und Spinoza.* Berlin: G. Reimer, 1890.

Strauss, Leo. *Spinoza's Critique of Religion.* Translated by E. M. Sinclair. New York: Schocken Books, 1965.

Taylor, A. E. "Some Incoherencies in Spinozism" (2 parts). In *Studies in Spinoza*, edited by S. P. Kashap, pp. 189–211, 289–309.

Vaughan, C. E. *Studies in the History of Political Philosophy Before and After Rousseau.* 2 vols. Manchester: University of Manchester Press, 1925.

Walker, Ralph. "Spinoza and the Coherence Theory of Truth." *Mind* 94 (1985): 1–18.

Wilson, Margaret Dauler. *Descartes.* The Arguments of the Philosophers. London: Routledge and Kegan Paul, 1978.

———. "Objects, Ideas and 'Minds': Comments on Spinoza's Theory of Mind." In *The Philosophy of Baruch Spinoza*, edited by R. Kennington, pp. 103–20.

Wolf, A. *The Life of Spinoza.* In *Spinoza's Short Treatise*, pp. xi–cii. New York: Russell and Russell, 1963.

Wolfson, H. A. *The Philosophy of Spinoza.* 2 vols. New York: Meridian Books, 1958.

Index